THE GERMAN IDEA

THE GERMAN IDEA

Four English writers and the reception of German thought
1800–1860

ROSEMARY ASHTON
Lecturer in English
University College London

CAMBRIDGE UNIVERSITY PRESS

CAMBRIDGE
LONDON   NEW YORK   NEW ROCHELLE
MELBOURNE   SYDNEY

Published by the Press Syndicate of the University of Cambridge
The Pitt Building, Trumpington Street, Cambridge CP2 IRP
32 East 57th Street, New York, NY 10022, USA
296 Beaconsfield Parade, Middle Park, Melbourne 3206, Australia

First published 1980

Printed in Great Britain by
Western Printing Services Ltd, Bristol

Library of Congress Cataloguing in Publication Data
Ashton, Rosemary D. 1947–
The German idea.
Bibliography: p.
Includes index.
1. English literature – 19th century – History and
criticism. 2. Literature, Comparative – English and
German. 3. Literature, Comparative – German and English.
4. Philosophy, German – 19th century. I. Title.
PR468.G4A8   820'.9'007   78–75254

ISBN 0 521 22560 4

FOR GERRY

CONTENTS

ACKNOWLEDGMENTS

Acknowledgments are due first to the British Academy for an award which enabled me to spend several weeks in the summer of 1976 consulting the collection of George Eliot and G. H. Lewes MSS in the Beinecke Rare Book and Manuscript Library at Yale University. I have also to thank the Librarian of the Beinecke for allowing me access to these papers, as well as to the Carlyle MSS and to the Speck Collection of Goetheana. To Professor Gordon S. Haight, of Yale University, go special thanks for his generosity in allowing me to consult and copy some of his collected Lewes material. The librarian of Jesus College, Cambridge, kindly allowed me access to copies of the Coleridge notebooks. Thanks are also due to the Folger Shakespeare Library for copies sent to me of G. H. Lewes's lists of his periodical publications. I thank the Trustees of Dr Williams's library for allowing me to consult Henry Crabb Robinson MSS and G. H. Lewes's library. I spent some weeks consulting the large collection of Blackwood Correspondence in the manuscript section of the National Library of Scotland, and would like to express my gratitude to the Trustees and the Keeper of Manuscripts for access to these and other collections. Other acknowledgments for permission to consult manuscript letters go to the Keeper of Western MSS at the Bodleian Library (for the Max Müller papers), the University of London Library and the Athenaeum Club (for Herbert Spencer material), the County Archivist at the Hertford County Records Office (for the Lytton Collection), the London Borough of Camden (for a manuscript at the Keats Memorial House, Hampstead), the Librarian at University College London (for the Robertson and Sully Collections), and the Librarians of Johns Hopkins University Library, Princeton University Library, and the Kestner Museum, Hanover (for MS letters of G. H. Lewes). I have also consulted Coleridge, Carlyle, and De Quincey MSS in the British Museum.
Some material from Chapter 1 on Coleridge and *Faust* and from

ACKNOWLEDGMENTS

Chapter 2 on Carlyle and Goethe has been published in slightly different form, in the *Review of English Studies* (May 1977) and the *Modern Language Review* (January 1976).

Dr Roy Park, Dr Elinor Shaffer, and Mr Michael Black have been helpful in conversation and correspondence during the preparing of this work. My thanks go to them, and also to Miss Susan Oldacre and her colleagues at University College London for fast and accurate typing of the work. Finally, I thank my husband Gerry Ashton most warmly for constant critical help and encouragement and for sharing the tedious task of proofreading with me. For any errors, of course, I alone am responsible.

I might add that all translations from the German in this book are, unless otherwise stated, my own. In the case of both English and German texts quoted in the course of the work, I have used modern scholarly editions where these exist. Otherwise I have quoted from appropriate nineteenth-century editions. This accounts for some variations in spelling and punctuation, which also occur in some of the manuscript material I have used.

ROSEMARY ASHTON

London 1978

x

Introduction

In a passage in a notebook of 1829, Coleridge showed his awareness of the idea his contemporaries had of him:

I have obtained, I hear, the soubriquet of the Ideomanist, or the *ideatic* (⚹ idiotic) Gentleman. Lord Byron, I remember, did me the honor of observing – that at my first rising on the literary horizon I gave hopes of becoming one of the Men of Genius in that generation – but that I went into Germany, studied metaphysics, and dosed away not [sic] a dreaming *Idiot*. To be an *Ideat* is therefore a preferment: for even Mania is less hopeless than idiocy.[1]

That this idea of Coleridge was not peculiar to Byron must be clear to readers of contemporary poetry, reviews, and memoirs. Wordsworth, De Quincey, Peacock, Jeffrey and others publicly and privately fostered the notion that Coleridge dealt, often obscurely, in 'ideas', and that the obscurest of his ideas were 'German'. Yet it was in a positive sense that the Victorian generation looked for ideas both to Coleridge and, often through his works, to German literature and philosophy. Carlyle, G. H. Lewes, and George Eliot were the most influential of many British thinkers who knew that in philosophy, aesthetics, and the higher criticism of the Bible Germany had produced more original and important writers than any other country. They count with Coleridge as the most important introducers to the British public of the best examples of German thought.

This book aims to study the way in which that introduction took place. After an early receptivity to Gothic and sentimental dramas and novels, British editors, reviewers, and readers settled down to ignorant contempt of individual German works like *Wallenstein* and *Faust* and *Wilhelm Meister* for their 'immorality' or 'absurdity' or 'obscurity', without deeming it proper to learn something of the cultural context, particularly as manifested in the important philosophical movement of Kant and his successors, to which such works belonged. A misinformed and negative idea of the Germans was prevalent. It is not too much to say that Coleridge alone in the period between 1800 and 1820 fully knew and drew on German culture for his own intellectual life. It was through his conversations, lectures, and writings, along with those of Carlyle in the late 1820s, that Victorians like George Eliot, Lewes, Mill, Arnold, Richard Holt Hutton, and the philosopher J. H. Stirling absorbed a culture which could no longer be simply English. Though France, particularly through the works of St Simon and Comte, was important for many Victorian thinkers, it was Germany, with its pioneering methods in philosophy, history, and aesthetics, which contributed most to English thinking in the later nineteenth century. This book does not attempt to deal with the whole range of German thought as it, to use John Sterling's word, 'leaked' into England.[2] It is hoped that it will illuminate the early stages of the phenomenon, with an equal eye to the 'ideas' which the four major English authors formed with reference to Germany and to the 'idea' of Germany which existed among the non-Germanised British reading and writing public. This second idea began as something to be combated and changed by persuasion and increased access to knowledge of Germany. Coleridge and Carlyle are the two most important single authors who undertook this difficult task. In Coleridge's case it was done sometimes grudgingly, often covertly, but that, I believe, is largely because of the uncaring and uncomprehending attitudes he encountered from friends, publishers, editors, and readers. In giving him credit for his contribution to the spread of interest and knowledge we must bear in mind also that he deferred to, and sometimes shared, the doubts and prejudices of his contemporaries. As Shelley wrote in the preface to *Prometheus Unbound* (1820), 'poets, not otherwise than philosophers, painters, sculptors, and musicians, are, in one sense, the creators, and, in another, the creations, of their age. From this subjection the loftiest do not escape.' Coleridge's sensitivity to public opinion, periodical reviews, and the views of his friends and fellow poets, and the plagiarism and denials connected with this sensitivity, are elements which must be taken into account when considering his writings in search of a coherent response to, or exposition of, Kant and Schelling and Schlegel.

Partly for these reasons, Coleridge's influence was diffusive rather than direct. When Mill re-read his works in preparation for his distinguished essay on Coleridge (1840), he realised that the writings were 'only one of the channels through which his influences have reached the age'.[3] The first historian of American Transcendentalism, O. B. Frothingham, looked back on England and America in the late 1820s and early 1830s and marvelled that Coleridge, 'the source of more intellectual life than any individual of his time', had 'disciples who never heard him speak even in print, and followers who never saw his form even as sketched by critics. His thoughts were in the air.'[4] Those thoughts were largely German. In the following pages there is a detailed discussion of Coleridge's relation to Kant, because in it we have the basis of much of his writing not only on philosophy, religion, and morality, but also on aesthetics, and because Coleridge, unlike any other Englishman of his time, knew his Kant. He studied the three great Critiques to the end, re-read them, criticised and absorbed them.[5] Henry Crabb Robinson, De Quincey, and Carlyle, who all wrote on Kant, only flirted with him by comparison. Whereas a great deal of scholarly work has been done on Coleridge's debts to A. W. Schlegel and Schelling, little has been said of the importance of Kant for Coleridge's critical formulations.[6] Apart from his early enthusiasm for Bürger's ballads and Schiller's dramas and some interest in Jean Paul, Novalis, and Fouqué,[7] Coleridge was generally less interested in the literature of Germany than its theory. However, he did translate *Wallenstein* and nearly translated *Faust*. The story of the poor reception of his *Wallenstein* and his neurotic fear two decades later for his reputation if he were to translate the much-condemned *Faust* needs telling in its context of public attitudes and Coleridge's desire to conform and win praise from his contemporaries. He was intellectually isolated in his study of German aesthetics and philosophy, and though he maintained his unfashionable interest, he got no encouragement to express it either from friends like Wordsworth and Southey or from critics like Jeffrey and Hazlitt.

It was Coleridge's fortune and misfortune to be nearly contemporary with the age of great intellectual activity in Germany. His English contemporaries ridiculed him for his interest, but the following generation, having learnt from him, could look on his German studies from the opposite point of view. Thus Pater wrote in 1866:

With an inborn-taste for transcendental philosophy, he lived just at the time when that philosophy took an immense spring in Germany, and connected itself with a brilliant literary movement. He had the luck to light upon it in its freshness, and introduce it to his countrymen. What an opportunity for one reared on the colourless English philosophies, but who feels an irresistible attraction towards metaphysical synthesis! How rare are such occasions of intellectual contentment![8]

By taking Coleridge's introduction of German philosophy and aesthetics alongside Carlyle's more literary (and more proselytising) essays and following their influence into the mid-nineteenth century, we can come to a nearer understanding of the widespread diffusion of German culture among the Victorians. Coleridge and Carlyle are the two most important figures in those fifty years of its reception in England during which they helped to produce a considerable shift in Britain's view of the Germans from small interest or misguided dismissal to discriminating acceptance and frankly avowed debts.

The four writers studied here were most important in changing and governing the British idea of what German culture was. Each was indebted to German writers for the formation of his own ideas: Coleridge to Kant and Schelling; Carlyle to Goethe, Fichte, and Novalis; Lewes to Hegel and Goethe; George Eliot to Goethe and the German higher criticism, particularly the work of Feuerbach. Between them they diffused to their readers, and in Coleridge's case to his hearers in the lecture hall and the salon, a comprehensive sense of how Germany, the 'land of ideas', could enrich English culture. In doing this, they all looked to the period of rich intellectual activity in Germany in the latter decades of the eighteenth century. With the philosophy of Kant, so important for Coleridge's philosophical education, had come also a new poetics in Germany. Questions were asked about the poet's perception and the nature of his creativity, its consciousness or unconsciousness. Schiller, Schelling, the brothers Schlegel, Jean Paul, and Hegel worked out theories about modern, 'Romantic', self-conscious poetry. The Imagination became for them the important faculty which reconciled the oppositions of man and nature, subject and object, mind and matter.[9] Coleridge's criticism used the same terms and belonged to the same post-Kantian aesthetic.

But Coleridge's interest in Germany had begun with the widespread enthusiasm in Britain for single works by German authors. The German literature which was noticed in England was itself largely influenced by English models. Percy's *Reliques of Ancient English Poetry* (1765) inspired imitations by Bürger; the melancholy 'Ossian' and Young's poetry excited the young Goethe. Indeed his *Leiden des jungen Werthers* (*Sorrows of Young Werter*, 1774) fitted so perfectly the mood of its English readers that, as Blake joked in 'An Island in the Moon' (1784–5), it was as much a necessary part of 'Miss Filligreework's' personal furniture as hats and gloves. Henry Mackenzie, author of the lachrymose novel *The Man of Feeling* (1771), introduced the newest German works in 1788 to an audience in Edinburgh which included Walter Scott. The latter, in his enthusiasm, translated Goethe's drama of chivalry, *Götz von Berlichingen* (1773), and Bürger's ballad 'Lenore' in the 1790s.[10] Schiller's play of the noble rebel, *Die Räuber* (1781, translated in 1792 by Francis Tytler), excited Coleridge, Wordsworth, and Hazlitt. Wordsworth's *Borderers* (1796–7) and 'Monk' Lewis's drama *The Castle Spectre* (1798) show its influence in plot and setting.

This early interest, particularly in the German drama, was short-lived, quickly giving way to negative ideas of what 'German literature' was like. Coleridge's translation of Schiller's *Wallenstein* in 1800 was a failure because Schiller's and Coleridge's names were associated with Jacobinism. In 1814 Coleridge hesitated to translate *Faust*, being afraid of a negative critical response. Yet by 1840 there were at least eight translations of *Faust* in England. One can hardly think of a Victorian author or critic who knew nothing of Goethe, either in the original or by way of Carlyle's translations and articles. Lewes and George Eliot, as translators and reviewers of German works and in their general frame of reference in their essays and novels, are the most important of the many inheritors of an Anglo-German culture which had its shaky beginnings in the early reception of, and the speedy revulsion from, German Gothic dramas and sentimental fictions.

Coleridge was there at this beginning. In 1794 he and his new friend Southey were full of talk about their domestic and democratic scheme of Pantisocracy. Coleridge wrote incoherently to Southey in September 1794, 'my God! how tumultuous are the movements of my Heart...America! Southey! Miss Fricker!'[11] Their ideas for a new society grew from their excitement about the French Revolution and their hopes for democracy in France. Southey had recently written his play in support of a people's revolt against tyranny, *Wat Tyler*, Coleridge collaborated with him on a pro-French, anti-English epic, *Joan of Arc*, and they had just published their tragedy, *The Fall of Robespierre*, in September 1794. When Coleridge read Schiller's *Räuber* in November 1794, it chimed in perfectly with his beliefs. Again he wrote to Southey:

'Tis past one o clock in the morning – I sate down at twelve o'clock to read the 'Robbers' of Schiller – I had read chill and trembling until I came to the part where Moor fires a pistol over the Robbers who are asleep – I could read no more – My God! Southey! Who is this Schiller? This Convulser of the Heart? Did he write his Tragedy amid the yelling of Fiends? . . .Why have we ever called Milton sublime?[12]

Thus *Die Räuber* belonged in the same context as the French Revolution in exciting that generation as a symbol of the struggle for freedom from oppression. Hazlitt recognised the connection when he looked back at his own experience in the 1790s:

For my part, I set out in life with the French Revolution, and that event had considerable influence on my early feelings, as on those of others. . .At that time, to read the 'ROBBERS' was indeed delicious, and to hear
'From the dungeon of the tower time-rent,
    That fearful voice, a famish'd father's cry,'
could be borne only amidst the fulness of hope, the crash of the fall of the strong holds of power, and the exulting sounds of the march of human freedom.[13]

However, by 1796, Coleridge, horrified by news of the Terror in France, had given up his Jacobinism, Wordsworth had been to France and experienced the new tyranny, and Southey had begun to settle down to the political and religious orthodoxy of which he later, as Poet Laureate and *Quarterly* Reviewer, became an important representative. Nevertheless, Coleridge and Southey were the chief victims of the satire of Canning, Ellis, Frere, and other supporters of Pitt's government in the influential *Anti-Jacobin; or, Weekly Examiner* (1797–8). This periodical had a primarily political aim:

We avow ourselves to be *partial* to the COUNTRY *in which we live*, notwithstanding the daily panegyrics which we read and hear on the superior virtues and endowments of its rival and hostile neighbours. . .Of JACOBINISM in all its shapes, and in all its degrees, political and moral, public and private, whether as it openly threatens the subversion of States, or gradually saps the foundations of domestic happiness, We are avowed, determined, and irreconcileable enemies.[14]

The method adopted by these writers to encourage patriotism and conservatism was to parody and satirise all those political poems and plays which seemed to support revolution. *Joan of Arc* was one such work, and Schiller's *Räuber*, known to be popular though as yet unstaged in England,[15] provided most of the stimulus for the successful satirical drama of the Anti-Jacobins, *The Rovers* (4 and 11 June 1798). Canning and his colleagues found in Schiller's play dangerous political ardour and anarchy (though in it the noble rebel, Karl Moor, finally gives himself up to punishment by the state, recognising the danger of anarchic action, however well motivated), represented with all the literary paraphernalia of the Gothic: the spilling of blood, the hooting of owls, and scenes in a ruined tower with secret dungeons. They could best attack the 'Jacobin' sentiments of the play by exaggerating its already heightened language and setting. Thus one scene is described as follows in *The Rovers*:

A Subterranean Vault in the Abbey of QUEDLINBURGH; with Coffins, 'Scutcheons, Death's Heads and Cross-bones. – Toads, and other loathsome Reptiles are seen traversing the obscurer parts of the Stage. – ROGERO appears, in chains, in a Suit of rusty Armour, with his beard grown, and a Cap of a grotesque form upon his head. – Beside him a Crock, or Pitcher, supposed to contain his daily allowance of sustenance. – A long silence, during which the wind is heard to whistle through the Caverns.[16]

The basis for this is Act iv, Scene v of *Die Räuber*, in which Karl Moor finds his father incarcerated in the underground dungeon of a ruined tower, where a diet of bread and water has left him 'ausgemergelt wie ein Gerippe', 'as emaciated as a skeleton'.[17]

Die Räuber stood conveniently for the whole German dramatic movement of the 'Sturm und Drang' (Storm and Stress), which celebrated not only democratic opinions but also formal freedoms, a revolt against the dramatic unities and, in its wider context, against the domination of German taste by French classical literature. It was not in the interests of the Anti-Jacobins to investigate the cultural conditions in which German theoreticians and dramatists like Lessing, Herder, Goethe, and Schiller sought to establish a truly German drama with Shakespeare, valued primarily for his ignoring of the 'rules', as its model.[18] The satirists were intent on drawing national lessons from foreign political and literary excesses. The supposed author of *The Rovers*, a Mr Higgins, introduces the play with a sweeping view of 'German drama':

I have turned my thoughts more particularly to the GERMAN STAGE, and have composed, in imitation of the most popular pieces of that Country, which have already met with so general reception and admiration in this, a Play: which, if it has a proper run, will, I think, do much to unhinge the present notions of men with regard to the obligations of Civil Society; and to substitute in lieu of a sober contentment, and regular discharge of the duties incident to each man's particular situation, a wild desire of undefinable latitude and extravagance; an aspiration after shapeless somethings, that can neither be described nor understood, a contemptuous disgust at all that *is*, and a persuasion that nothing is as it ought to be – to operate, in short, a general discharge of every man (in his own estimation), from every thing that laws divine or human; that local customs, immemorial habits, and multiplied examples impose upon him; and to set them about doing what they like, where they like, when they like, and how they like – without reference to any Law but their own Will, or to any consideration of how others may be affected by their conduct.[19]

In pursuit of this object, *The Rovers* parodied, along with the politics and Gothicism of Schiller, the domestic mores – seen to be part of the same dangerous influence of 'the German drama' – of Goethe's *Stella* (1776) and the sentimental plays of August von Kotzebue. *Stella*, subtitled 'Ein Schauspiel für Liebende' ('A Play for Lovers'), became known as the chief example of the immorality of German domestic drama. It concerns Fernando and his relationships with his estranged wife Cezilie and his noble mistress Stella. The two women meet, become instant good friends, and on discovering their mutual interest in Fernando, agree to share him. The situation is ridiculed in *The Rovers*, where Matilda and Cecilia share their intimate secrets within minutes of meeting and a footnote draws attention to the 'genteel German comedy which ends with placing a man *bodkin* between *two wives*, like *Thames* between his *two Banks*, in the CRITIC'.[20] Of the many plays of Kotzebue which were translated and adapted for the English stage in the 1790s,[21] the Anti-Jacobins chose to satirise the dubious moral conclusions and the excessive coincidence of the plots. The last entry in the list of Dramatis Personae in *The Rovers* reads: 'Several Children; Fathers and Mothers unknown'. Here the authors might well have had in mind *Menschenhass und Reue*, adapted by Benjamin Thompson as *The Stranger* and staged successfully at Drury Lane in 1798, in which a 'reformed housekeeper', living a quiet philanthropic life after having been seduced as a young woman, meets a quiet misanthropic stranger who turns out to be her wronged husband. In the final scene their children appear as if from nowhere to complete the family reconciliation.[22]

Whether as a direct result of the Anti-Jacobin ridicule of 'German drama' or not, English interest in German dramas ceased abruptly around 1800. Periodicals like the *Monthly Review* and *Monthly Magazine* had published regular notices of translations and produc-

INTRODUCTION

tions of German plays in the 1790s, but by 1800 the reviewers were complaining of the 'trash' they had been 'obliged to swallow' in the form of more plays by Kotzebue.[23] In October 1800, after a year of increasingly unfavourable reviews of plays by Kotzebue, Schiller, and Iffland, Coleridge's translation of Schiller's *Wallenstein* was reviewed negatively in the *Monthly Review*.[24] The combination of Schiller and Coleridge, both known as 'Jacobins', was not one to be encouraged in 1800. The periodicals largely lost interest in German works, and Francis Jeffrey made the first of his many sweeping statements against German literature in a review of Goethe's 'Hermann und Dorothea', translated by Thomas Holcroft, in the *Monthly Review* in 1802. He wrote with reassuring hindsight of the temporary loss of taste in Britain: 'We have always been persuaded, in spite of many alarming appearances to the contrary, that the poetical taste of this nation was fundamentally different from that of our neighbours in Germany.' Jeffrey here picked up the two broad characteristics of German drama which the Anti-Jacobins had selected for attention, suggesting that they were representative of German literature as a whole:

['Hermann und Dorothea'] is a performance purely and characteristically German and cannot possibly be admired by those who have not a true German taste. It is proper, however, to observe that the Teutonic poetry has two characteristic qualities, and either astonishes by its boldness and sublimity, or engages by its familiarity and plainness. In the lofty way, it deals largely in suicides, adulteries, castles, and enchantments; in the other, it accomplishes its purposes by the assistance of hair dressing, post waggons, boiled mutton, and tobacco.[25]

In the matter of chastising English enthusiasts for German literature, too, Jeffrey took over from the Anti-Jacobins. In the first issue of the *Edinburgh Review*, of which he was editor, he took Southey's *Thalaba* as his subject. Introducing Southey as belonging to a 'sect' of poets who were '*dissenters* from the established systems in poetry and criticism', he thought their 'doctrines' to be undoubtedly 'of *German* origin', especially in adopting the 'simplicity and energy (*horresco referens*) of Kotzebue and Schiller'.[26] Jeffrey's unfavourable reviews of the works of all the so-called 'Lake Poets', particularly Coleridge, contributed to the latter's feeling that he was unlucky with the press, and that this had much to do with his being known for his German mania. Jeffrey went on generalising about German literature, always adopting the role of watchdog of national

9

taste and morality. In 1806 he called Lessing's drama *Nathan der Weise* (translated by William Taylor as *Nathan the Wise*) 'genuine sour kraut', more absurd even than 'the celebrated German play in the poetry of the Antijacobin'.[27] Nearly twenty years later he reviewed Carlyle's translation of *Wilhelm Meisters Lehrjahre* (*Wilhelm Meister's Apprenticeship*) in strikingly similar terms.

One of the few enthusiasts for German literature who carried on publishing translations and reviews of German works in the years after 1800, when Coleridge had been so discouraged, was Southey's friend William Taylor of Norwich. The interest of the first Anglo-Germanist (so called by George Borrow, to whom he had taught German[28]) had begun, naturally enough, with *Werther, Die Räuber*, and Kotzebue.[29] In 1791 he translated *Nathan*, in 1793 Goethe's *Iphigenie*, and in 1796 Bürger's ballad 'Lenore'. It was on Taylor's version that Walter Scott drew for his own.[30] According to Crabb Robinson Taylor encouraged his own 'growing taste for German literature', and Southey almost learned German at his friend's instigation.[31]

Taylor wrote essays on German authors from the 1790s to the 1820s, and was the first to write on Herder and Lessing. Indeed, his fortunes as a translator and reviewer of Lessing provide a good example of the unfavourable conditions for German literature in the first years of the nineteenth century. On the face of it, Lessing should have been an author to appeal to British taste. His critical works, important as throwing off German dependence on French literary theory and preparing the way for a new German theory and practice, were written with a precision, logic, and clarity of style which Taylor, and later Lewes,[32] praised as an un-German, almost British quality. Carlyle, in his survey of the 'State of German Literature' (1827), wondered why 'more of this man is not known among us'.[33] It was not for lack of trying on Taylor's part that Lessing remained largely unknown even in the 1820s. Apart from translating *Nathan*, Taylor planned in 1805 to collect his German essays for a larger work, of which essays on Lessing would form an important part:

I believe I shall now set about a 'Sketch of the Life and Writings of Lessing.' It was a project of Coleridge's, never begun I suspect. A volume of 'Lives of the German Poets' I shall one day put together, and employ my reviewals of Wieland, Klopstock, &c., as the tailpieces to the biographies. This of Lessing will be manuscript in store, or more probably will appear progressively in the Monthly Magazine.[34]

The sketch did appear in the *Monthly Magazine*, in eight articles from 1805 to 1809. The object, apart from recounting the life, was to illustrate Lessing's skill as a polemicist, that 'felicity, which persuades a reader that he (Lessing) could better have executed the work he is criticizing'.[35] Taylor here shared his appreciation of Lessing's method with Coleridge, who had planned to write a life of Lessing on his return from Germany in 1799. Coleridge 'made a point of re-perusing' Lessing's works 'as masterpieces of Style and argument', and his own essay on the freedom of the press in *The Friend* (1809 and 1818) takes its cue from Lessing's argument and method.[36]

Nathan der Weise formed part of Lessing's polemics, his long controversy with the theologian Goeze. Lessing had written eleven 'anti-Goeze' pamphlets on the question of freedom of the press in religious discussion. In order to express his views without incurring the very censorship he was arguing against he used the less obviously controversial form of the drama to carry on the argument. Knowing this, Friedrich Schlegel called *Nathan* the twelfth anti-Goeze.[37] Not knowing this, Jeffrey complained of the play's lack of dramatic qualities in his article in 1806, the only article on German literature in the *Edinburgh Review* between 1803 and 1813.[38] Jeffrey made no allowances for the clumsiness of the plot on the grounds of its primary function as a piece of argument, an argument which anyway he found unacceptable. Lessing's plea was for religious tolerance, or as Jeffrey put it 'absolute indifference, or infidelity'.[39] When Taylor came to discuss *Nathan*, he stressed the non-dramatic nature of the play, calling it 'rather a dramatic metrical romance than a play', 'evidently intended for readers, more than for hearers'.[40] Unfortunately, instead of pursuing this argument, as Lewes was to do in his article on Lessing,[41] Taylor chose to defend the play on Jeffrey's terms. He wasted his energies in a weak apology for the theme of near-incest: 'Surely that critic [Jeffrey] has little claim to moral taste, who would have a man give vent to expressions of disappointment, because he cannot climb the bed of his sister...'[42] Without a more positive evangelistic attitude, Taylor could not hope to attract or keep readers for his subject. It was to be Carlyle's strength that he adopted the right lecturing tone in his first essays on German literature. Taylor, meanwhile, even gave in privately to Jeffrey's hostility over Lessing. He made a curious remark to Southey: 'I agree with Jeffrey in most things about 'Nathan,' and am well satisfied with his reviewal.'[43]

William Taylor carried on with his articles, informative but not adventurous, on Lessing. Obviously he failed to make Lessing known, for De Quincey took up the task of 'introducing' Lessing in *Blackwood's Magazine* in 1826 as if Taylor's articles had not existed. Indeed, the articles only just kept on going. Taylor's editor and publisher, Sir Richard Phillips, wrote gloomily in 1808 of both the Lessing articles and the second edition of Taylor's translation of *Nathan* (1805): 'Lessing is not a popular subject, but it shall proceed ... 'Nathan' has done very little, and yet I have done my best for him'.[44] As for Jeffrey, Taylor had failed to make an impression on him. Referring to Lewes's article in the *Edinburgh* in 1845, he wrote to his successor as editor, Napier, that it was 'over-praised, and yet it is soberly and cleverly written. I rather think I wrote a review of Nathan the Wise some half-century ago, and have retained, I suppose, a vile prejudice against the author ever since.'[45] Taylor, like Coleridge, was thus made to feel the unfashionableness, indeed the absurdity, of his German interest. He was looked on as an eccentric bachelor who taught the young men of Norwich atheism, wine-drinking, and German.[46]

The only other regular enthusiast for German literature during the early years of the century was Crabb Robinson, who, like Taylor, belonged to the Norwich circle of intellectuals and dissenters, and who was also a friend of Wordsworth, Coleridge, and Southey. He sent articles on German subjects to the *Monthly Register* from Germany in 1802–3, where he was a student of philosophy and the confidant of Madame de Staël. The Unitarian *Monthly Repository* also published some German articles by him in 1808 and again in 1832.[47] His essays were undistinguished and failed to arouse interest. Indeed, he was most important as a friend and lender of German books to those who were more ambitious or more gifted than he. Coleridge appealed to him constantly, Carlyle sought his help when translating stories for *German Romance* (1827), Hayward, translator of *Faust* in 1833, asked him for an introduction to Eckermann,[48] and Lewes wrote to him for data for the *Life of Goethe* (1855). His large correspondence and diaries, written over a long lifetime of reading and talking about German literature, beginning simultaneously with Coleridge's discovery of Germany in the 1790s and lasting into the 1840s and 1850s when Lewes and George Eliot were beginning their careers, offer useful comments on all four authors studied here. His was a social rather than an intellectual contribution to the spread of interest in German culture, and he knew it: 'I early found that I had not the literary ability to give me such a place among English authors as I should have desired; but I thought that I had an opportunity of gaining a knowledge of many of the most distinguished men of the age, and that I might do some good by keeping a record of my interviews with them.'[49]

It was through his personal contact with leading authors in England and Germany that Crabb Robinson helped in a small way to bring about a second, more permanent, growth of interest in German literature. In 1813 he acted as legal adviser to Madame de Staël in the publication in England of her book *De L'Allemagne*.[50] A political exile from Napoleonic France, where her book was banned, Madame de Staël could be sure of a favourable reception in England.[51] Undoubtedly also, though, the time had come for a fresh look at German intellectual activities. The many reviewers of *De L'Allemagne* were now able to look back at the early rage for certain kinds of German works and see them in their cultural and political context:

Thirty years ago, there were probably in London as many Persian as German scholars.

Dramas, more remarkable for theatrical effect than for dramatic genius, exhibited scenes and characters of a paradoxical morality...These moral paradoxes, which were chiefly found among the inferior poets of Germany, appeared at the same time with the political novelties of the French Revolution, and underwent the same fate. German literature was branded as the accomplice of freethinking philosophy and revolutionary politics.[52]

Even Jeffrey, though still not willing to be influenced, realised in 1814 that German literature was again a subject of which a periodical like the *Edinburgh Review* ought to take notice. He wrote to Thomas Moore asking him to 'hunt me up a good smart German reviewer', one who 'knows that literature thoroughly, without thinking it necessary to rave about it'.[53]

More influential even than Madame de Staël's work was that of her friend and adviser, A. W. Schlegel, whose lectures *Über dramatische Kunst und Literatur* (1809–10) were translated by John Black in 1815 as *Dramatic Lectures*. Schlegel provided a fine blank verse translation, which is still widely read, of most of Shakespeare's plays from 1797 to 1810, and had been writing and lecturing on literature since he and his brother Friedrich produced their joint periodical,

Athenäum (1798–1800). The Schlegels were important as critics who responded both to the excited 'discovery' by Lessing and Herder of Shakespeare as a Promethean and Protean genius, disdainful of mere dramatic rules, and to the philosophical framework provided by Kant and Schelling for aesthetic discussion of the nature of genius and the Imagination as a receptive and productive faculty. English critics, becoming acquainted with A. W. Schlegel in translation only in 1815, found much to praise in the German's appreciation of Shakespeare. Wordsworth gave favourable mention to Schlegel's lectures in the preface to *Poems* (1815), and in his work on Shakespeare, Hazlitt agreed that Schlegel's lectures gave 'by far the best account of the plays of Shakespear that has hitherto appeared'. The only thing Hazlitt felt he could offer which Schlegel had omitted was to bring 'illustrations from particular passages of the plays themselves, of which Schlegel's work, from the extensiveness of his plan, did not admit'.[54] But Hazlitt and Wordsworth lacked a knowledge of the intellectual context in which Schlegel wrote. Only Coleridge was intimate with the complex cultural activity of which Schlegel's work was an example, and he tried to conceal his close acquaintance with Schlegel's lectures. His dishonesty in this respect is not unconnected with the lack of interest and special knowledge of such friends as Wordsworth and Hazlitt.

The last of Schlegel's lectures dealt briefly with the German drama up to the time of writing, but the work seems to have been read in England only for what it had to say about Shakespeare. Thus, though the *Dramatic Lectures*, with *De L'Allemagne*, found general appreciation in England,[55] the old prejudices against 'German drama' persisted. Hazlitt lectured on 'the German Drama' in 1819 as if nothing had appeared in the genre since *Die Räuber*.[56]

On the other hand, some new enthusiasts appeared at this time to increase the attention given by the periodical press to German literature. *Blackwood's Magazine*, begun in 1817, included from 1819 a regular series called 'Horae Germanicae', in which new German works were the subject of knowledgeable attention. Most of the works reviewed, with many translated extracts, were dramas, and most of the translating and reviewing was done by R. P. Gillies. An accurate translator, Gillies provided a useful introduction of the very latest German plays, and he soon became quite well known to his contemporaries as the Germanist of *Blackwood's*.[57] When Carlyle began work on his translation of *Wilhelm Meister* in 1824, he knew of Gillies as 'a great German Scholar', from whom he hoped to borrow books.[58] But Gillies, like William Taylor, was less able as a critic. He chose to introduce to his readers mostly second-rate works in the genre 'Schicksalsdrama' (Fate Drama), which had as its chief representatives Werner, Müllner, the early Grillparzer, Houwald, and the Danish author Oehlenschlaeger. These authors took their inspiration from Schiller's rather academic attempt to write a classical tragedy in his *Braut von Messina* (*Bride of Messina*, 1803), in which Schiller forgot the practical requirements of the theatre in his desire to carry out a theoretical experiment.[59] His less theoretical imitators adopted the familiar 'classical' themes of incest, unwitting murder, and the idea of a relentless fate regulating the lives of the characters. Werner's *Der 24. Februar* (1809) was the first and most imitated example. Inspired by the coincidence of the death of his mother and a close friend on 24 February 1804, the play concerns three generations of a family in which hasty and accidental murders take place, always on the same date. Müllner acted in this play in 1812 (appropriately in February), and three months later his 'companion piece', *Der 29. Februar*, was completed. The plot copies Werner's, but Müllner goes further, choosing a date which occurs only every four years for his births, deaths, and curses. While audiences, particularly in Vienna, enjoyed this and Müllner's other popular play, *Die Schuld* (*Guilt*, 1816, also reviewed by Gillies in *Blackwood's*), several of the more serious German periodical critics complained of their 'barbarity'.[60]

Gillies praised these plays extravagantly in his articles. His colleagues on *Blackwood's Magazine* tried to persuade him to leave them alone and attend to better examples, such as Goethe's and Schiller's mature works. J. G. Lockhart wrote to Blackwood: 'Try whether [Gillies] wd not submit to sit down composedly and translate six or seven of the best scenes of Schiller's William Tell – Carlos – or B. of Messina.'[61] Gillies's uncritical enthusiasm led to his being caricatured in *Blackwood's*. In the regular 'Noctes Ambrosianae', a series of literary conversations at 'Ambrose's', Gillies appears as Kempferhausen, a cloddish German figure who contributes little to the talk, only venturing occasionally to say something about German literature, always irrelevant and tedious and always ignored or ridiculed by the wits around the table.[62]

One of the wits was Lockhart, who also contributed occasionally on German subjects. He translated Friedrich Schlegel's lectures,

Geschichte der Alten und Neuen Literatur (*History of Ancient and Modern Literature*, 1815), for Blackwood in 1818, and in two of his best articles in the magazine he reminded readers of the forgotten Coleridge translation of the ignored *Wallenstein* and of the less undeservedly forgotten Walter Scott translation of *Götz*. In the former article he was able to set *Wallenstein* in its historical context and to explain the failure of Coleridge's translation, 'by far the best translation of a foreign tragic drama which our English literature possesses':

Mr. Coleridge's translation from Schiller appeared just when the apathy had attained that depth which was, although no one dreamed of it, the sure prelude to a burst of revivification. Had it been an English original, it might have done wonders; but we were at our darkest too proud to be kindled by a foreign torch; and the WALLENSTEIN had, like the first publication of Wordsworth's Lyrical Ballads, the fate to delight the few, and to be totally neglected by the many.[63]

'Christopher North's' boast in the 'Noctes Ambrosianae' in 1832 that German literature was 'all very well in its way, and Maga was the first periodical work in this country that did anything like justice to it', was not altogether idle.[64] Gillies became the first editor of the new *Foreign Quarterly Review* in 1827, and Lockhart encouraged an interest in German subjects when he took over the editorship of the *Quarterly Review* in 1826.

Though De Quincey had learnt German in 1803, it was not until the 1820s, in *Blackwood's* and its rival the *London Magazine*, that he too began to make known his interest. Like Crabb Robinson, he was a close observer of Coleridge's German studies; indeed he was the first of Coleridge's contemporaries to point out, in articles written soon after Coleridge's death in 1834, some of the latter's plagiarisms from German authors. His main interest was in Lessing, from whose *Laokoon* he translated extracts in *Blackwood's* in 1826, and in the romantic humorist, Jean Paul, of whom he wrote in 1821 the first important critical article in England.[65] Thomas Beddoes, the Bristol chemist and friend of Coleridge, had shown an acquaintance with Jean Paul's works in the 1790s, and William Taylor had reviewed him briefly in the *Monthly Magazine* in 1801.[66] But it was De Quincey who first translated passages from Jean Paul and enthused about his work.[67] Carlyle heard of this and De Quincey's subsequent articles on Jean Paul from Crabb Robinson, and noted that they had helped to draw his attention to the German author.[68] De Quincey wrote on Jean Paul with a sympathetic insight which made his evaluation much more perceptive than were his comments on Goethe, whose works he abhorred. The Sterne-like humour and expansiveness, the quizzical wit, the irony, and the pious sentiment of Jean Paul accorded with De Quincey's own. It was natural that De Quincey, with his 'constitutional determination to reverie' and his belief that dreams possess a potential grandeur, should be attracted by the visionary writings of Jean Paul.[69] He found Jean Paul so difficult to translate that he only managed to prepare one of several proposed 'Analects from Richter' (*London Magazine*, February 1824), and that, he complained to the editor, took him twenty-four hours to do, so slowly did he proceed.[70] Carlyle produced much more, including two of Jean Paul's stories in his *German Romance* (1827), but De Quincey's articles provided a pointer which Carlyle was to follow in his own articles.

De Quincey's interest in German literature, however, was not sustained or consistent. He was uncomprehending in his articles on Kant,[71] and wrote a stupidly angry review of Goethe's *Wilhelm Meisters Lehrjahre* in Carlyle's translation. His conclusion, that the work showed 'depraved taste and defective sensibility', was no more enlightened than Jeffrey's, who found now, as twenty years before, that the German work before him was 'eminently absurd, puerile, incongruous, vulgar, and affected'.[72] In the same year, 1825, Coleridge complained to his nephew, not without reason, that he carried no weight with publishers because of his 'German' reputation: 'The prejudices excited against me by Jeffray [sic], combining with the mistaken notion of my German Metaphysics to which (I am told) some passages in some biographical Gossip-book about Lord Byron have given fresh currency, have rendered my authority with the TRADE worse than nothing.'[73]

Thus, though many more periodicals were now paying attention to German literature than at the beginning of the century, and though authors like De Quincey, Lockhart, and Gillies wrote regularly on the subject, prejudices and misunderstandings still existed. The history of Anglo-Germanism in the 1820s is further complicated by the mixed quality of the interest in German subjects. Enthusiasts were often, as in Gillies's and sometimes in De Quincey's case, unreliable. Carlyle summed up the situation boldly in the preface to his 1824 translation of *Wilhelm Meisters Lehrjahre*:

Whether it be that the quantity of genius among ourselves and the French, and the number of works more lasting than brass produced by it, have of late been so considerable as to make us independent of additional supplies; or that, in our ancient aristocracy of intellect, we disdain to be assisted by the Germans, whom, by a species of second-sight, we have discovered, before knowing any thing about them, to be a tumid, dreaming, extravagant, insane race of mortals; certain it is, that hitherto our literary intercourse with that nation has been very slight and precarious. After a brief period of not too judicious cordiality, the acquaintance on our part was altogether dropped: nor, in the few years since we partially resumed it, have our feelings of affection or esteem been materially increased. Our translators are unfortunate in their selection or execution, or the public is tasteless and absurd in its demands; for, with scarcely more than one or two exceptions, the best works of Germany have lain neglected, or worse than neglected, and the Germans are yet utterly unknown to us. Kotzebue still lives in our minds as the representative of a nation that despises him; Schiller is chiefly known to us by the monstrous production of his boyhood; and Klopstock by a hacked and mangled image of his *Messias*, in which a beautiful poem is distorted into a theosophic rhapsody, and the brother of Virgil and Racine ranks little higher than the author of *Meditations among the Tombs*.[74]

To the old Anti-Jacobin complaints of the absurdity and immorality of German literature was now added, mostly in connection with Coleridge and what was understood to be 'German philosophy', that of obscurity and mysticism. Carlyle's great achievement was to meet these criticisms head-on in his famous polemical article for the doubting Jeffrey, 'The State of German Literature' (1827). Goethe noticed in 1828 that the *Edinburgh*, which had carried two sarcastic articles by Palgrave on his *Dichtung und Wahrheit* in 1816–17, had suddenly changed its attitude:

Wenn ich bedenke, wie die Edinburger vor noch nicht langen Jahren meine Sachen behandelt haben, und ich jetzt dagegen Carlyles Verdienste um die deutsche Literatur erwäge, so ist es auffallend, welch ein bedeutender Vorschritt zum Besseren geschehen ist.

When I think how the Edinburgh Reviewers treated my works not many years ago, and when I now consider Carlyle's merits with respect to German literature, I am struck by the significant improvement.[75]

Jeffrey, as we have seen, had been unkind about Coleridge's German interest, and reviewed Carlyle's translation of *Wilhelm Meisters*

Lehrjahre severely in the *Edinburgh*. Yet when he met Carlyle in 1827 he recognised his literary talent, and welcomed his articles for the *Edinburgh*, though still stubbornly maintaining that German literature was 'absurd' and 'vulgar'. Nevertheless, Carlyle felt grateful enough for Jeffrey's kindness to him at the beginning of his career to give him, rather incongruously, one of the medals Goethe sent him for distribution among British lovers of German literature.[76]

Like Coleridge, Carlyle first looked to the Germans for a satisfactory philosophy, one which refuted scepticism and materialism. Coleridge's writings and reputation helped to shape Carlyle's response to German philosophy, and he brought an independent defiance of public opinion (and even of his editor Jeffrey's hostility) and an affecting enthusiasm which made him a more immediate and successful populariser than Coleridge could be. Though his understanding of the German philosophers was deficient compared to Coleridge's, his authoritative championship of them in his *Edinburgh Review* essays was better able to excite his generation than were Coleridge's more accurate but more difficult and diffident writings. Through Carlyle's essays, which were soon published in American magazines,[77] Ralph Waldo Emerson, Margaret Fuller, and other Americans absorbed a 'German philosophy' which was the result of some misunderstanding and exaggeration by Carlyle, being far removed from its roots in Kant, but which bloomed in its new soil as 'Transcendentalism'. Carlyle joined with Coleridge as the chief mediator of German ideas to America as to England. Unlike Coleridge's, Carlyle's influence can be perceived directly, since so many of his readers described the effect on them of the most 'German' of English works, *Sartor Resartus* (1833–4). Hardly a young person survived the 1830s without being struck by *Sartor* and by it inspired to read – even if only in Carlyle's English translation – *Wilhelm Meister* in the light of Teufelsdröckh's praise of Goethe as the 'Wisest of our Time'. Francis Espinasse remembered

the joy with which, in a thumbed volume of *Fraser's Magazine*, he lighted on *Sartor Resartus*, and with what intensity of interest he followed the spiritual autobiography of Diogenes Teufelsdröckh – the *Pilgrim's Progress*, it seemed to him, of the nineteenth century, from doubt and despair to 'blessedness' and belief...Carlyle had in his own case reconciled reason with faith; this, above all things, it was that attracted to him those two stripplings [i.e. Espinasse and his brother]. And he had indicated that for others this consummation so devoutly to be wished was attainable through a right study of German literature.[78]

By his translations and articles, and through *Sartor*, Carlyle persuaded his readers of the value, spiritual as well as literary, of reading German literature, and Goethe in particular. As he wrote in his preface to *Wilhelm Meister*:

...of all these people [i.e. German authors] there is none that has been more unjustly dealt with than Johann Wolfgang von Goethe. For half a century the admiration, we might almost say the idol of his countrymen, to us he is still a stranger. His name, long echoed and reëchoed through Reviews and Magazines, has become familiar to our ears: but it is a sound and nothing more; it excites no definite idea in almost any mind. To such as know him by the faint and garbled version of his *Werter*, Goethe figures as a sort of poetic Heraclitus; some woe-begone hypochondriac, whose eyes are overflowing with perpetual tears, whose long life has been spent in melting into ecstasy at the sight of waterfalls, and clouds, and the moral sublime, or dissolving into hysterical wailings over hapless love-stories and the miseries of human life. They are not aware that Goethe smiles at this performance of his youth; or that the German Werter, with all his faults, is a very different person from his English namesake; that his Sorrows are in the original recorded in a tone of strength and sarcastic emphasis, of which the other offers no vestige, and intermingled with touches of powerful thought, glimpses of a philosophy deep as it is bitter, which our sagacious translator has seen proper wholly to omit. Others again, who have fallen-in with Retzsch's *Outlines* and the extracts from *Faust*, consider Goethe as a wild mystic, a dealer in demonology and osteology, who draws attention by the aid of skeletons and evil spirits, whose excellence it is to be extravagant, whose chief aim it is to do what no one but himself has tried...

Now, it must no doubt be granted, that so long as our invaluable constitution is preserved in its pristine purity, the British nation may exist in a state of comparative prosperity with very inadequate ideas of Goethe: but, at the same time, the present arrangement is an evil in its kind; slight, it is true, and easy to be borne, yet still more easy to be remedied, and which therefore ought to have been remedied ere now. Minds like Goethe's are the common property of all nations; and, for many reasons, all should have correct impressions of them.[79]

It was Goethe who was of most interest, and who was at first most mistaken in Britain during the whole period from the late eighteenth century to the later Victorian period, when Arnold modelled his idea of culture and Weltliteratur partly on Goethe's and quoted Goethe in almost every essay he wrote.[80] The reception of his works over fifty years offers the best single example of the general changes in attitude wrought by Coleridge, Carlyle, Lewes, and George Eliot. Schiller, who had died in 1805, was thought in both England and Germany to be less important than the still living and writing Goethe until the Jungdeutschland (Young Germany) movement for political reform took him as their literary hero in the mid-nineteenth century. Goethe enjoyed a long life of astonishingly varied literary activity and influence. After his death in 1832, countless works of memoirs, correspondence, and conversations were published by those who had known him, and many of these were translated into English by Sarah Austin in the 1830s. The history of changing attitudes to Goethe in Britain is largely representative of that of the whole complex response to German literature. It forms the most important theme of this book.

Carlyle was the chief cause of the new attention to Goethe in the 1820s and the following decades. Readers of *Sartor* and of Carlyle's *Wilhelm Meister* translation began with an idea of Goethe which, though preferable to the ignorant prejudice of the earlier period, was idiosyncratic. It was of an altogether rhapsodic, didactic, and mystic writer. John Sterling's 'education' through German literature is typical for his age. He first read Carlyle's articles on the Germans in the early 1830s, then met Carlyle through their mutual friend Mill, and began to read Goethe, reporting his impressions to Carlyle in 1836.[81] He praised Carlyle in an article in 1839 for having written 'almost all the just appreciation of Goethe now existing in England', but he also felt, as he wrote privately to Blackwood, that Carlyle 'mixes a good deal too much of his own potent brandy with Goethe's pure wine'.[82] As with the German philosophers, Carlyle had found Goethe often puzzling and sometimes abhorrent, yet he believed enough in his wisdom to refashion him in an image more congenial to himself and his English readers.

His response to Kant and post-Kantian philosophy and to Goethe requires to be studied in detail, for it largely dictated the notions of German literature and philosophy adopted by English and American readers of his works. There was in the decade following Carlyle's essays and *Sartor* a much increased desire to read Goethe, and a number of translators, most of whom named Carlyle as their model and were in correspondence with him, provided the English texts. Sarah Austin translated biographical memoirs of Goethe in 1833, in which she praised Carlyle, 'to whom all lovers of German literature are so deeply indebted'.[83] She also taught German to Mill. Most of those who now translated *Faust* in the 1830s – Hayward, Blackie, Syme, Anster, and Talbot – mentioned Carlyle's example as decisive. Coleridge had decided not to translate the play, and Lord Leveson Gower's version of 1823, the first, had omitted the Prologue in Heaven 'from considerations of decency', judging that its representation of God bargaining with the irreverent Mephistopheles over Faust's soul was unedifying.[84] All the new translations included it, though a residual doubt about Goethe's morality, or perhaps a prudent caution about public reaction, led Hayward to put it in an appendix and Anster to express unease in his preface.[85] But by 1840 German literature was on the whole both acceptable to British taste and accessible to those who knew no German. Carlyle, who did so much to make this so, announced in 1838 that 'readers of German have increased a hundredfold', and that Germany was no longer that 'vacant land, of grey vapour and chimaeras' which it had been in Coleridge's time twenty years before.[86] His essays and *Sartor* contributed to this progress. George Eliot spoke for herself and for her generation when she wrote in 1855:

There is hardly a superior or active mind of this generation that has not been modified by Carlyle's writings; there has hardly been an English book written for the last ten or twelve years that would not have been different if Carlyle had not lived. The character of his influence is best seen in the fact that many of the men who have the least agreement with his opinions are those to whom the reading of *Sartor Resartus* was an epoch in the history of their minds.[87]

They 'fell under the influence' of Carlyle's rhetoric at least as much as under that of Coleridge's conversation and later works.[88] In particular, they wrote on Carlyle's model their novels of 'apprenticeship', their own *Wilhelm Meisters*. Lewes's early novels, *Ranthorpe* (1847) and the unfinished 'Apprenticeship of Life' (1850), are crudely imitative of Goethe. Bulwer's *The Disowned* (1828) borrows from Goethe the young man who has to learn to be patient before his artistic genius can mature, who finds culture and self-culture in Italy, and Bulwer himself adopts a debased Goethean stance, a mixture of the prudent and the moral, towards the crowded scenes in which his hero acts and is acted upon. Froude's *Nemesis of Faith* (1849) is the most remarkable of the many novels inspired by Goethe via Carlyle. As Kingsley said of Froude, he took his 'distemper of Werterism' late,[89] displaying it feverishly in this novel of disillusion, loss of

faith, adulterous love, and irresolution. In it, Carlyle appears, with
Newman, as the chief thinker of consequence; the plot of Goethe's
Die Wahlverwandtschaften (Elective Affinities) is closely imitated: a
young man visits a married couple, there is mutual attraction between
him and the wife; the husband obligingly goes away, leaving them
together, there is an episode in a boat during which moral resolu-
tions fail, and a child is neglected and subsequently dies; remorse on
the woman's part leads her to go into a convent.[90]

Lewes learnt German and visited Germany in 1838, knowing that
the study of German literature was now almost a necessary activity
for an aspiring author and critic. And he knew, from reading
Coleridge, Carlyle, and their successors, that Germany was predominantly the land of ideas. He found what he was seeking in
Hegel – a science of literature, a systematic aesthetic. Lewes was the
first to write on Hegel, and also on Spinoza; he contributed a new
interest to the mass of Goethe literature by attending to Goethe's
achievements in botany and optics; and he wrote the first complete
Life of Goethe in any language. The pressure to condemn Goethe's
works as immoral no longer applied, thanks to Carlyle's emphasis on
Goethe's wisdom and earnestness, but Lewes changed that emphasis
towards seeing Goethe as primarily interested in art, not ethics. In
doing so, he had to contend with objections to his tolerance of the
tendency of the works and of Goethe's not so wise and earnest relationships in life. Nevertheless, a frank description of Goethe's love
affairs would have been unthinkable in 1820, where now it was
merely controversial. Critics like Sarah Austin and Richard Holt
Hutton, even if they objected to Lewes's openness about the life,
were able to assess his criticisms of the works themselves without
prejudice.

Lewes also equipped himself with a knowledge of the German philosophers, in order to write his popular *Biographical History of Philosophy* (1845–6), and though he was antagonistic to their *a priorism*,
he was able, unlike De Quincey or Hazlitt or Mill,[91] to argue with
their conclusions from direct experience of their works. Germany
was for George Eliot and Lewes almost a second home. Coleridge
had visited Germany only once, Carlyle did not go until 1852, and
neither could speak the language competently.[92] Lewes and George
Eliot travelled several times in Germany, spent their first few difficult
months together in Weimar and Berlin, and made friends with celebrated Germans.

Of course, some prejudices against 'the Germans' still existed. Now the main controversial area of German thought was its post-Hegelian higher criticism of the Biblical texts, in particular the works of Strauss and Feuerbach. George Eliot's freethinking and openness to foreign thought first found expression in her translation of Strauss's *Leben Jesu* (*Life of Jesus*) in 1846, and subsequently in her essays and novels. Like Coleridge, she was alive to what was most important in German thought and desired to help Britain assimilate and not simply ignore new ideas.[93] On Lewes's advice, she translated Spinoza's *Ethics* from Latin; no English translation of the work was available in 1854. Spinoza counts as 'German' for our purposes. Schelling's *Naturphilosophie* would be unintelligible without reference to Spinoza's pantheism; he was, as Arnold said, 'the lonely precursor of German philosophy'.[94] He was also, properly speaking, the first historical critic of the Bible. It was with the new movement in German literature and philosophy, particularly with Lessing and Goethe, that Spinoza was rescued from neglect and respected for his strength of logic and his humanity in ethics. Coleridge was attracted to Spinoza as he was to Schelling; Lewes became uncharacteristically autobiographical about Spinoza's effect on him. George Eliot translated him, and her novels indicate how closely she agreed with his determinism but also with his belief in the possibility of human choice and improvement. George Eliot gave English readers the new higher critical texts, and in more than one article she insisted that no British philosopher, historian, or theologian dared call himself an expert until he had read the German contributions to his subject. Germany was now recognised in Britain for what it had been since the 1780s, the most important European country for theory, for ideas.

The aim of this book is to study these most important interpreters of German thought without wrenching them from the cultural, social, even political conditions in which they worked. Elements as disparate as the Napoleonic Wars, opium, the Church of England, as well as his need for the approval of his non-Germanised friends, help to make up the complex conditions of Coleridge's response to German culture. With Carlyle, his Scottishness, his impatient taking up or dismissing of certain writers, his prophetic stance, and Jeffrey's opposition go towards determining both his merits and the special kind of effect he had on readers. Lewes and George Eliot absorbed German culture under less fraught conditions.

It is interesting that in George Eliot's case, as in Coleridge's (and William Taylor's and Crabb Robinson's), her acquaintance with new and important German works was made in a provincial centre. It was among her freethinking friends in Coventry that Strauss came to her notice, just as Coleridge's advanced Bristol circle of friends, including Thomas Beddoes, helped to stimulate his German interest.

In spite of false starts, like the short-lived cult of German plays around 1790, and the idiosyncracies of those mediating between Germany and Britain, there was an important continuity of interest during the period between 1800 and 1850. Coleridge exercised a power over Carlyle which the latter recognised as 'German' in its character, and Coleridge and Carlyle together influenced a genera-tion – Mill talked of his response to Coleridge, Carlyle, and Goethe as if they constituted a single cultural phenomenon.[95] Coleridge, Lewes, and George Eliot revered Spinoza; Carlyle, Lewes, and George Eliot saw Goethe as the greatest German of the age; Coleridge and George Eliot shared an interest in the higher criticism; and all of them recognised Kant's importance. All four writers translated from German, all but Coleridge wrote on German literature in the periodi-cals. Others, from William Taylor to Bulwer Lytton and beyond, translated and reviewed German works, but none so consistently or influentially as these. Their contemporaries testified again and again to their importance. It is not possible to judge their efforts for German thought without direct knowledge of the German works they read and wrote about. For this reason, detailed descriptions and assessments are given here of the most important German writers and their works in the context of their reception in Britain. As Coleridge was undoubtedly the most important interpreter of Kant, Kant's *Critiques* are discussed with reference primarily to Coleridge. Hegel appears most prominently in connection with Lewes, Strauss and Feuerbach with George Eliot. The writer of most constant, though changing, interest in Britain was Goethe, from the *Anti-Jacobin* parody of *Stella* in 1798 to the rush of *Faust* translations, Lewes's *Life*, and beyond. His works are therefore discussed in every chapter; they act as a test of prevailing attitudes on questions of art and morality. Reviewers, editors, and readers figure here as necessary elements in the discussion. If Coleridge diffused and Carlyle popular-ised German culture, their audiences require to be viewed too. Finally, one might adapt Goethe's aphorism, quoted by George Eliot more than once, that there are so many echoes for every real

1

Coleridge

Coleridge and Germany (1794–1800)

Coleridge outlined one of his many unfulfilled plans[1] for promoting
an interest in German literature in two letters to the publisher Boosey
in 1816:

I shall probably attempt to realize a Plan which I have long had in
agitation – viz – a fortnightly or monthly Letter to my literary Friends in
London and elsewhere concerning the real state and value of the German
Literature from Gellert and Klopstock to the present Year, as to all points
in which the German Literati are at all peculiarized. . .Two or three prefa-
tory Letters would give a brief but clear and discriminating History of
German Literature before Gellert, Bodmer &c – 1. from Otfried, nearly
contemporary with our Alfred, to the Minnesingers and Meister singers;
and 2. from Hans Sachs to Opitz, including the fugitive Literature,
Ballads, Songs &c: – and from Opitz to Gellert. – 3. the Theology and
Metaphysics from Luther, Melanchthon, and Ulrich von Hutten to Leibnitz and Wolf – and the interval of the popular & eclectic philosophy to
the famous controversy of Lessing with Goetz [Goeze] – which will con-
clude the preliminary information. – After these I propose to take each great
name by itself, beginning with Klopstock, & attaching a short biographical
Sketch to each. – My object is to remove the cloud of Ignorance & Prejudice which to a disgraceful and even inhospitable and ungrateful excess
overglooms the mind of the learned Public with regard to German
Literature.

It might appear presumptuous and arrogant if I should say that *I* know of
no literary man but myself fitted for the conduct of a periodical Work, the
Object of which should be to create an enlightened Taste for the genuine
productions of German Genius in Science, and the Belles Lettres; but the
arrogance would disappear on a closer view. – There may be, or rather,
there *are, many* who have a much more extensive knowledge of German
Literature than myself; but that is only one of the Requisites. It is an
indispensable Condition, that the person should be equally familiar with
the past History and the present State of the Taste and Philosophy of
Great Britain. . .Not therefore in Learning or Talent do I claim the least

superiority; but in the united knowledge of German and English Literature, without over or under valuing either.[2]

Coleridge made these claims in that spirit of defensive, even desperate, boastfulness familiar to readers of his letters and of the *Biographia Literaria*, where personal and professional grievances are aired, often but not always in footnotes.[3] The injured tone and the insistence on the special nature of his knowledge and ability are especially evident where he refers to his relationship with German culture. That relationship, particularly as it concerns his borrowings and denials of borrowings, has been celebrated by a series of prosecutors from De Quincey to Norman Fruman and another line of defenders from Hare and Sara Coleridge to modern students of Coleridge, notably Thomas McFarland.[4] Readers of Coleridge and Coleridge scholarship may well feel that more than enough has been said on the subject. It might now be helpful to drop the courtroom stance and see Coleridge's interest, in its positive and negative aspects, in terms of his relationship with his publishers, his public, and other authors of his day. That way, it might be possible to extend our critical vision and begin to assess Coleridge's place in the complex history of the reception of German literature and philosophy in England in the nineteenth century, rather than concentrate only on the minutiae of direct and indirect borrowings of 'ideas' or of verbal nuances.[5] After all, the question of influence, foreign or not, on any writer must remain indeterminable. Shelley, defending his own *Revolt of Islam* against charges of imitating Wordsworth, wrote indignantly in 1819:

It may as well be said that Lord Byron imitates Wordsworth, or that Wordsworth imitates Lord Byron, both being great poets, and deriving from the new springs of thought and feeling, which the great events of our age have exposed to view, a similar tone of sentiment, imagery, and expression. A certain similarity all the best writers of any particular age inevitably are marked with, from the spirit of that age acting on all.[6]

Of Coleridge's many attempts to acquit himself of borrowings, that in the 1816 Preface to *Christabel* strikes a similar tone. Here Coleridge is in the unusual position of forgiving another, Walter Scott, for his 'imitation' of *Christabel* in the *Lay of the Last Minstrel* (1805). He does so by means of a telling metaphor of the organic versus the mechanical:

For there is amongst us a set of critics, who seem to hold, that every possible thought and image is traditional; who have no notion that there are such things as fountains in the world, small as well as great; and who would therefore charitably derive every rill they behold flowing, from a perforation made in some other man's tank.[7]

It is not necessary to form moral judgments on Coleridge's public honesty as to his sources in order to assess his interest in German thought, his intelligence in absorbing what was new and exciting, or even his contribution towards making German philosophy, in particular, known in Britain.[8]

Henry Crabb Robinson, who was well qualified to judge, fully supported Coleridge's claims to be unique in the united knowledge of English and German literature. In 1826 he described *Aids to Reflection* accurately as 'exhibit[ing] the best adaptation of Kantian principles to English religious sentiment', and in 1829 he wrote to Goethe that Coleridge was 'the only living poet of acknowledged genius who is also a good German Scholar'.[9] Crabb Robinson, in spite of his reputation as a garrulous hanger-on of the Wordsworth circle, was an astute observer of Coleridge's German activities. Moreover, his stay in Germany as a university student all but coincided with Coleridge's own, and his German reading during the first few years of the nineteenth century matched Coleridge's closely. While Coleridge, returned from Germany, was beginning his study of Kant in 1801, Crabb Robinson was reading Kant in Jena and hearing Schelling lecture.[10] He was an early contributor on German subjects to English periodicals, and later, at least by 1811, became Coleridge's main lender of German books.[11] Though not himself an important thinker, he was able by the closeness of his interest to comment shrewdly on Coleridge, and provides useful comparisons with Coleridge in the extent and quality of that interest which they shared.

Coleridge first became acquainted with German literature in the heady days of the Pantisocracy scheme and his post-French Revolution radicalism. He read Schiller's *Die Räuber* in 1794. With its misunderstood, lonely, outlawed hero and its indictment of tyranny, parental and political, the play appealed to Coleridge. He wrote excitedly to his fellow Pantisocrat Southey of Schiller's ability to convulse the heart and make Coleridge 'tremble like an Aspen leaf', and he recorded his admiration of the 'Bard tremendous in sublimity' in his sonnet addressed to Schiller.[12] In May 1796 came his announcement to Poole that he was learning German and planning 'a proposal to Robinson, the great London Bookseller, of translating all the works [of] Schiller, which would make a portly Quarto, on the conditions that he should pay my Journey & wife's to & from Jena, a cheap German University where Schiller resides'.[13] No doubt he planned to meet the like-minded Schiller and discuss liberal politics. But it was only one of the many early schemes which were not carried out. Pantisocracy proved unpalatable to most of those involved, and attitudes towards France – Coleridge's own, Wordsworth's, Southey's, and, though Coleridge did not then know it, Schiller's – changed. In the course of a few years their support for post-Revolution France gave way to horror and uneasiness about France's intentions at home and abroad. Coleridge settled down to marriage, parenthood, and more orthodox political views. By March 1798 he had 'snapped [his] squeaking baby-trumpet of Sedition & the fragments lie scattered in the lumber-room of Penitence'.[14]

Meanwhile the attitude of British politicians and public towards libertarian literature, English and foreign, hardened. Canning, Frere, and other Tories, alarmed at 'Jacobin' enthusiasm in England and fearful of the progress of events in France, satirised the most obvious examples of enthusiastic literature. In *The Anti-Jacobin Review* (1797–8) they cleverly parodied in their play *The Rovers* the excesses, artistic as well as political, of *Die Räuber*, and in poems like 'The Friend of Humanity and the Knife-Grinder' the democratic sentiments of early poems by Southey, Wordsworth, and Coleridge.[15] Their success extended beyond stemming enthusiasm for *Die Räuber*, which had affected other young men than Coleridge: in 1820 Hazlitt recalled that 'The Robbers was the first play I ever read: and the effect it produced upon me was the greatest. It stunned me like a blow.'[16] German literature generally now lost its readers, for it seemed vaguely synonymous with 'Jacobinism' or any political and moral radicalism, and also with bad literary taste. Not only Schiller's play but also Goethe's early works, Kotzebue's hitherto popular domestic dramas, and even Bürger's British-inspired ballads lost favour by the association.[17] A glance at the subject-matter of, say, the *Monthly Review* and *Monthly Magazine* from 1790 to 1800 shows how complete the reversal was. After regular reviewing of German works early in the decade, they had almost stopped discussing them by 1800. Unfortunately for Coleridge, his fine translation of Schiller's *Wallenstein* in 1800, a work not dangerous to national safety or taste, came at the wrong time. It fell, as Coleridge recalled, 'dead-born from the Press'.[18] It was reviewed adversely in the

Monthly Review, to which Coleridge wrote denying the pejorative description of him as a 'Partizan of the German Theatre'.[19] His name, with Southey's and Wordsworth's, continued to be linked by reviewers with 'Jacobinism' and 'German literature' for a surprisingly long time after the Anti-Jacobins. Jeffrey, whom Coleridge had constantly in mind as the murderer of his reputation, dismissed Coleridge, Southey, and Wordsworth in 1802 for their 'doctrines' which Jeffrey had no hesitation in denouncing as 'of German origin'.[20] Southey, even more anxious to assert his orthodoxy than Coleridge, reviewed *The Ancient Mariner* rather treacherously in 1798, describing it as 'a Dutch attempt at German sublimity'.[21]

This generalised view of 'German literature' was widespread and lasting. Much of Thomas Love Peacock's wit in his humorous novels *Headlong Hall* (1815) and *Nightmare Abbey* (1817) is directed against 'German tragedy'.[22] Hazlitt wrote in 1820 that Goethe, Schiller, and Kotzebue were 'incorrigible Jacobins, and their school of poetry is the only real school of Radical Reform'.[23] His use of the present tense to describe the 'German drama' of more than thirty years before and his assigning the German authors to a 'school' of literature are typical of the general undiscriminating attitude towards German literature in England. Coleridge, himself so often described as a member of the infamous 'Lake School', had every reason to be annoyed at such critical insensitivity:

...the School of Rafael – what did that mean? – The Flemish School – the Venetian School – the School of Milan & c. – but now! The Southeian *School*, the Wordsworthian /&c !! – O the spirit of envy & baseness & more than all, indolence of heart & mind amounting to & manifesting itself in an impotence of *intelligent* admiration...[24]

Coleridge himself early on discerned the difference between Kotzebue's 'pantomimic Tragedies and weeping Comedies' and Schiller's and Goethe's more lasting works.[25] In 1805 he reminded himself in his notebook of the need to avoid falling into unfair generalisations about the character of German (or any other) literature:

Schiller disgusted with Kotzebueisms deserts from Shakespere. What? cannot we condemn a counterfeit, & yet remain admirers of the Original? ...And now the French Stage, is to be re-introduced / O Germany! Germany! – Why this endless Rage of Novelty! Why, this endless Looking-out of thyself? – But stop! let me not fall into the Pit, I was about to warn others of – let me not confound the discriminating character & genius of a nation with the conflux of its individuals, in *Cities & Reviews*/ Let England be ⟨Sir P Sidney,⟩ Shakespere, Spenser, Milton, Bacon, Harrington, ⟨Swift,⟩ Wordsworth, and never let the names of Darwin, Johnson, Hume, *furr* it over! – If these too must be England, let them be another England ...even so Leibnitz, Lessing, Voss, Kant, shall be *Germany* to me, let whatever Coxcombs rise up, & *shrill* it away in the Grasshopper-vale of Reviews/ and so shall Dante, Ariosto, Giordano Bruno be my Italy/ Cervantes my Spain...[26]

Unfortunately the undiscriminating and wholesale change of attitude in the press to German works had begun just as Coleridge set out for Germany in 1797. He was now a sober citizen, anxious to learn enough German to read works of philosophy and science, no longer a revolutionary keen to meet like-minded Germans like Schiller. Indeed, one of the first things he noticed in Germany was that Schiller and other German authors had also retracted their early republicanism: 'It is absolutely false that the literary Men are Democrats in Germany – Many *were*; but like me, have *published* Abjurations of the French – among which number are Klopstock, Goethe (the author of the Sorrows of Werter), Wieland, Schiller & Kotzebu [sic]'.[27] Instead of visiting Schiller in Jena or settling in Weimar – he had heard that travel and the cost of living in Weimar were expensive – his new plan was to study 'Physiology, Anatomy & Natural History' at Göttingen. He was also collecting materials for a life of Lessing, and buying books, 'chiefly metaphysics'.[28] He and Wordsworth had already taken different directions. Wordsworth and Dorothy had gone to Goslar, where they spoke English together and Wordsworth 'work[ed] hard, but not very much at the German'.[29] He wrote the Lucy poems, among others, while in Germany. Meanwhile Coleridge laboured 'at nothing else, from morning to night',[30] but German. He had come to Germany largely unprepared in the language. His tongue-tied shyness in the interview with Klopstock and Wordsworth's saving of the situation by talking in French are well known from Coleridge's own humorous account.[31] His notebook in Germany records lists of basic vocabulary rather than the detailed notes from German authors – Goethe, Herder, Schiller – which we might have expected. The trip seems to have been most valuable in giving him a thorough grounding in the language which enabled him to come to grips with the works of the philosophers, theologians, and historians of Germany. It also signalled a change in direction from the interests he had hitherto shared with Wordsworth and

Southey, for whom German literature and philosophy were of no importance.

On his return in July 1799 Coleridge still planned to make a work out of his notes on Lessing. In fact the only German business he completed was his translation of *Wallenstein* in 1800. Unfortunately for Coleridge, both his own and Schiller's names betokened 'Jacobinism', and the translation apparently lost its publisher, Longman, £250.[32] Coleridge, already seeing his contributions to *Lyrical Ballads* being omitted from Wordsworth's second edition (1800) because Wordsworth blamed them for the relative failure of the first edition, was sensitive about this second injury to his pride, his reputation, and his pocket. He replied petulantly to criticism in the *Monthly Review*, assuring its editors and readers that 'the mere circumstance of translating a manuscript play is not even evidence that I admired that one play, much less that I am a general admirer of the plays in that language'.[33] In his extreme sensitivity, he came to believe that he had not really wanted to translate *Wallenstein*, but had done so only at Longman's pressing request, indeed that he had protested to Longman about the futility of the project.[34] His touchiness was not wholly unwarranted. Henry Crabb Robinson, in Frankfurt in 1801, received a letter from his brother Thomas, giving him up-to-date news on the German interest in England:

You promise me some account of the German stage. We are acquainted with many of their Plays – Of what description are those which are the most popular in Germany? it has been said not exactly the same which have had the greatest run with us. But this rage is evidently abated, and I think I observe an opposite prejudice rising against the German drama. You speak highly of Wallenstein, I have not the means at present of turning to the review, but I have an imperfect recollection that Coleridge's translation was a good deal ridiculed by the Reviewers.[35]

Only when he heard that his translation had been publicly praised by others did Coleridge feel able to make claims for it and for the original. Thus in *The Friend* (1818) he felt encouraged to quote some lines from his translation and add a footnote:

I return my thanks to the unknown Author of Waverly, Guy Mannering, &c. for having quoted this free Translation from Schiller's best (and *therefore* most neglected) Drama with applause: and am not ashamed to avow, that I have derived a peculiar gratification, that the first men of our age have united in giving no ordinary praise to a work, which our anonymous critics were equally unanimous in abusing as below all criticism: though

33

they charitably added, that the fault was, doubtless, chiefly if not wholly, in the Translator's dullness and incapacity.[36]

He still smarted about the unkind reception his translation had had,[37] and cherished, probably also exaggerating, the praise which came reportedly from, among others, Scott, Lockhart, Tieck, and A. W. Schlegel.[38] Added to Scott's use of a passage from the translation was the favourable review of it by Lockhart in 1823.[39]

In fact, the translation is very good indeed. Although Coleridge has a tendency to expand the original, he writes in excellent blank verse, and often catches the mood and situation precisely, as in his rendering of Wallenstein's famous speech recognising that he has compromised himself and is no longer the proud, free man he was:

> Wärs möglich? Könnt ich nicht mehr, wie ich wollte?
> Nicht mehr zurück, wie mirs beliebt? Ich müsste
> Die Tat vollbringen, weil ich sie gedacht,
> Nicht die Versuchung von mir wies – das Herz
> Genährt mit diesem Traum, auf ungewisse
> Erfüllung hin die Mittel mir gespart,
> Die Wege bloss mir offen hab gehalten? –
> Beim grossen Gott des Himmels! Es war nicht
> Mein Ernst, beschlossne Sache war es nie.
> In dem Gedanken bloss gefiel ich mir;
> Die Freiheit reizte mich und das Vermögen.
> Wars unrecht, an dem Gaukelbilde mich
> Der königlichen Hoffnung zu ergötzen?
> Blieb in der Brust mir nicht der Wille frei,
> Und sah ich nicht den guten Weg zur Seite,
> Der mir die Rückkehr offen stets bewahrte?
> Wohin denn seh ich plötzlich mich geführt?
> Bahnlos liegts hinter mir, und eine Mauer
> Aus meinen eignen Werken baut sich auf,
> Die mir die Umkehr türmend hemmt!

Coleridge's version is five lines longer, but contains nothing unnecessary:

> Is't so? I *can* no longer what I *would*?
> No longer draw back at my liking? I
> Must *do* the deed, because I *thought* of it,
> And fed this heart here with a dream? Because
> I did not scowl temptation from my presence,
> Dallied with thoughts of possible fulfilment,
> Commenced no movement, left all time uncertain,
> And only kept the road, the access open?

By the great God of Heaven! It was not
My serious meaning, it was ne'er resolve.
I but amus'd myself with thinking of it.
The free-will tempted me, the power to do
Or not to do it. – Was it criminal
To make the fancy minister to hope,
To fill the air with pretty toys of air,
And clutch fantastic sceptres moving t'ward me?
Was not the will kept free? Beheld I not
The road of duty close behind me – but
One little step, and once more I was in it!
Where am I? Whither have I been transported?
No road, no track behind me, but a wall,
Impenetrable, insurmountable,
Rises obedient to the spells I mutter'd
And meant not – my own doings tower behind me.[40]

The welcome publicity from Scott and Lockhart sparked off a new interest in *Wallenstein* in Coleridge's translation. The work was included in the 1828 collection of his poems, and it became customary for translators of German works to defer to Coleridge's as a model translation, one which got the balance between free and literal translation exactly right.[41] It may be seen from this and other instances in Coleridge's relations with German culture that no assessment can be correct which does not take into account the circumstances, financial and psychological, under which Coleridge made his statements or hid his sources. The particular audience he addressed – correspondent, friend, himself in a notebook or marginal comment, publisher, or fickle public – in each case played a part in deciding his tone and attitude towards his subject matter.

In the case of Schiller, Coleridge undoubtedly went on reading him with pleasure and profit after 1800. There is evidence that he read at least some of Schiller's important essays in aesthetics, written in the 1780s and 1790s.[42] Indeed some of his conclusions about literature and philosophy were similar to Schiller's, a fact that is hardly surprising when both read Kant's three Critiques with care, both declared that Kant had been the greatest influence on their approach to metaphysics, and both built up a theory of literature on the basis of the new philosophy. Without suggesting that Coleridge borrowed from Schiller, an assumption for which there is no basis in Coleridge's writings, it might be instructive to bear in mind Schiller's response to Kant when considering Coleridge's, similar in many respects.

Coleridge and Kant (1801–25)

Coleridge and Schiller responded immediately to their reading of Kant, and for both the study of his philosophy stretched over several years. In February 1793 Schiller wrote to his friend Körner:

Es ist gewiss von keinem Sterblichen Menschen kein grösseres Wort noch gesprochen worden, als dieses Kantische, was zugleich der *Innhalt* seiner ganzen Philosophie ist: Bestimme Dich aus Dir selbst: So wie das in der theoretischen Philosophie: Die Natur steht unter dem Verstandesgesetze. Diese grosse Idee der Selbstbestimmung strahlt uns aus gewissen Erscheinungen der Natur zurük, und diese nennen wir Schönheit.

Certainly no mortal man has ever spoken a greater word than this Kantian one, which represents the content of his whole philosophy: Determine yourself out of yourself. So also the word in his theoretical philosophy: Nature is subject to the law of the understanding. This great idea of self-determination appears to us again in certain phenomena of Nature, and this we call Beauty.[43]

Coleridge told Robinson in 1812 that he had learnt more from Kant than from any other philosopher:

To Kant his obligations are infinite, not so much from what Kant has taught him in the form of doctrine as from the discipline Kant has taught him to go through.[44]

In *Biographia*, Coleridge pays tribute to Kant's influence on him, again stressing that it was Kant's method which most instructed him, 'invigorat[ing] and disciplin[ing]' his understanding.[45]

It was precisely this method, assigning to itself a new and special meaning of 'critical', that was most misunderstood by those in England who attempted to keep up with the new philosophy from Germany. Coleridge, probably alone among his contemporaries, resisted falling into one of two opposite errors about Kant's epistemology – assuming him to be a sceptic (more or less like Hume) clearing a path to atheism, or taking him to be a dogmatic rationalist upholding the doctrine of innate ideas and holding no brief for the life of the senses in experience. De Quincey provides an example of the former error. In one of his many articles on Kant, an autobiographical essay of 1836, he tells us that he learnt German in Oxford in 1805 and undertook a study of Kant, but quickly found his to be a 'philosophy of destruction', in effect atheistic.[46] We find the second mistake more frequently, for example in Henry Crabb Robinson, who was dipping into Kant in Frankfurt early in 1801, exactly when Coleridge began his serious study of the philosopher. Robinson wrote to his brother Thomas in January 1801, 'of Kant I dare say you would be glad to know something'. He then gave a loose 'résumé' of the important ideas in the *Critique of Pure Reason*, attributing to Kant a belief in 'the existence of Innate Ideas' and calling his system 'mystical in its fundamental Principles'.[47] William Drummond, in his survey of philosophy from Plato to the present day (1805), included Kant, whom he knew only in a French version (by Villers) and a Latin translation. He, too, assumed Kant to be a mystic, 'contemplat[ing] the laws of nature *in visions of pure reason*'.[48]

The contradictory labels both stuck. By 1820 'Kantism' was on all sides an object of scorn. Peacock ridiculed 'the sublime Kant' at every opportunity in his satirical novels, and Hazlitt accused 'the great German oracle' of 'wilful and monstrous absurdity'. The former seems to have objected most to the 'mental chaos' and 'mystical jargon' of 'transcendental philosophy', but it is clear that Kant is little more than a name to Peacock, whose real target is Coleridge ('Mr Flosky'), particularly in his capacity as thinker and reader of German philosophy.[49] As for Hazlitt, his chief complaint is that Kant's system is 'an enormous heap of dogmatical and hardened assertions, advanced in contradiction to all former systems'.[50] Certainly Kant did advance his system in contradiction to all previous ones, but Hazlitt's description ignores Kant's attempt, by means of the 'Copernican Revolution' of proving the existence of objects by analysis of the subject,[51] to avoid the pitfalls of dogmatism on the one hand and scepticism on the other. Kant, far from wilfully ignoring the methods of these two traditional approaches, carefully points out their limitations and then uses them as stepping-stones to his own 'critical' method. The Dogmatist is 'unkritisch', never questioning the limits of possible knowledge, and is thus unarmed against the attacks of the Sceptic, his 'Zuchtmeister' (task master). The sceptical system, particularly of Hume, is useful for correcting dogmatism but it cannot, by its denial of causality, include universal and necessary principles. It is Kant's own method, the 'critical' one, which alone can go beyond scepticism and demonstrate from principles the limits of our knowledge:

Der erste Schritt in Sachen der reinen Vernunft, der das Kindesalter derselben auszeichnet, ist dogmatisch. Der eben genannte zweite Schritt ist skeptisch, und zeugt von Vorsichtigkeit der durch Erfahrung gewitzigten Urteilskraft. Nun ist aber noch ein dritter Schritt nötig, der nur der gereiften und männlichen Urteilskraft zukommt, welche feste und ihrer Allgemeinheit nach bëwahrte Maximen zum Grunde hat; nämlich, nicht die Facta der Vernunft, sondern die Vernunft selbst, nach ihrem ganzen Vermögen und Tauglichkeit zu reinen Erkenntnissen a priori, der Schätzung zu unterwerfen; welches nicht die Zensur, sondern Kritik der Vernunft ist, wodurch nicht bloss Schranken, sondern die bestimmten Grenzen derselben, nicht bloss Unwissenheit an einem oder anderen Teil, sondern in Ansehung aller möglichen Fragen von einer gewissen Art, und zwar nicht etwa nur vermutet, sondern aus Prinzipien bewiesen wird.

The first step in matters of pure Reason, its childhood, is dogmatic. The second step is sceptical, and shows our judgment has been made more cautious by experience. But now a third step is necessary, which is possible only to the mature judgment, and which is based on proved principles of universality. Namely, to examine not the facts of Reason but Reason itself, in all its power and aptitude for pure a priori modes of knowledge. This is not the censorship but the criticism of Reason, by means of which not just its limits but its determined limits, not just its ignorance of this or that but its ignorance with regard to all possible questions of a certain kind, are not simply supposed but are proved from principles.[52]

Thus Kant believed, with Locke, Hume, and the empiricists, that knowledge *begins* with experience, but found himself in company with Descartes, Leibnitz, and the rationalists, that knowledge can never *arise* out of experience.[53] He adopted a middle course by means of our 'transcendental' mode of knowledge, by synthetic *a priori* judgments. That is, we have the materials of knowledge in objects which we intuit with our senses, but in order to *think* them we apply categories of the understanding which are *a priori*, independent of sense experience.[54] The new terminology caused problems. It is easy to see that the common confusion between 'transcendental' (of our application of *a priori* categories of the understanding to experience) and 'transcendent' (beyond experience and for Kant explicitly illegitimate in the field of knowledge) led to the view of Kant as an idealist, a mystic who floated in realms of pure idea, scorning all basis in experience.[55] This kind of misunderstanding could only be avoided by a proper registering of the term 'Critique'. The very title of Kant's first *Kritik* indicated that he was, by means of criticism, denying to Pure Reason any validity in our speculative knowledge. For Kant the very proof of the impossibility of our knowing theoretically such transcendent concepts as God, free will, and immortality makes way for a proof of our practical (i.e. ethical) knowledge of them.[56]

Kant himself felt it necessary to spell out his position more explicitly to those who had misunderstood the *Kritik* on its first appearance in 1781. In his preface to the second edition of 1787 he claimed that only the critical method could avoid the extremes of idealism and scepticism:

Durch diese [die Kritik] kann nun allein dem Materialism, Fatalism, Atheism, dem freigeisterischen Unglauben, der Schwärmerei und Aberglauben, die allgemein schädlich werden können, zuletzt auch dem Idealism und Skeptizism, die mehr den Schulen gefährlich sind, und schwerlich ins Publikum übergehen können, selbst die Wurzel abgeschnitten werden.

Only by means of criticism can we cut off at the roots materialism, fatalism, atheism, freethinking unbelief, fanaticism and superstition, which may be a general danger, and also idealism and scepticism, which are more dangerous to the schools than to the general public.[57]

Mistakes like De Quincey's about Kant's 'scepticism' arose out of viewing the *Kritik der reinen Vernunft* as if it were a moral and philosophical system in itself, instead of being an epistemological investigation – clearing the ground of past systems and getting out of the blind alleys into which they had led – of the limits of possible knowledge. There is nothing 'destructive' or 'atheistic'[58] about the *Kritik der praktischen Vernunft* which followed in 1788, showing that we can know, though not by pure speculative reason, the existence of God and immortality by means of our experience of moral duty.[59]

Coleridge followed Kant right through the Critiques, and where he dissented, he generally did so from a dislike, not a misunderstanding, of Kant's conclusions.[60] His most explicit public statement on Kant came in his 'Philosophical Lectures' in 1819. There he undertook to explain that what he knew was too commonly taken to be Kant's 'scepticism' was really 'a modest humility with regard to the powers of the intellect'. Kant's great achievement for philosophy was 'that he examined the faculties critically before he hazarded any opinions concerning the positions which such faculties had led men to establish'. Having prepared the theoretical ground, Kant carried his conclusions into ethics:

...for while he admitted that there was a power in the reason of producing ideas to which there were no actual correspondents in outward nature, and

39

therefore they were only to be regarded as regulative, he was then asked or rather he asked himself, what would become of the ideas of God, of the free will, of immortality? For these too were the offspring of the reason, and these, too, it would be said, were merely regulative forms to which no outward or real correspondent could be expected. Here, then, he disclosed what I may call the proof of his Christianity, which rendered him truly deserving the name philosopher – and not the analysis of the mind. He says, 'In my [Critique of the Pure Reason we have not entered] into the whole human being. There is yet another, and not only another but a far higher and nobler constituent of his being, his will, the practical reason, and this does not announce itself by arguing but by direct command and precept: thou shalt do to others as thou wouldst be done by: thou shalt act so that there shall be no contradiction in thy being.' And from this he deduced a direct moral necessity for the belief, or the faith of reason; and having first shewn that though the reason could bring nothing positively coercive in proof of religious truths, which if it could it would cease to be religion and become mathematical, yet he demonstrated nothing could be said with reason against them; and that on the other hand there was all the analogy, all the harmony of nature, all moral interests, and last of all there was a positive command which, if he disobeys, he is at once a traitor to his nature – nay, even to his common nature.[61]

Two years earlier, in *Biographia*, Coleridge used Kant and his method to refute Locke's empiricism and in particular Hartley's necessitarianism, which he had once adopted enthusiastically. In fact *Biographia* was Coleridge's equivalent effort to Wordsworth's *Prelude* in detailing the growth of the author's mind up to the point at which he was able (in *Biographia* itself) to record that growth in preparation for a future speculative work.[62] He reflectively rehearses step by step in the early chapters his progress since the turn of the century from Hartleianism via Kant and Schelling to his present position as 'transcendental philosopher'.[63] In Chapters 7 and 9 he reconstructs his questioning of eighteenth-century philosophy and his triumph over empiricism in terms of 'necessary conditions' of knowledge and synthetic *a priori* judgments, not so named by Coleridge but obviously culled from Kant's *Kritik der reinen Vernunft*:

After I had successively studied in the schools of Locke, Berkeley, Leibnitz and Hartley, and could find in neither of them an abiding place for my reason, I began to ask myself; is a system of philosophy, as different from mere history and historic classification, possible? If possible, what are its necessary conditions? I was for a while disposed to answer the first question in the negative, and to admit that the sole practicable employment for the human mind was to observe, to collect, and to classify. But I soon felt, that human nature itself fought up against this wilful resignation of intellect; and as soon did I find, that the scheme taken with all its consequences and cleared of all inconsistencies was not less impracticable than contra-natural. . .How can we make bricks without straw? Or build without cement? We learn all things indeed by *occasion* of experience; but the very facts so learnt force us inward on the antecedents, that must be presupposed in order to render experience itself possible.

Here is Kant's transcendental mode of knowledge. Twice in *Biographia* Coleridge gives it a fine illustration, unfortunately without naming Kant:

This phrase, *a priori*, is in common, most grossly misunderstood, and an absurdity burthened on it, which it does not deserve! By knowledge, *a priori*, we do not mean, that we can know anything previously to experience, which would be a contradiction in terms; but that having once known it by occasion of experience (that is, something acting upon us from without), we then know, that it must have pre-existed, or the experience itself would have been impossible. By experience only I know, that I have eyes; but then my reason convinces me, that I must have had eyes in order to the experience.[64]

These are the most positive contributions to a proper introduction of Kant to English readers and audiences which we have in the early nineteenth century, Coleridge's unsatisfactory camouflage notwithstanding. We need only compare Coleridge's grasp of Kant's doctrine with that of others who wrote about Kant for the instruction of the reading public – like De Quincey. De Quincey wickedly undermined Coleridge's contribution, both during and after the latter's lifetime. The spate of essays on or including Coleridge which began in *Tait's Magazine* in 1834 are themselves interesting psychological documents. In them, as in the two versions of the *Confessions of an English Opium-Eater* (1821 and 1856), De Quincey seemed mesmerised by Coleridge. He devoted perhaps more attention to Coleridge in his writings than to any other subject, always claimed to be his greatest admirer, yet invariably began some verbal skirmishing about opium, conversation (i.e. Coleridge's monologues), and Kant. In an article on Kant in the *London Magazine* in 1823 he blustered: '. . .so far from assisting Kant's progress in this country, Mr. Coleridge must have retarded it by expounding the oracle in words of more Delphic obscurity than the German original could have presented to the immaturest student'.[65] Yet, despite this belligerence, and his plea in an earlier article that Coleridge 'leave transcendentalism to me and other young men: for, to say the truth, it does not prosper in his hands',[66] he carefully avoided attempting to 'expound the oracle' himself. His own way of distinguishing between the key words 'transcendent' and 'transcendental' leaves his readers no wiser: 'Let this be A, and that be D: let this notion be called *transcendent*, and that be called *transcendental*.'[67] We have seen that he assumed, on mistaken grounds, that Kant denied the existence of God, where in fact he merely denied the possibility of proving it by speculative reason. De Quincey might well have taken issue with Kant's *method* of proving it in the second *Kritik*. He could have argued, as both Coleridge and Schiller did, that Kant's God was impersonal and his concept of duty too rigorous, leaving no room for natural affections, love, and charity.[68] But he remained vague and ill-informed about Kant.

Carlyle, who fell victim to an equally erroneous conclusion (though of the opposite kind from De Quincey), namely finding Kant an antidote to atheism and materialism, an idealist who 'annihilated' Time and Space,[69] also complained of Coleridge. In his *Life of Schiller* (1825) he appealed for help from Coleridge on Kant. His request was for a translation or exposition of Kant. 'Are our hopes from Mr. Coleridge always to be fruitless?' he asked. 'Sneers at the commonsense philosophy of the Scotch are of little use: it is a poor philosophy, perhaps, but not so poor as none at all, which seems to be the state of matters here at present.'[70] This may seem strange, since *Aids to Reflection* was published in 1825, and *Biographia*, *Lay Sermons*, and *The Friend* had long been available. De Quincey and Carlyle, two of the more interested observers of German culture, behaved as though Coleridge had done nothing to promote or diffuse that culture. The fault is, of course, largely Coleridge's for obscuring his sources. Yet Coleridge must receive credit for being the only thinker actively engaged in studying and in some sort introducing and explaining the Kantian philosophy in England at the time.

To be able to suggest why Coleridge, though giving Kant honourable mention in scattered places in *Biographia* and elsewhere as the 'illustrious' and 'venerable Sage of Königsberg',[71] did not give him explicit or adequate credit for his discoveries, we have to retrace Coleridge's dealings with Kant back to the beginning of the century. Although Coleridge mentioned plans to study 'the great german Metaphysician' as early as 1796, and noticed in Germany that all around him were Kantians,[72] it is likely that he only began to read Kant at first hand early in 1801 (in any case, his German would not have been advanced enough before or even during most of his trip[73]). His first notes, as we might expect from our backward glimpse from *Biographia*, concerned the overcoming of empiricism by showing that 'to *think* of a thing is different from to *perceive it*, as "to walk" is from "to feel the ground under you"', being 'a succession of perceptions accompanied by a sense of *nisus* & purpose'.[74] Coleridge wrote to Poole in February 1801 that he was reading Leibnitz and Kant and becoming a 'purus putus Metaphysicus'.[75] Next came his celebrated four 'philosophical' letters to Josiah Wedgwood, with copies to Poole, in which he stated (exaggeratedly) that Locke, far from being the innovator he had been thought to be, had owed much to the rationalist method of Descartes.[76] On the face of it, these letters have little directly to do with his concurrent study of Kant. But they were followed by an excited letter to Poole in March, declaring:

If I do not greatly delude myself, I have not only completely extricated the notions of Time, and Space; but have overthrown the doctrine of Association, as taught by Hartley, and with it all the irreligious metaphysics of modern Infidels – especially, the doctrine of Necessity.

Here Coleridge disingenuously claimed the discovery as his own, but several sentences further on he made an oblique reference to Kant, leaving his correspondent to infer if he would the connection between Coleridge's new position and the Kantian philosophy he had admitted to studying a month before:

I shall propose to Longman to accept. . .a work on the originality & merits of Locke, Hobbes, & Hume/ which work I mean as a *Pioneer* to my greater work, and as exhibiting a proof that I have not formed opinions without an attentive Perusal of the works of my Predecessors from Aristotle to Kant.[77]

We cannot doubt that Kant was the chief source of Coleridge's freedom from his 'imprisonment' in necessitarianism, according to which all knowledge springs from sense experience ('the soul is present only to be pinched or *stroked*'[78]) and the mind is a mere register of external impressions. The reference to Time and Space points, I think, to Kant's difficult discussion of them early on in the *Kritik der reinen Vernunft*. He calls them forms of intuition which are applied, like the other categories of the understanding, by the mind in perception, rather than adhering in the objects of experience themselves.[79] Thus time and space do not tyrannise over man in his spiritual aspect; neither are they, on the other hand, mere illusions, invalidating the experience of the senses. Here, as all through the *Kritik*, Kant was steering a course between atheistic empiricism and enthusiastic idealism. He did so largely by means of a thorough-going dualism, by which each object is to be understood as having a twofold nature – as phenomenon (given to us in experience and thought by the categories of the understanding, such as quality, quantity, and relation) and noumenon (the transcendent thing-in-itself, unknown and unknowable by us).[80] Man as phenomenon is subject to the laws of nature applying to all phenomena, but he also has a supra-sensuous nature, by which he 'knows', not speculatively, as a constitutive idea, but ethically, by a moral imperative which is a regulative idea, freedom of will, the existence of God, and immortality:

[Die Vernunft] gibt...auch Gesetze, welche Imperativen, d.i. objektive Gesetze der Freiheit sind, und welche sagen, was geschehen soll, ob es gleich vielleicht nie geschieht, und sich darin von Naturgesetzen, die nur von dem handeln, was geschieht, unterscheiden, weshalb sie auch praktische Gesetze genannt werden.

[Reason] also gives laws, which are imperatives, i.e. objective laws of freedom, which say what should happen, even if perhaps it never does happen, and in this respect they differ from laws of nature, which only deal with what does happen. For this reason they are called practical laws.[81]

Why does Coleridge in his letters to Poole avoid direct acknowledgment of Kant? Why are there so few references to Kant in his letters from 1801 to 1803, when we know from the notebooks that he was working on Kant then? There is no certain or single explanation. Part of the reason must lie in Coleridge's isolation in both his knowledge of and his warmth towards Kant in the early years of the century. He was sensitive about his unhappy reputation as a 'partizan of the German theatre'; there was widespread ignorance and scorn of Kant in England. Even Josiah Wedgwood, the recipient of Coleridge's metaphysical letters, was unresponsive to Coleridge's philosophical studies.[82] He certainly had no encouragement to broadcast his interest in the 'unintelligible' Kant. As G. H. Lewes wrote in 1866:

Indignation, scorn, and ridicule are poured forth with all the greater freedom because usually unhampered by any first-hand knowledge. It is with [Comte] as it used to be with Kant, who not many years ago was a standing butt: many who had never opened the "Kritik," and more who would have understood nothing if they had read it, laughed at the "dreamer" and his "transcendental nonsense," without any misgivings that they were making themselves ridiculous in the eyes of those who knew something about Kant.[83]

When Coleridge came to record in *Biographia* his progressive philosophical education, he was more, not less, embittered after successive failures to gain a creditable reputation or make a financial success of his publishing ventures. German literature and particularly philosophy still commanded little general interest. Coleridge's hiding his sources for long passages in *Biographia* (especially Schelling's direct contributions to Chapter 12) in footnotes or general commendations placed just far enough away from the text itself not to be connected by the reader forms a part both of Coleridge's own personal psychological history and of the history of the reception of German culture in England.

While Kant was extremely important for Coleridge's development as a thinker, there were aspects of his philosophy which repelled him. Already in 1803 Coleridge began to distinguish certain points in which he could not agree with Kant.[84] Throughout his life, with all its re-readings of Kant (ca. 1809, 1817–18, and again in the mid 1820s), his quarrel was with Kant's 'stoic' legalism in his system of morality. In his notebook in December 1803 he noted Kant's insistence on obedience to the moral law for the sake of the law, and added a qualification of his own, 'it must not only be our Guide, but likewise our Impulse':

Does even the sense of Duty rest satisfied with mere *Actions*, in the vulgar sense, does it not demand, & therefore may produce, Sympathy itself as an Action/? – This I think very important/ – Nay, it is proved by Scripture / & Kant therefore, p. 13 Metap. der Sitten, very unfairly explains away the word Love into Beneficence.[85]

In later years he often returned to question the ethics of doing our duty solely because it is our duty, and of Kant's rigid separation in the *Kritik der praktischen Vernunft* of inclination and duty, where he assumed them to be necessarily hostile.[86] In *Aids to Reflection* he located the difference between Stoicism and Christianity in terms

45

which, though applied here to the Greeks, suggest that he had Kant in mind also:

Of the sects of ancient philosophy the Stoic is, perhaps, the nearest to Christianity. Yet even to this sect Christianity is fundamentally opposite. For the Stoic attaches the highest honour (or rather, attaches honour solely) to the person that acts virtuously in spite of his feelings, or who has raised himself above the conflict by their extinction; while Christianity instructs us to place small reliance on a virtue that does not begin by bringing the feelings to a conformity with the commands of the conscience. Its especial aim, its characteristic operation, is to moralize the affections.[87]

In one respect it is not surprising that Coleridge exasperated De Quincey and Carlyle. It would have been difficult enough for them if he had rested content to expound Kant's views as if they were his own. This he often did, but he was as often guilty of a contradictory tendency – to offer as 'Kantian' concepts which had undergone a major change by means of his own response to, and criticism of, Kant.[88] We may sympathise with Carlyle in his memory of a visit to Highgate in 1824: '[I] tried hard to get something about *Kant* and Co. from him, about 'reason' versus 'understanding' and the like, but in vain. Nothing came from him that was of use to me that day, or in fact any day'.[89] Carlyle had not read enough of the *Kritik der reinen Vernunft* to have grasped the significance of 'Vernunft' and 'Verstand'. His confusion was doubtless heightened by the fact that Coleridge meant something different by *his* 'reason' and 'understanding'. In his study of Kant he objected to the important cognitive function assigned to 'Verstand' (the faculty by which we think concepts and the only one by which we have valid knowledge of phenomena) and Kant's insistence that 'Vernunft' can give us no knowledge in the realm of speculation, that the 'Ideas' of reason merely operate regulatively in the moral sphere, but have no constitutive function in our knowledge. Coleridge tended to keep reason as the faculty of ideas that are constitutive, having epistemological validity. As early as 1806 he answered Thomas Clarkson's question about the difference between the two faculties in vocabulary which owes a great deal to Kant, is attributed by Coleridge to 'the Ancients'[90] (though he uses Kant's German terms 'Vernunft' and 'Verstand'), and is really a modification of his own:

I would reply, that that Faculty of the Soul which apprehends and retains the mere notices of Experience, as for instance that such an object has a triangular figure, that it is of such or such magnitude, and of such and such a color, and consistency, with the anticipation of meeting the same under the same circumstances, in other words, all the mere φαινόμενα of our nature, we may call the Understanding. But all such notices, as are characterized by UNIVERSALITY and NECESSITY, as that every Triangle *must* in all places and at all times have it's two sides greater than it's third – and which are evidently not the effect of any Experience, but the condition of all Experience, & that indeed without which Experience itself would be inconceivable, we may call Reason – and this class of knowledge was called by the Ancients Νοούμενα in distinction from the former, or φαινόμενα.[91]

'Mere' phenomena are all that we can know, according to Kant. Coleridge uses Kant's valuable *a priori* conditions of experience, but assigns them to Reason, where for Kant the Understanding applies such conditions to the phenomena which are the only source of our knowledge. The terms are difficult, both in Kant and in Coleridge, and the latter does not always use them in the one sense only. Yet on the whole, and increasingly as he pressed metaphysics into the service of religion,[92] Coleridge depreciated the Understanding to a more mechanical intellectual faculty and adopted an idealist view of Reason. Thus the confessed aim of *Aids* is:

...to substantiate and set forth at large the momentous distinction between Reason and Understanding. Whatever is achievable by the Understanding for the purposes of worldly interest, private or public, has in the present age been pursued with an activity and a success beyond all former experience, and to an extent which equally demands my admiration and excites my wonder. But likewise it is, and long has been, my conviction, that in no age since the first dawning of Science and Philosophy in this island have the truths, interests, and studies that especially belong to the Reason, contemplative or practical, sunk into such utter neglect, not to say contempt, as during the last century. It is therefore one main object of this volume to establish the position, that whoever transfers to the Understanding the primacy due to the Reason, loses the one and spoils the other.[93]

Here is a debasing of Kant's carefully built-up system which was probably the source of much of the nineteenth century's ideas of Kant. For instance, Carlyle's refutation of the eighteenth-century mentality – its empiricism, materialism, and its nineteenth-century heir Utilitarianism – followed on from Coleridge's Reason and Understanding, owing less to Kant's than Carlyle thought.[94] James Marsh republished *Aids* in America in 1829, where it greatly influenced theologians and other thinkers.[95] American 'Transcendentalism', so much more idealist in tendency than Kant's, arose in response to the joint 'German' influence of Coleridge and Carlyle. Mill's intelligent but generalising definition of the 'Germano-Coleridgean doctrine' in its revolt against eighteenth-century philosophy also gives evidence of this transference:

[Coleridge] distinguishes in the human intellect two faculties, which, in the technical language common to him with the Germans, he calls Understanding and Reason. The former faculty judges of phenomena, or the appearances of things, and forms generalizations from these: to the latter it belongs, by direct intuition, to perceive things, and recognize truths, not cognizable by our senses.[96]

Coleridge certainly became more and more impatient both of Kant's limitation of Reason and of his impersonal ethics.[97] As for the 'critique' of Reason, Coleridge became increasingly disenchanted with what had at first seemed an exciting release from empiricism. There is an angry entry in a late notebook (probably 1823) which classifies Kant's system as 'Philokrisy', 'the preponderative inquisition of the Weights & Measures of the human Mind'.[98] In 1832 'Reason is *subjective* Revelation, Revelation *objective* Reason. . .If I lose my faith in *Reason*, as the perpetual revelation, I lose my faith altogether.'[99] Coleridge absorbed Kant's doctrines, rejecting those parts which were incompatible with his religious needs. But he did so largely by using the Kantian method of criticism, defining the categories of the mind and assigning functions to them.[100] And whatever his mistakes of commission or, more often, omission with regard to Kant, he was alone in his time in the dimensions of his knowledge of Kant and the quality of his interest in him.

Coleridge and German 'aesthetics' (1802–18)

In 1821 Coleridge sent a set of half-facetious metaphysical letters to *Blackwood's Magazine*. He took as his topic the subject–object relationship, which he discussed in a series of 'scholia' which were, on his own admission, obscure.[101] In the course of these letters he volunteered a description of *Blackwood's* as 'a Philosophical, Philological, and Aesthetic Miscellany'. Deeming the third adjective to need explaining, he added a footnote:

I wish I could find a more familiar word than aesthetic, for works of taste and criticism. It is, however, in all respects better, and of more reputable origin, than belletristic. To be sure, there is *tasty*; but that has been long

ago emasculated for all unworthy uses by milliners, tailors, and the andro-
gynous correlatives of both, formerly called *its*, and now yclept dandies. As
our language, therefore, contains no other *useable* adjective, to express
that coincidence of form, feeling, and intellect, that something, which, confirming the inner and the outward senses, becomes a new sense in itself, to
be tried by laws of its own, and acknowledging the laws of the understanding so far only as not to contradict them; that faculty which, when
possessed in a high degree, the Greeks termed φιλοκαλία, but when spoken
of generally, or in kind only, τὸ αἰσθητικόν; and for which even our sub-
stantive, Taste, is a – not inappropriate – but very inadequate metaphor;
there is reason to hope, that the term *aesthetic*, will be brought into common use as soon as distinct thoughts and definite expressions shall once
more become the requisite accomplishment of a gentleman.[102]

The term was already a commonplace in German criticism and
philosophy, as meaning the criticism of taste considered as a
science.[103] It was important for Coleridge to include the creation
and study of literature in his thorough-going scrutiny of the faculties,
just as Kant had followed his critiques of the mental and moral
faculties with a third Critique, that of 'Judgment', the faculty of
'purposiveness' in nature and of 'purposeless purposiveness' in
art.[104] Without doubt this is the most obscure of Kant's three
Critiques, dubious in its attempt to place Judgment as an inter-
mediate faculty between Understanding and Reason, one which
'thinks the particular as contained in the universal'.[105] As one
nineteenth-century commentator observed, Kant almost dissolved
his realistic dualism into an idealistic monism by asserting a faculty
which mediates between the theoretical consciousness (the realm of
Understanding) and the practical (the realm of Reason).[106] In art
this mediation occurs through the 'free purposive play' of the
Imagination, which follows nature but is free from the constraints of
the mechanical law governing nature.[107] This deduction, though
looked on askance for its sophistry by Goethe,[108] was enormously
influential on Schiller's aesthetic essays of the 1790s. Coleridge, too,
warmed to this application of principles to the 'sensuous' activity of
poetry. As early as 1802 he wrote to Sotheby about his desire that
poetry should combine the life of the spirit (which corresponds to
Kant's unconditioned spirit in the *Kritik der praktischen Vernunft*)
with that of nature (the conditioned world of Kant's first *Kritik*):

Nature has her proper interest; & he will know what it is, who believes &
feels, that every Thing has a Life of it's own, & that we are all *one Life*. A
Poet's *Heart* & *Intellect* should be *combined, intimately* combined &

unified, with the great appearances in Nature...It must occur to every Reader that the Greeks in their religious poems address always the Numina Loci, the Genii, the Dryads, the Naiads, &c &c – All natural Objects were *dead* – mere hollow Statues – but there was a Godkin or Goddessling *included* in each – In the Hebrew Poetry you find nothing of this poor Stuff – as poor in genuine Imagination, as it is mean in Intellect –/ At best, it is but Fancy, or the aggregating Faculty of the mind – not *Imagination*, or the *modifying*, and *co-adunating* Faculty.[109]

Much of this foreshadows the description of the poetic activity in *Biographia*, and while it is not possible to know whether Coleridge had read the *Kritik der Urteilskraft* in 1802 – he owned an edition of 1799 – he may have found his desire for the marriage of nature and spirit sympathetically voiced by Kant.[110]

Coleridge was not consistent in his distinction between Imagination and Fancy, sometimes using them synonymously, though often suggesting, as here and usually in *Biographia*, that the Fancy belongs to that part of our minds which is done to rather than doing. It is part of the dreaded 'association', and 'equally with the ordinary memory [it] must receive all its materials ready made from the law of association'.[111] Coleridge, in spite of his anger at the attempt of Hume and Hartley to reduce *all* knowledge to 'mechanical' accidental impressions on the senses, did not deny that *psychologically* it is true that we are a prey to unbidden memories and associations.[112] He wished only to free the creative imagination from such 'slavery'. So also did Kant. There is a passage tucked away in the 'Deduction of the Pure Concepts of Understanding' in the *Kritik der reinen Vernunft* which may be important for Coleridge's formulation of his theory:

So fern die Einbildungskraft nun Spontaneität ist, nenne ich sie auch bisweilen die produktive Einbildungskraft, und unterscheide sie dadurch von der reproduktiven, deren Synthesis lediglich empirischen Gesetzen, nämlich denen der Assoziation, unterworfen ist, und welche daher zur Erklärung der Möglichkeit der Erkenntnis a priori nichts beiträgt, und um deswillen nicht in die Transzendentalphilosophie, sondern in die Psychologie gehört.

Inasmuch as the Imagination is spontaneous, I call it the productive Imagination, and distinguish it thus from the reproductive Imagination, which is subject to empirical laws of association, and which therefore contributes nothing to the explanation of the possibility of *a priori* knowledge, and therefore belongs, not to transcendental philosophy, but to psychology.[113]

In Chapter 5 of *Biographia* Coleridge states his aim 'to shew, by what influences of the choice and judgement the associative power becomes either memory or fancy; and, in conclusion, to appropriate the remaining offices of the mind to the reason, and the imagination'.[114]

As with his Imagination–Fancy distinction, Coleridge expressed his aesthetic in terms of pairs of opposites: naive, objective, finite, 'classic' versus reflective, subjective, infinite, 'romantic'.[115] Most of the German Romantic theorists also wrote in such terms – the two Schlegels and Jean Paul in particular.[116] These classifications, as well as references to the creative imagination and to organic unity in literature were commonplaces in Germany from the 1790s on. As Coleridge said in a defence of himself against the charge of plagiarism from A. W. Schlegel, 'Schlegel & myself had both studied deeply & perseverantly the philosophy of Kant'.[117] A more or less scrutinising, dialectic method is observable in all the German writers of the time.[118] They tended to veer between the prescriptive and descriptive use of their antithetical terms. In 'Über naive und sentimentalische Dichtung' ('On naive and reflective Poetry') Schiller explicitly tells us not to confuse 'naiv' and 'sentimentalisch' with 'classical' and 'modern'. The distinction is one of manner, not of age.[119] Yet he seems to forget this difference himself when he takes it for granted that Homer is the norm of the 'naiv' genius. And his view varies from a historical one, in which he takes certain great writers – Homer, Horace, Shakespeare, Goethe – and classifies them according to their observed features, to a theoretical one, in which it is made clear that there never has been a perfectly 'naiv' nor a perfectly 'reflective' poet, and furthermore, that what we must hope for in the future is a perfect blending of the two sets of characteristics. Schiller writes here in terms of a Kantian dialectic of categories:

Das Gegentheil der naiven Empfindung ist nehmlich der reflektirende Verstand, und die sentimentalische Stimmung ist das Resultat des Bestrebens, auch unter den Bedingungen der Reflexion die naive Empfindung, dem Innhalt nach, wieder herzustellen. Diess würde durch das erfüllte Ideal geschehen, in welchem die Kunst der Natur wieder begegnet.

The opposite of the naive sensibility is the reflective understanding, and the reflective mood is the result of the effort to reinstate the naive sensibility, by means of the content, under the conditions of reflection. This would happen by means of the Ideal, in which art meets nature again.[120]

Hegel, in his lectures on aesthetics in the 1820s, represents the culmination of the dialectic approach, with its embracing of all history yet its 'head in the clouds' ahistoricism.[121]

It may be that the dissatisfaction readers have felt with Coleridge's definition of the poetic activity in *Biographia* arises in part from the initial difficulty of his having on the one hand an example of a fine poet in whom he seeks to see the creative imagination at work (Wordsworth), and on the other a deductive theory of 'the Poet' contemplated 'in *ideal* perfection' in the exercise of that faculty.[122] The diversity of his aims, one descriptive and the other prescriptive, resulted in Coleridge's failure to apply the hard-proved theory of the Imagination in any detail to Wordsworth's poetry. Both *Biographia* and Coleridge's Shakespeare criticism show him from time to time embarrassed by the irreducibility of his favourite writers to a consistent theory. Like Schiller, he confessed that he was puzzled by Shakespeare's seeming unconcern for sustaining a high moral tone, while *feeling* that Shakespeare was nevertheless in the right. Schiller wrote in 'Über naive und sentimentalische Dichtung':

> Wie die Gottheit hinter dem Weltgebäude, so steht er hinter seinem Werk: Er ist das Werk und das Werk ist Er...So zeigt sich z. B. Homer unter den Alten und Shakespeare unter den Neuern; zwey höchst verschiedene, durch den unermesslichen Abstand der Zeitalter getrennte Naturen, aber gerade in diesem Charakterzuge völlig eins. Als ich in einem sehr frühen Alter den letztern Dichter zuerst kennen lernte, empörte mich seine Kälte, seine Unempfindlichkeit, die ihm erlaubte, im höchsten Pathos zu scherzen, die herzzerschneidenden Auftritte im Hamlet, im König Lear, im Makbeth u.s. f. durch einen Narren zu stören, die ihn bald da festhielt, wo meine Empfindungen forteilte, bald da kaltherzig fortriss, wo das Herz so gern stillgestanden wäre.

> He [the naive genius] stands behind his work like God behind the universe; he is the work and the work is he...This is what, for example, Homer among the Ancients and Shakespeare among the Moderns are like; two very different natures, separated by an immeasurable gulf of years, yet in just this characteristic exactly similar. When, as a young man, I first became acquainted with the latter, I was horrified by his coldness, the insensitivity which allowed him to joke in the midst of deep pathos, to let a fool disturb the heart-rending scenes in *Hamlet, Lear, Macbeth*, etc., an insensitivity which made him stop just where my feelings rushed ahead and move on relentlessly when my heart would so gladly have rested.[123]

In the same spirit Coleridge complained of the 'disgusting passage of the Porter [in *Macbeth*], which I dare pledge myself to demonstrate an interpolation of the actors'.[124] Schiller had so disapproved of the same scene that he omitted it in his adaptation and production of the play at Weimar in 1800. And of *Venus and Adonis* Coleridge commented on 'the alienation, and, if I may hazard such an expression, the utter *aloofness* of the poet's own feelings, from those of which he is at once the painter and the analyst'.[125]

Coleridge, like Schiller, saw himself as a hybrid, caught between nature and spirit, between poetry and philosophy. He bemoaned his adherence to 'abstruse researches' long before he studied the German philosophers who were supposed by his friends to have killed the poet in him. As early as December 1796 he mused, 'I *think* too much for a *Poet*.'[126] Schiller, too, was confessedly a 'Zwitterart', half philosopher, half poet, and was to himself the type of the modern, self-conscious, endlessly striving, reflective spirit.[127] Both formulated their theories about literature primarily in response to Kant.

In Coleridge's case, Schelling also played an important part in the formation of his ideas on art, a part which has been well documented.[128] Crabb Robinson observed in 1811:

[Coleridge] soon mounted his hobby, and I was not a little surprised to find him very much of a Schellingianer, of which I had no idea. At least, his mode of comparing the fine arts and of antithetically considering all their elements appeared to me very similar...

A few months later in 1812:

Coleridge spoke of Schelling in terms of greater praise than I ever heard him use before, but without giving up any part of Kantianism to him. Yet he says Schelling alone understands Kant...But I suspect Coleridge himself is now floating between Kant and Schelling with a greater uncertainty than he is himself aware of.[129]

Certainly Coleridge became busy with Schelling, borrowing his works from Robinson in 1813; and, as is well known, the theses in Chapter 12 of *Biographia* are Schelling's.

What Schelling added to Kant's hints was a thorough study of the Imagination as the supreme mental power, reconciling subject with object, mind with matter, spirit with nature in a way that Coleridge found 'alluring'. Schelling offered in particular a breath of fresh philosophical air after Kant's difficult and rather dry logic and the extreme subjectivism which Fichte had built (illegitimately) upon Kant's system. Coleridge found Fichte absurd in his assumption of the 'I' as the first principle, an act (not a state of being) positing the existence of the 'Not-I' or Nature for its own progres-sion.[130] It is as if Coleridge began *Biographia* thinking that via the history of his philosophical progress from Hartleianism through Kant, Fichte, and Schelling to his present position he could apply his 'transcendental' theories to literature in the promised deduction of the creative imagination. At some point he found that his further urge, to link reason and imagination with faith and thus present a unified system of philosophy, aesthetics, and religion, could not be satisfied by following Schelling all the way.[131] For Schelling ended in pantheism; Nature was 'absolute' and Mind only Nature made conscious;[132] what was infinitely fruitful for poetry – organic whole-ness, reconciliation of opposites, etc. – was inauspicious for Christian-ity. So in *Biographia* he works his way through Schelling to the point where there is 'absolute identity of subject and object, which it calls nature, and which in its highest power is nothing else than self-conscious will or intelligence'.[133] The consequences for religion are clear, and on this brink Coleridge draws back, inserts the 'joke' letter about the obscurity of the work so far, then offers the famous definition pat, and significantly at the end of a chapter. The 'infinite I AM' (i.e. God),[134] has crept into the definition, contributing to confuse an already difficult deduction. Coleridge's great urge to balanced wholeness has been frustrated and gives way to the contra-dictory desire for a hierarchical order of faculties, of which faith is the last and the highest.[135] Schelling could not satisfy that urge any more than Kant did when he severely restricted the validity of theoretical reason.

Increasingly after *Biographia* Coleridge subordinated Nature with her 'phantom purposes' and her 'dread activity' to the human spirit. Schelling's position was represented horrifically as suggesting that Nature 'formed with restless hands unconsciously / Blank accident! nothing's anomaly!'[136] He told his student J. H. Green in 1818, soon after Green had begun working with him on the 'Logosophia', that he regretted having been so much a Schellingian in *Biographia*:

The inconsistency Schelling has contrived to hide from himself by the artifice of making all knowledge bi-polar, Transcendental Idealism as one Pole and Nature as the other – and from the tendency of my mind to confidence in others I was myself *taken in* by it, retrograding from my own prior and better Lights, and adopted it in the metaphysical chapters of my Literary Life – not aware, that this was putting the Candle horizontally and burning it at both ends.

To Tulk he admitted two months later that Schelling's Naturphilosophie was 'plausible and alluring at a first acquaintance', but that
he had discovered it to be 'little more than Behmenism', 'reduced at
last to a mere Pantheism', a sort of 'Plotinized Spinozism'.[137] Of
course Coleridge had found Schelling, and for that matter Boehme
and Spinoza, attractive. They all allowed for the life of the senses
and gave Nature meaning and dignity. They were, however, incompatible with spiritual Christianity, and Coleridge rejected them,
albeit with a sense of loss.[138]

The fact that all this went on (and goes on for us) in the text of
Biographia makes for some of the difficulties we have in understand-
ing and assessing the work. Coleridge's contemporaries were im-
patient of its waywardness. Hazlitt, almost as two-minded about
Coleridge as De Quincey, came down heavily against it in the
Edinburgh Review:

With chap. IV begins the formidable ascent of that mountainous and
barren ridge of clouds piled on precipices and precipices on clouds, from
the top of which the author deludes us with a view of the Promised Land
that divides the regions of Fancy from those of the Imagination, and
extends through 200 pages with various inequalities and declensions to the
end of the volume. The object of this long-winding metaphysical march,
which resembles a patriarchal journey, is to point out and settle the true
grounds of Mr. Wordsworth's claim to originality as a poet; which, if we
rightly understand the deduction, turns out to be, that there is nothing
peculiar about him; and that his poetry, in so far as it is good for any thing
at all, is just like any other good poetry...We shall dismiss the whole of
this metaphysical investigation...by shortly observing, that we can by no
means agree with Mr. C. in refusing to Hobbes the merit of originality...
and that we totally dissent from his encomium on Kant and his followers.[139]

It is worth remembering that Schelling was first translated into
English only in 1845,[140] that Coleridge's contemporaries knew little
or nothing about him. Coleridge's struggle with the Naturphilosophie
could be said to be 'obscure' in both uses of the word.

As for the concept of 'Ästhetik', that might still be thought too
obscure to be the subject of attention in the *Edinburgh Review* in
1842, when Lewes tried to interest the periodical in an article based
on Hegel's lectures on aesthetics. Of Coleridge's contemporaries,
Hazlitt and De Quincey came nearest to having aesthetic theories.
The former's aim as a critic was, however, to apply an inductive,
experiential method, not a deductive one. He tried 'to feel what was

55

good, and to "give a reason for the faith that was in me"'.[141] De Quincey's distinction between the 'literature of knowledge' and the 'literature of power' – 'the function of the first is – to *teach*; the function of the second is – to *move*; the first is a rudder; the second, an oar or a sail' – was formed partly in response to Coleridge, but still bears the stamp of traditional notions of rhetoric.[142] As Tieck recognised in 1818, the English public was not ready for 'manche philosophische und kritische Ansicht, manche Grundsätze über Schönheit und Kunst' ('certain philosophical and critical views, certain principles of beauty and art') which were familiar to German readers.[143]

Coleridge and Faust (*1814–20*)

Coleridge's interest in German literature, after his youthful enthusiasm for the Gothic works of Bürger and Schiller, centred chiefly in its philosophical and critical works. No doubt partly because of the early critical reaction against German literature, he never wrote an essay on any work of German literature. His flirtation with *Faust* is indicative in its details both of Coleridge's continuing interest and of the thwarting of it by his fear of public, and particularly periodical, censure.

The first part of *Faust*, though published in Germany in 1808, was not translated into English until 1823, when John Murray published Lord Francis Leveson Gower's version. There was, however, a plan for Coleridge to translate the play for Murray in 1814, but after a brief correspondence between them, the plan, for reasons not altogether clear, was dropped.[144] It may be that Lamb helped to dissuade Coleridge, for he, like Wordsworth and Southey, disapproved of Goethe: 'How canst thou translate the language of cat-monkeys? Fie on such fantasies!'[145] Yet the play continued to interest Coleridge. In 1820 he approached it again, with the intention of writing an introduction to Retzsch's illustrations to *Faust*. That, too, came to nothing.

Coleridge's comments on *Faust*, private and public, ranged back and forth from hostility (on the grounds of the play's lack of unity and morality) to enthusiasm. They generally had an uncertainty or ambivalence of tone, which suggests that he was undecided on the merits of the work, but also that he was much concerned with the likely reception of it by those distinct but interacting institutions which he regarded with mingled awe and scorn, the Periodical Press and the reading public. Coleridge, we know, was sensitive to the 'Taste of the Age', which it was his misfortune never to gratify in his own writings, and which he half despised for its unadventurousness. Thus, in a notebook he characterised Southey as the type of poet who exhibits 'a correspondence to the Taste of the Age, which Taste is the Index and as it were the effluvium & fragrancy of the collective or average Intellect of the Reading World – above many, below a certain few – but yet the *average* – & still however *reflective*, *echoing*, not projectile, not creative'.[146] He was also sensitive to what was original, stimulating, 'ahead' of the age, to be judged aesthetically, according to ideal 'Principles' rather than by current fashion or the arbitrary judgment of a reviewer. He was caught between his desire for immediate financial success and celebrity, though aware that these were open only to the Scotts, Byrons, and Southeys, whom he thought of with envy and contempt, and his wish to approach a universal Ideal in his own endeavours. His ambivalence towards *Faust*, as a work of enduring literary value and as a subject for translation, is traceable to this conflict of attitudes and emotions.

As Coleridge was also a man of his age, sharing some of its tastes and preoccupations, his comments on *Faust* are an uneasy partial reflection of prevailing views of *Faust* in England. These views changed within two decades from quiet but disparaging ignorance before 1820 to violent rejection, then in the 1830s and after to enthusiasm. For example, Lamb's remarks in his letter of 1814 were based on ignorance of the work. What idea he had of it came from an unreliable source – 'Madame de Stael on Germany'.[147] When Gower's translation appeared in 1823 critics were unanimous in deploring *Faust* as 'immoral', though Gower had taken the precaution of omitting the 'blasphemous' Prolog im Himmel (Prologue in Heaven) from 'considerations of decency'. Yet by 1835 five more translations had found publishers and were welcomed by reviewers. These changes of response in the particular case of *Faust* represent the complex reception of German literature generally in the early nineteenth century. The question of Coleridge's place in its history is a vexed one. Though he was known in his lifetime, and can be known with greater accuracy and fairness now that his complete works are being published, as the greatest student and interpreter of German thought in his time, he published no essay specifically on

the subject, and only one translation, of *Wallenstein*. The fact that
the translation was, as we have seen, abused in the *Monthly Review*
and subsequently ignored for fifteen years has some bearing on the
question of his attitude to *Faust*, as does his constant concern with
the fickle taste of the English public. The plan to translate *Faust*,
and the shelving of it, are not merely another example of his fertile
but unfulfilled planning, though they are that. They should also be
seen in the context of attitudes to German literature at the time and
Coleridge's sensitivity to them.

Although Coleridge maintained his study of the best and most
original examples of German thought in the low period which
followed the failure of *Wallenstein*, he felt it prudent (as we have
seen with Kant) to deny it or keep quiet, fearing that it was a chief
reason for his unfavourable reputation. Indeed, he was known
loosely as a 'German mystic', with Byron and Peacock, among
others, caricaturing him as such in their works. While Jeffrey, Hazlitt,
and other Edinburgh Reviewers talked dismissively about 'German
literature' – meaning Kotzebue and the 'Storm and Stress' plays of
the 1770s and 1780s – into the 1820s, Coleridge read and re-read
Kant, Fichte, Schelling, the Schlegels, and was keeping up with the
contemporary productions of German novelists.[148] But, being aware
of the general view, he did not broadcast the fact. This explains why
his interest in, say, Jean Paul Richter, is reflected fully in his notebooks around 1810 but scarcely at all in his published writings.[149]
Coleridge wrote a bitter note on a copy of his *Statesman's Manual*
(1816): 'Give a Dog a bad name: and you hang him or worse, have
him hunted with a black kettle at his tail. So has it been with me in
relation to the black charge of *Metaphysics* – and then 'his jargon
about Ideas!...'' Even in 1825 he wrote a harassed denial to his
nephew that he was a 'German transcendentalist'.[150] Much of his
detailed knowledge and absorption of German ideas was denied to
contemporaries outside an interested circle (which included De
Quincey, Henry Crabb Robinson, Green, and John Sterling), and the
cause is rooted as much in his discouragement from the 1790s as in
his celebrated fragmentariness and weakness of will. We can assign
to a different cause from the one suggested by Coleridge his decision
in 1814 not, after all, to translate *Faust*. He recalled rather pompously in 1833:

I was once pressed – many years ago – to translate the Faust...I debated
with myself whether it became my moral character to render into English

– and so far, certainly, lend my countenance to language – much of which I thought vulgar, licentious, and blasphemous. I need not tell you that I never put pen to paper as a translator of Faust.[151]

It is likely that his memory of the failure of *Wallenstein* and the fear of being labelled 'German' played at least as persuasive a part as strictly moral scruples in his decision. The public was not ready for *Faust.*

The correspondence with Murray about translating it should be seen against this background. When Coleridge first mentioned it to Murray on 23 August 1814, he had heard from Lamb, who had heard from Robinson, that Murray wished 'to have the justly cele-brated FAUST of Goethe translated' and that he was the man 'most likely to execute the work adequately'.[152] The rest of the letter was devoted to promoting himself as the man for the job, while assuring Murray at the same time that his ideals were so high, and so far in advance of the public's, that the undertaking would be a long and demanding one:

Language is the sacred Fire in the Temple of Humanity; and the Muses are it's especial & Vestal Priestesses. Tho' I cannot prevent the vile drugs, and counterfeit Frankincense, which render it's flame at once pitchy, glowing, and unsteady, I would yet be no voluntary accomplice in this Sacrilege. With the commencement of a PUBLIC commences the degra-dation of the GOOD & the BEAUTIFUL – both fade or retire before the accidentally AGREEABLE...I thought it right to state to you these opinions of mine, that you might know that I think the Translation of the 'FAUST' a task demanding (from *me*, I mean) no ordinary efforts – & why.

The unspoken suggestion is that the effort should be adequately remunerated, though Coleridge hastens to protest his lack of interest in the financial terms:

...I bow to the all-wise Providence, which has made me a *poor* man & therefore compelled me by other duties inspiring yet higher feelings, to bring *even my Intellect* to the *Market* – And the Finale is this – I should like to attempt the Translation – if you will mention your Terms, at once & irrevocably (for I am an Ideot at Bargaining & shrink from the very Thought) I will return an answer by the next Post, whether in my present Circumstances I can or cannot undertake it.

With a final flourish of contradictoriness he expresses little hope of the venture being a commercial success, since it is unlikely to suit the 'General Taste'.[153]

Murray replied on 29 August, skilfully appealing to Coleridge's vanity – 'I suspect that no one could do justice to [*Faust*] besides yourself' – and making his offer, a generous enough one of £100.[154] Coleridge thought the offer low and wrote back on 31 August, revealing a confusion of motives which might have been partly due to Lamb's warnings of a few days before (26 August) but which also suggests the complex concerns of principle, reputation, and success which weighed so heavily with him:

Considering the necessary Labor, and (from the questionable nature of the original work, both as to it's fair claims on *Fame* (the dictum of the good & wise according to unchanging Principles) and as to its Chance for *Reputation*, as an accidental result of local and temporary Taste) the risk of character on the part of the Translator, who will assuredly have to answer for any disappointment of the Reader, the Terms proposed are humiliatingly low.

Nevertheless, he accepted the offer, though grudgingly. His real concern, though, was not so much the questionable nature of *Faust* (adduced chiefly to stress the 'risk' involved) as the low opinion of his merits to which he attributed the meanness of the terms. Thus he went on to bewail his lack of success and insist on his ability – 'I have received testimonials from men not merely of genius according to *my* belief, but of the highest *accredited* reputation, that my Translation of the Wallenstein was in language & in metre superior to the original.' The mention of the *Wallenstein* experience is unfortunate, being hardly an example calculated to encourage Murray to offer more for *Faust*, but, as we have seen, it was an experience which encapsulates Coleridge's feelings of having been ill-used, his sense of superiority to mere celebrity, yet outrage and self-pity at his consistent failure to attain it:

...tho' I know that executed as alone I can or dare do it, that is, to the utmost of my powers (for which the intolerable Pain, nay, the far greater Toil & Effort of doing otherwise, is a far safer Pledge than any solicitude on my part concerning the approbation of the PUBLIC), the Translation of so very difficult a work, as the Faustus, will be most inadequately remunerated by the Terms, you propose; yet they very probably are the highest, it may be worth your while to offer to *me*. I say this, as a philosopher: for tho' I have been much talked of, & written of, for evil & – not for good, but – for suspected Capability – yet none of my works have ever sold.

Murray must have replied coolly, for Coleridge's next letter contained protestations of his opinion that 'the "Faust"' was 'a work of genius, of genuine and original Genius', and of his willingness to do the translation.[155] Nothing came of it. By spring 1815 Coleridge had rationalised the correspondence with Murray until its elements appeared in a different relation, favourable to himself and dubious on Murray's part. He wrote to Byron, complaining that Murray had not responded: .

...whether because I had the open-heartedness to dissuade him from hazarding any money on the translation of the Faust of Goethe much as I myself admired the work on the whole, and tho' ready to undertake the translation – from the conviction that the fantastic character of its Witcheries, and the general tone of the morals and religious opinions would be highly obnoxious to the taste and Principles of the present righteous English public, I know not.[156]

His own position as to the morality of the play is not made clear, but there is a suggestion of irony about 'the present righteous English public' which leads one to suppose that he had no strong objections on that score. Certainly Henry Crabb Robinson recorded Coleridge's opinion of *Faust* in 1812 as chiefly favourable: 'he acknowledged the genius of Goethe in a manner he never did before', though he thought Goethe lacked 'religion'.[157]

Coleridge remained interested enough to take up *Faust* again in 1820 with a view to writing the 'preliminary Essay' for Boosey, to accompany Retzsch's drawings. (These sketches, accompanied not by Coleridge's but by an anonymous introduction, became so widely known that George Eliot could appeal to her readers' memory of them in Chapter 37 of *Daniel Deronda*.) Coleridge was now more direct about his fears for his reputation than he had been with Murray. He expressed his objection to Boosey thus: 'I scarce know how to ward off the notion, that I am connecting my name with a work in bad repute with the religious part of the Community without having space or opportunity to explain myself.'[158] However, he got as far as making an initial plan for the essay which shows that he would have tried to reconcile his admiration for the play's originality with his own, and what he deemed would be his readers', moral scruples:

A preliminary Essay, stating *briefly* the peculiar character of Goethe, as man, philosopher, & poet; more at large, the specific character of his Faust, including it's *purposes*, & the tone of mind presupposed in the Reader as well as it's form of *Style*, Humor of Pathos, Imagery, &c. Then to explain it's *Nationality* as a German Poem, with it's high merit on this very account – it is, perhaps, the only properly *original* work of German Poesy, & with the Louisa of Voss the most *national* – but from these very causes, especially the state of mind in those, whom Goethe had a right to calculate on as his readers, & the *inclosed* number of those Readers, often most unfit, & in large portions uninteresting to the English Public.[159]

Had such an essay been written and read by the large public which we know became acquainted with Retzsch, Coleridge would have begun to do openly for German literature much what Carlyle succeeded in doing from 1827 on, namely introducing 'that strange literature' in terms of its literary merit, originality, and puzzling, un-English, but rewarding 'philosophy'.[160] As it was, someone else wrote the text to Retzsch. Shelley read it in Italy in 1822, and wrote to his friend Gisborne with unconscious irony: 'We have just got the etchings of 'Faust'. The painter is worthy of Göthe...The translations...are miserable. Ask Coleridge if their stupid misintelligence of the deep wisdom and harmony of the author does not spur him to action.' Shelley also tried to translate a piece of *Faust*, choosing the very Prologue in Heaven about which there was so much discussion and the witches' Walpurgisnacht. His difficulties in translating Goethe led him to endorse Crabb Robinson's view that Coleridge's German knowledge and talent were unique: 'I feel how imperfect a representation, even with all the licence I assume to figure to myself how Göthe wd. have written in English, my words convey. No one but Coleridge is capable of this work.'[161] Coleridge's discouragement and dismay at not being fairly assessed in his lifetime and his half defiant, half ingratiating attitude towards making a good name with the public outweighed any desire he might have to introduce *Faust* or any other German work to it. Carlyle, a decade later, had no reputation, good or bad, to consider, and opinion had changed sufficiently to tolerate his enthusiasm. For, Jeffrey and Hazlitt notwithstanding, a new interest in German literature did begin in some quarters in the second decade of the century.

Coleridge was certainly aware of the new interest. His half willingness to translate *Faust* for a largely 'philistine' public probably relates to the widespread interest in Madame de Staël, who visited England in 1813 and whom Coleridge met, and her associate A. W. Schlegel, with whose lectures on Shakespeare he was but too well acquainted.[162] The European situation now worked in favour of allowing attention to German affairs. Buonaparte was the common enemy, and British sympathy was with those German states under his control. Madame de Staël and her book, *De L'Allemagne* (1813), were banned from Napoleonic France, and were welcomed in England because of it. Schlegel's lectures on Shakespeare pleased the English with their appreciation of Shakespeare's genius and judgment and their depreciation of French classical drama. The Schlegel lectures were quickly translated into English, by John Black in 1815, and were widely read. Even Wordsworth and Hazlitt, usually hostile to German literature, by which they meant the 'sickly and stupid German Tragedies' of the 1790s, praised Schlegel for his sympathetic criticism of Shakespeare.[163] 'All the world', said Lockhart in 1826, 'is acquainted with these two works' by Schlegel and Madame de Staël.[164]

In spite of the positive response to Schlegel and the increase in acceptance of some German literature in the 1820s, *Faust*'s claims to greatness were unclear to most observers, even those who thought of translating it. Gower omitted the Prologue in Heaven, in which God and Mephistopheles bargain over Faust's soul. And John Anster, a Dublin barrister and for a short time a protégé of Coleridge,[165] translated extracts from *Faust* for *Blackwood's* in 1821, but expressed disapproval of the 'light' and 'irreverent' tone of the Prologue. Even William Taylor, who alone had noticed *Faust* at the time of its publication in Germany, had reacted adversely, finding the play 'pure trash' and unsuitable for translation, though, interestingly, his private opinion was much higher.[166] Byron shrewdly predicted the reaction in England:

What would the Methodists at home say to Goethe's 'Faust'? His devil not only talks very familiarly *of* Heaven, but very familiarly *in* Heaven. What would they think of the colloquies of Mephistopheles and his pupil, or the more daring language of the prologue, which no one will ever venture to translate?[167]

Even the avowed Germanists – Taylor, Anster, Gower – agreed in finding *Faust* immoral. How much more predictable was it that those who expected nothing but bad taste and immorality from the Germans should find their prejudices confirmed in this case. Hazlitt complained in *The Plain Speaker* (1826) of its perversity and absurdity.[168] Against such a background Coleridge's half doubts about *Faust* seem relatively mild. As it happens, *Faust* was the subject of Carlyle's first essay on German literature. He tackled it uneasily in the *New Edinburgh Review* in 1822, and found, like the others, 'a want of unity in the general plan' and 'numerous sins against taste in the execution of it'.[169] Carlyle's fame as the 'Germanist' of the *Edinburgh Review* and the champion of Goethe, dating from 1827, came after some years of revulsion and puzzlement regarding Goethe.

Despite – or because of – the disapproval of *Faust* in the early 1820s, it enjoyed a notoriety in a debased form, as *The Devil and Dr Faustus*, presented at Drury Lane in 1825–6, with an overture by Weber. Like Kotzebue's plays thirty years before, it helped to fill a gap in contemporary drama in England. The London stage in the 1820s relied chiefly on dramatisations of Scott's novels, and some Kotzebue plays were still presented. An object of critical disapproval was required. Byron and Shelley could not, after 1824, provide new material for scandal. Goethe, with God and 'the Devil' on stage and with his famous liaison in life with Christiane Vulpius, served instead. The outcry over *Faust* (and *Wilhelm Meister* and *Dichtung und Wahrheit*) was partly an extension of the Anti-Jacobin accusations directed against earlier German works, but it was also an accurate reflection of the 'moral squeamishness' which prevailed in the 1820s.[170]

Only Lockhart among critics then took an enlightened view. He insisted on the integral importance of the Prologue and was 'at a loss to comprehend' the reasons for the moral objections made by his fellow critics.[171] The increase in general attention to German literature in the later 1820s may be attributed in part to Lockhart's discussions, of *Wallenstein* and *Faust* particularly. They combined with Carlyle's authoritative reviews and the less measurable influence of Coleridge in his written works, his lectures, and his conversations. John Sterling recorded his debt to both Coleridge and Carlyle for his introduction to German literature, and even such an unlikely subject as Mill was led by Coleridge and Carlyle to read and admire Goethe in the early 1830s:

The influences of European, that is to say, Continental, thought, and especially those of the reaction of the nineteenth century against the eighteenth, were now streaming in upon me. They came from various quarters: from the writings of Coleridge, which I had begun to read with interest even before the change in my opinions; from the Coleridgians [i.e. Sterling and F. D. Maurice] with whom I was in personal intercourse; from what I had read of Goethe; from Carlyle's early articles in the Edinburgh and Foreign Reviews. . .[172]

Goethe became acceptable to English taste in the course of a decade. Carlyle, in notes for an article he never published on Hayward's *Faust* translation, while finding some faults in it and regretting that a prose translation could give only 'the naked trunk and boughs' of the original, recognised the change that had taken place:

On the whole therefore is not this Book and the reception it seems to meet with a thing we can honestly look upon with welcome? A satisfaction that German Literature (which in one best sense may be said to mean Literature itself, in this epoch) spreads vigorously both in height and breadth, has its interpreters its critics, and ever-increasing public; that one of the chief Products of G Literature need no longer be misknown, may now begin to be in some small degree known. Ten years that do much in many cases have in this worked wonders: a new influence may be said to have added itself to British Thought; where, as is easy to predict, its effects deep enough in their character can nowise be wanting.[173]

Publishers brought out translations of *Faust* in such numbers that James White, reviewing in *Blackwood's* in 1839, exclaimed:

Faust! Faust! – every human being, from about eighteen up to five-and-twenty, and some, even, who have come to years of discretion, have got into a perpetual sing-song of wonder and awe about the depth, grandeur, sublimity, and all the rest of it, of this inimitable performance.[174]

The second part of *Faust*, published posthumously in 1832, naturally aroused critical interest at the same time. Its symbolisms were bewildering to many critics, yet it was seen to solve the problem of fragmentariness posed by the first part. Also, moral, social, and even religious conclusions could without difficulty be drawn from the sequel. Adaptations of the two parts, no longer travestied, began to appear successfully on the London stage.

The question of the unity and morality of *Faust*, which had exercised Coleridge, Carlyle, and the early critics and translators, became one of positive rather than negative importance. Coleridge had not translated the play or written his introductory essay, and had not lived long enough to take much interest in the second part. But an interest in German culture had been established partly through his personal and posthumous influence. Crabb Robinson described him fairly to Goethe in 1829 as 'the only living poet of acknowledged genius who is also a good German Scholar'. That Coleridge's name cannot be linked directly with *Faust* is a regrettable fact of literary history, due not merely to his dilatoriness and not entirely, regardless of some of his utterances, to moral considerations, but in large part to his sensitivity to the confused attitudes prevailing in England towards *Faust* and German culture as a whole, and to his nervous desire for financial success, celebrity, and excellence. Attitudes changed positively within a few years. It is a curious fact that Coleridge did a great deal, in private and roundabout ways, to encourage interest, while feeling unable to assume publicly, as Carlyle did in the 1820s, the role of advocate. There is no doubt, however, that he was the first and most important interpreter of Kant, and the first theorist of literature to respond to the new aesthetic movement in Germany which followed Kant's philosophy. His own generation, apart from a few interested acquaintances like Crabb Robinson and Shelley, deplored his German interest; the next generation responded to it in their reading of his later works and conversations. It was Carlyle who drew their attention forcibly to German thought, thus creating a more favourable intellectual atmosphere in which Coleridge could be reassessed and properly celebrated.

2

Carlyle

In 1827 there appeared in the *Edinburgh Review* a long article
defending German literature from misunderstandings and false
criticisms, entitled 'The State of German Literature'. Insofar as any
one effort to popularise German literature in England could be said
to have revolutionised attitudes, this was it. Here was Carlyle
arguing for it in the periodical which for over twenty years had
most fostered stereotyped ideas about the bad taste, immorality, and
absurdity of German literature both generally and in the few particular examples which it reviewed. Jeffrey's article on Carlyle's
translation of *Wilhelm Meisters Lehrjahre* in 1825 was a good
example of this. He took *Wilhelm Meister* to be representative of
German literary taste, and concluded that German taste was far
inferior to British. The latter being the only true standard, he judged
Wilhelm Meister to be 'almost from beginning to end, one flagrant
offence against every principle of taste, and every just rule of
composition'. It was 'absurd, puerile, incongruous, vulgar, and
affected'.[1] Lewes probably had this very article of Jeffrey's in mind
when he caricatured the pre-Carlyle attitude to Goethe in 1843:

'Ah! now do you really think Göthe was not a *charlatan?*' asked a smart
dogmatical critic, with that complacent smile, which, while it indicates a
tender pity for the weakness of another, reflects so serenely on one's own
superiority. The speaker was ignorant of German – 'but that's not much!'
The speaker was also quite incapable of seeing into the significance of such
a man as Göthe, whatever knowledge he might have of the language –
n'importe! The one thing definitely settled in his conviction was this curious
fact of Göthe's being a charlatan.[2]

Yet in 1827 Jeffrey encouraged Carlyle, rather cautiously, to
'Germanize the public'.[3] Carlyle did so with such success that Henry
Crabb Robinson wrote to Goethe, 'the most noted of our Reviews
has on a sudden become a loud eulogist', and Goethe welcomed the

event in his periodical, *Ueber Kunst und Alterthum* (*On Art and Antiquity*).[4]

Carlyle began the article by dismissing the ostensible subject of his review, two books on the history of German literature by Franz Horn:

But our chief business at present is not with Franz Horn, or his book; of whom, accordingly, recommending his labours to all inquisitive students of German, and himself to good estimation with all good men, we must here take leave. We have a word to say on that strange Literature itself; concerning which our readers probably feel more curious to learn what it is, than with what skill it has been judged of.

He notices that there has been, since Madame de Staël's book on Germany, an increased attention to the Germans, but finds that they are 'perhaps not less mistaken than before'. The two chief errors of the British idea of the Germans are those of 'bad taste' and 'mysticism'. Of the first, Carlyle writes:

Their literature, in particular, is thought to dwell with peculiar complacency among wizards and ruined towers, with mailed knights, secret tribunals, monks, spectres, and banditti: on the other hand, there is an undue love of moonlight, and mossy fountains, and the moral sublime; then we have descriptions of things which should not be described; a general want of tact; nay, often a hollowness and want of sense.[5]

We recognise this idea of the Germans as precisely that of the Anti-Jacobins thirty years before, in their criticism of *Die Räuber*, *Götz*, and other Sturm und Drang works. Carlyle gives the sensible reply that there is more to recent German literature than those early examples of it, and that to think only in terms of Gothic extravagance would be equivalent to a German critic judging English literature by *The Monk* or *The Mysteries of Udolpho*. The question that arises here is whether Carlyle was right to suggest that there had been no improvement in British knowledge and attitudes to German literature since the 1790s. He concedes that the Germans are now 'much more attended to', but dismisses the translators of German works in a body as 'the same faithless and stolid race that they have ever been'.[6] Of the more favourable critics like Gillies and Lockhart in *Blackwood's*, of De Quincey and Coleridge, Carlyle makes no mention in the article. In the interests of making a strong impression, he gives a generalised view of British neglect of the Germans, naming no names in the process.

Yet he was not unaware of the recent history of German studies in Britain. He knew of Gillies's translations and articles, for while translating *Wilhelm Meister* in 1824 he wrote: 'There is one Pearse Gillies, an advocate here [i.e. in Edinburgh], who knows of me, and whom I am to see on the subject of this book; he being a great German Scholar, and having a fine library of books, one or two of which I wish to examine.'[7] He was also aware of Lockhart's interest, for he chose him as the recipient of one of the medals which Goethe sent him for distribution among the most important Germanists in England. He wrote to Sir Walter Scott (also a recipient of a medal) in 1828, 'Perhaps Mr. Lockhart, whose merits in respect of German Literature, and just appreciation of this its Patriarch and Guide, are no secret, will do me the honour to accept of one.'[8] As for De Quincey, Carlyle later mentioned the influence of his criticisms of Jean Paul[9] on his own. 'Perhaps', he wrote in 1866, 'it was little De Quincey's reported admiration of Jean Paul...that first put me upon trying to be orthodox and admire.'[10] It was, in fact, Crabb Robinson, as generous with books and advice to Carlyle as he was to Coleridge, who told him of De Quincey's articles in a letter of 1825.[11] Carlyle was rather mean-spirited about William Taylor, the first 'Anglo-Germanist', minimising Taylor's usefulness as a translator and early reviewer of German works in an article on the 'clever old *Philister*' in the *Edinburgh Review* in 1831.[12] He wrote to Goethe: 'A certain William Taylor of Norwich, the Translator of your *Iphigenie* has written what he calls a Historic *Survey of German Poetry*; the tendency of which you may judge of sufficiently by this one fact, that the longest article but one is on August von Kotzebue.'[13] Certainly, Taylor's taste in German literature was not impeccable. Lockhart pointed out in 1843 that 'even in his old age [he] talks of Kotzebue as the greatest of all dramatists next to Shakspeare – and we might mention not a few equally preposterous decisions'. But Lockhart also saw that Taylor 'must be acknowledged to have been the first who effectually introduced the Modern Poetry and Drama of Germany to the English reader', both by his translations and by his reviews, his achievement being all the more remarkable because 'the mere possession of the German language was in those days a great rarity'.[14] Carlyle made no allowance for the change in critical perspective since Taylor's first work of more than thirty years before.

What Jane Carlyle described as his tendency to 'hope the worst'[15] shows itself in Carlyle's remarks on his fellow critics. He felt it necessary to warn Goethe in advance about the expected review of the recently published *Briefwechsel zwischen Schiller und Goethe* (*Correspondence between Schiller and Goethe*) by William Empson, adding reassuringly that he would right the balance himself in his own article on the correspondence in *Fraser's Magazine*.[16] In his next letter, Carlyle admitted that Empson's review was better than he had expected.[17] The same happened with Hayward's 1833 translation of the first part of *Faust*. Writing to Mill, Carlyle said that he had been told that Hayward 'has out his poor Translation of *Faust*'. He forecast that ' "the cleverest of our second-rate men", I doubt, will but have made a bungle of that business'. When he read it, he found that Hayward had in fact done it 'most handsomely'.[18] The impression Carlyle gave in his article may have been partly tactical; if he exaggerated the mistakes and ignorance about German literature, he could make all the stronger his appeal for fairness. Part of it, however, must have been true of his own experience. He had translated *Wilhelm Meisters Lehrjahre* and several German stories for *German Romance* (1827) and had published a *Life of Schiller* in 1825. None of these sold well or was well reviewed.[19] When he met Jeffrey in Edinburgh in 1827, the latter was no more interested in German literature than he had ever been, so that his encouragement took the form of teasing. He admired Carlyle's abilities, but reminded him in almost every letter that his taste was 'vicious', his articles had too much 'mystical jargon', and his 'idolatry' of the Germans was foolish.[20] Carlyle's geographical isolation in Craigenputtoch must have contributed to his sense of being almost unique in his literary tastes.

The second 'grand objection against German literature' which Carlyle tackled in the article was its 'mysticism':

Mysticism is a word in the mouths of all: yet, of the hundred, perhaps not one has ever asked himself what this opprobrious epithet properly signified in his mind; or where the boundary between true science and this Land of Chimeras was to be laid down. Examined strictly, *mystical*, in most cases, will turn out to be synonymous with *not understood*.[21]

This was a much more real problem. Peacock, Shelley, Byron, and others used the phrase indiscriminately about Kant and 'the Germans'. Carlyle himself was in two minds about whether to deny that the German writers, particularly the philosophers, were mystics or to expand and correct the British notion of a mystic and praise the Germans as the only true mystics:

Let the reader believe us, the Critical Philosophers, whatever they may be, are no mystics, and have no fellowship with mystics.

Nevertheless, after all these limitations, we shall not hesitate to admit, that there is in the German mind a tendency to mysticism, properly so called...

Endeavouring, by logical argument, to prove the existence of God, a Kantist might say, would be like taking out a candle to look for the sun; nay, gaze steadily into your candle-light, and the sun himself may be invisible. To open the inward eye to the sight of this Primitively True; or rather we might call it, to clear off the Obscurations of Sense, which eclipse this truth within us, so that we may see it, and believe it not only to be true, but the foundation and essence of all other truth, – may, in such language as we are here using, be said to be the problem of Critical Philosophy.[22]

This last passage comes close to describing Carlyle's own notion as expressed in *Sartor Resartus* and in letters to Mill in 1833 of that 'mysticism' which he thought the only true philosophy. Here it follows uneasily a precarious critique of Kant, or as Carlyle revealingly puts it, 'the Kantists', which started out as a denial of their 'mysticism'.[23]

Carlyle had first turned to German literature and philosophy, as Coleridge had done, for relief from the materialism of Hume and the Utilitarians. German literature seemed, on his introduction to it in 1820, already to reveal 'a new Heaven and new Earth'.[24] Its best examples offered a secularised spirituality, a 'natural supernaturalism'.[25] As for the philosophers, Carlyle read them only fitfully, and, as Leslie Stephen noticed, 'sympathised with the general tendency without caring to bewilder himself in any of the elaborate systems evolved by Kant or his followers'.[26] Heine's witty generalisation about 'German philosophy' broadly describes Carlyle's idea of it. Heine explains for the benefit of his French readers:

Als man den Geist hier in Frankreich leugnete, da emigrierte er gleichsam nach Deutschland und leugnete dort die Materie.

When spirit was denied here in France, it immediately emigrated to Germany and there denied matter.[27]

For Carlyle, 'German philosophy' meant not only anti-materialism but thoroughgoing idealism. He looked to Coleridge for guidance with the Germans, but was disappointed both in his conversation, which Carlyle experienced in 1824, and in his failure to write systematically and clearly on German philosophy, particularly Kant's, to which he was said to hold the 'key'. His most famous description of Coleridge is not flattering:

His talk, alas, was distinguished, like himself, by irresolution: it disliked to be troubled with conditions, abstinences, definite fulfilments. . .He had knowledge about many things and topics, much curious reading; but generally all topics led him, after a pass or two, into the high seas of theosophic philosophy, the hazy infinitude of Kantean transcendentalism with its 'sum-m-mjects' and 'om-m-mjects'.[28]

Yet he took much of his own 'German philosophy' pre-digested from Coleridge. His unfinished novel 'Wotton Reinfred' (1827), some of which was absorbed into *Sartor* three years later,[29] reflects his reading of the 'Germano–Coleridgean' philosophy, as well as his annoyance at Coleridge's indolence and obscuring tactics. Dalbrook in the novel is a philosopher with a 'huge whirlpool of a mind, with its thousand eddies and unfathomable caverns', who 'pour[s] forth floods of speech, and the richest, noblest speech, only that you find no purpose, tendency, or meaning in it!. . .And yet it is a thousand pities, for there is finest gold in him if it could be parted from the dross.' He described the real Coleridge even more vehemently in 1825 as 'a mass of richest spices, putrified into a dunghill'.[30] Although handicapped in this way, Dalbrook speaks in terms not just reminiscent of Coleridge, but even closer to the oracular utterances of Carlyle himself in his celebrated essays in the *Edinburgh Review* on the 'condition of England' a few years later in 'Signs of the Times' (1829), and 'Characteristics' (1831). He attacks the 'mechanical philosophy':

'Why do we not in good earnest set up Gulliver's poetical turning-loom', said Wotton, 'and produce our poetry in Birmingham by steam?'

'It is surely a false theory', said Dalbrook, 'but of a piece with our other false mechanical philosophy. All things must be rendered visible or they are not conceivable: poetry is an internal joiner-work, but what of that? Virtue itself is an association or perhaps a fluid in the nerves; thought is some vibration, or at best some camera-obscura picturing in the brain; volition is the mounting of a scale or the pressing of a spring; and the mind is some balance, or engine, motionless of itself, till it be swayed this way and that by external things. Good Heavens! Surely if we have any soul there must be a kind of *life* in it? Surely it does not hang passive and inert within us, but acts and works; and if so, acts and works like an immaterial spirit on spiritual things, not like an artisan on matter. Surely it were good, then, even in our loosest contemplations, to admit some little mystery in the operating of a power by its nature so inscrutable. With our similitudes, we make the mind a passive engine, set in motion by the senses; as it were a sort of thought-mill to grind sensations into ideas, by which figures also we conceive this grinding process to be very prettily explained. Nay, it is the same in our material physiology as in our mental; animal life, like spiritual, you find is tacitly regarded as a quality, a susceptibility, the relation and result of other powers, not itself the origin and fountain-head of all other powers; but its force comes from without by palpable transmission, does not dwell mysteriously within, and emanate mysteriously in wonder-working influences from within; and man himself is but a more cunning chemico-mechanical combination, such as in the progress of discovery we may hope to see manufactured at Soho. Nay, smile not incredulously, John Williams! It is even as I say; and thus runs the high road to Atheism in religion, materialism in philosophy, utility in morals, and flaring, effect-seeking mannerism in Art. Art do I call it? Let me not profane the name! Poetry is a making, a creation', added he, 'and the first rising up of a poem in the head of the poet is as inexplicable, by material formulas, as the first rising up of nature out of chaos.'[31]

Thought as vibration, volition as the pressing of a spring, the soul as passive and inert, sensations as primary – these are Carlyle's own expression of the Coleridgean indignation with Hume and Hartley. To this Carlyle adds with his 'thought-mill' a characteristic pun on Mill's name (repeated in *Sartor*), he heightens and generalises with his insistence on the importance of mystery and wonder (again a theme in *Sartor*), and runs all the modern evils together – Atheism, materialism, utility, mannerism in Art – as one great symptom of the condition of England. Similarly in his 'Signs of the Times' article he described the age as 'the Mechanical Age' in its philosophy as well as its industry. 'Hartley's vibrations and vibratiuncles' are a symptom of this, as are 'the Millites', and Carlyle urges as an antidote the cultivation of the 'dynamic' forces of love, faith, and wonder.[32]

Though Carlyle grumbled thus about Coleridge's reticence and fragmentariness, he saw his importance as an ally against the materialists, and knew him to be 'Germanised'. He was also well aware of Coleridge's difficulties with uncomprehending critics. In an article on Novalis in 1829, nervous of interesting an English audience in such a 'mystical' writer, he thought naturally of Coleridge as a parallel case:

Our Coleridge's *Friend*, for example, and *Biographia Literaria* are but a slight business compared with these *Schriften*; little more than the Alphabet, and that in gilt letters, of such Philosophy and Art as is here taught in the form of Grammar and Rhetorical Compend; yet Coleridge's works were triumphantly condemned by the whole reviewing world, as clearly unintelligible; and among readers they have still but an unseen circulation; like living brooks, hidden for the present under mountains of froth and theatrical snow-paper, and which only at a distant day, when these mountains shall have decomposed themselves into gas and earthy residuum, may roll forth in their true limpid shape, to gladden the general eye with what beauty and everlasting freshness does reside in them.[33]

And just as Coleridge objected to being labelled a 'mystic', but at the same time feelingly excused such a mystical writer as Boehme from unsympathetic criticism,[34] so Carlyle defended Novalis's mysticism and even thought of himself in such terms, yet resented the description when it was applied to him by others. In 1833 he wrote to Mill, whom he was keen to convert, about the comparatively small significance of mere logic (by which he meant something very like what Coleridge increasingly indicated by 'Understanding' – i.e. the eighteenth-century, 'mechanical' frame of mind), as compared to intuitive vision:

My similitude was always: Who is he with a pair of *stout legs* that cannot *walk*, whether he anatomically know the mechanism of the muscles or not? The grand difficulty, I think, with us all is to *see* somewhat, to *believe* somewhat; a quite mystic operation, to which Logic helps little, to which, proclaim what laws of vision you will, nothing but an *eye* will be of service.[35]

But Carlyle was not insensitive to the fact that others disapproved. It was thus no coincidence that he chose as his main theme in the 'State of German Literature' article the defence of that literature against the frequently made charges of bad taste and mysticism. It was lucky that Jeffrey had taken to him ('I feel at once that you are a man of Genius – and of original character and right heart – and shall be proud and happy to know more of you'[36]), but this did not prevent him from reminding Carlyle constantly of the dubiousness of his German interest. Through Jeffrey's good offices Carlyle was considered for the chair of philosophy at the new London University. He joked – 'Perhaps they may want a Professor of Mysticism' – but he also let Carlyle know that Brougham and the rest of the board were really 'alarmed at [his] German predilections'.[37] Carlyle found himself, like Coleridge, denying the title of 'mystic':

Charles Buller, a good pupil of mine, had, as he informed me, been endeavouring to strengthen my interest with Mill; but was met by the information that 'I was a mystic, and *altogether* inadmissible.' Now, God knows I am no mystic, but have a clear Scotch head on my shoulders, as any man need, and too strong in logic and scepticism rather than too weak: however once for all these good souls. . .are possessed with this notion; and how can I or any mortal influence drive it out of them?[38]

Carlyle's solution was, in *Sartor*, to allow himself full rein with the rhapsodic visionary Teufelsdröckh, while cannily retaining a commonsense, deflating presence in the form of the professor's English editor. The critical atmosphere Carlyle entered in the mid-1820s, and his relationship with Jeffrey, explain in some degree his hesitancy about how far to follow Coleridge down an unpopular path. Jeffrey's constant irony about his pretensions and his melodramatic indulgence of Carlyle's wish to convert the readers of the *Edinburgh Review* to 'Germanism' may also excuse his sense of himself as special, a lone voice 'introducing. . .that strange Literature', the German, in England.

If Carlyle was in the 'State of German Literature' article not wholly accurate in the particulars of his assessment of 'Kantism' and kept silent about those who shared his German interest, he nevertheless offered a broadly correct historical view of the new movement in German literature, criticism, and philosophy at the end of the eighteenth century:

Far from being behind other nations in the practice or science of Criticism, it is a fact, for which we fearlessly refer to all competent judges, that they are distinctly and even considerably in advance. We state what is already known to a great part of Europe to be true. Criticism has assumed a new form in Germany; it proceeds on other principles, and proposes to itself a higher aim. The grand question is not now a question concerning the qualities of diction, the coherence of metaphors, the fitness of sentiments, the general logical truth, in a work of art, as it was some half-century ago among most critics; neither is it a question mainly of a psychological sort, to be answered by discovering and delineating the peculiar nature of the poet from his poetry, as is usual with the best of our own critics at present: but it is, not indeed exclusively, but inclusively of those two other questions, properly and ultimately a question on the essence and peculiar life of the poetry itself.

In Germany criticism was a science, 'remotely or immediately' connected 'with the subtlest problems of all philosophy', not the parochial business it was in Britain.[39] The article's strength consists in its sweeping gesture of approval for the Germans, its insistence on a new positive response, and its certitude of tone. With this Carlyle became famous as the 'Germanist' of the *Edinburgh Review*. He wrote proudly to Goethe of his success in converting Jeffrey and the *Edinburgh* to tolerance:

> The Editor of the *Edinburgh Review*, who himself wrote the Critique on *Wilhelm Meister*, and many years ago admitted a worthless enough Paper on your *Dichtung und Wahrheit*, is thought hereby to have virtually re-canted his Confession of faith with regard to German Literature; and great is the amazement and even consternation of many an "old stager," over most of whom this man has long reigned with a soft yet almost despotic sway. Let it not surprise you if I give one of your Medals even to him; for he also is a "well-wisher," as one good man must always be to another, however distance and want of right knowledge may, for a time, have warped his perceptions, and caused him to assume a cold or even unfriendly aspect.[40]

Other articles in several periodicals followed, with the aim of converting ignorant hostility into admiration, particularly for Goethe.

Carlyle and Goethe (1822–32)

By means of his translation of *Wilhelm Meister*, his *Life of Schiller*, and his *Edinburgh Review* articles, Carlyle became known to Goethe, who helped to spread his reputation as a German scholar in Germany. In fact, he was the only student of German literature to communicate regularly with Goethe, and after Goethe's death with his secretary, Eckermann, and his most enthusiastic critic, Varnhagen von Ense. The correspondence between them from 1824 till Goethe's death in 1832 encouraged Carlyle's sense of mission and importance as a mediator of German literature as much as Jeffrey's more negative advice.

In 1824 Carlyle had sent a copy of his translation of *Wilhelm Meisters Lehrjahre* to Goethe. A reply came four months later, politely thanking Carlyle for his effort, and enclosing a few poems. Although not much more could be expected from Goethe, who was constantly being visited by admirers, including several English travellers,[41] Carlyle's pride at receiving a letter from him was not untempered by some disappointment at the 'kind nothings' Goethe had written.[42] Soon, however, Carlyle meant more to Goethe than yet another correspondent who had to be politely flattered. Goethe, already over seventy, was unable to keep pace with all that was being done in England to spread his name. He found Carlyle a useful correspondent, who could keep him up to date. As his English was not good, it is unlikely that he read Carlyle's translations very closely. Indeed, William Allingham, on being shown round Goethe's house in Weimar in 1859, made a note in his diary about the 'book-room, narrow and dark, row of shelves in the centre. Carlyle's *German Romances* (uncut), with C.'s writing descriptive of sketches of his house in Scotland'.[43] But if Goethe never read *German Romance*, he almost certainly did read Carlyle's *Life of Schiller*. This homage to Goethe's friend and fellow poet was one of two things which probably contributed most to his high regard for Carlyle. He wrote in praise of the work in his periodical, *Ueber Kunst und Alterthum* (1828), and he also sent a letter to the gratified author, expressing the 'great esteem' in which he held the biography:

Lassen Sie mich vorerst, mein Theuerster, von Ihrer Biographie Schillers das Beste sagen: sie ist merkwürdig, indem sie ein genaues Studium der Vorfälle seines Lebens beweist, so wie denn auch das Studium seiner Werke und eine innige Teilnahme an denselben daraus hervorgeht.

Let me first of all, my dear Sir, praise your biography of Schiller. It is remarkable for its detailed study of the events of his life, and equally for the study of his works and the fervent sympathy with them which it displays.[44]

He went on to talk of 'Weltliteratur', and his hopes for a greater understanding between nations through the general human element in literature, ending by calling every translator a 'prophet' to his countrymen. No wonder Carlyle, who had written to his mother in 1826 that he felt he had 'much to do in this world', not in 'the vain pursuit of wealth and worldly honours' but in 'the search and declaration of Truth', was thrilled with this particular expression of praise.[45]

Enclosed with this letter of Goethe's was a poem, and also a translation of the Scottish ballad, 'The Barring of the Door', called by Goethe 'Gutmann und Gutweib'. This suggests a second reason which probably lay behind Goethe's interest in Carlyle. His imagination was roused by the idea of Carlyle working alone in the wilds of Scotland. Perhaps he still felt some of the old romantic interest in 'Ossian', documented in his early novel, *Die Leiden des jungen Werthers* (1774), where he had quoted pages of the sombre Highland poetry. At any rate, he was pleased to think of a special Scottish–German relationship. He mentioned it in a letter to Carlyle of June

1828 and in his introduction to the German translation of the *Life of Schiller* in 1830. His readiness to believe that Carlyle was his only champion in Britain may well have been due in part to his romantic notion of the 'mountain solitude' of Craigenputtoch.[46] The building was sketched, at Goethe's request, and its picture appeared on the frontispiece of the German *Life of Schiller*, while Goethe in his preface wrote eloquently of Carlyle's lonely Scottish home. The letters seldom went unaccompanied by some homely token of Scottish or German life. Jane worked at 'tammies' for Goethe's daughter-in-law, Ottilie, and Goethe sent presents of medals, as well as necklaces and little poems for Jane.

This polite correspondence makes strange reading, but it indicates real pleasure on Goethe's part and pride on Carlyle's. No other contemporary British author except Byron appealed to Goethe's imagination as Carlyle did. Goethe often mentioned him in his periodical, and he sent a testimonial for Carlyle's (unsuccessful) candidature for the chair of moral philosophy at St Andrews in 1828. As a result of Goethe's attentions, Carlyle became known and respected in Germany. The Berlin Society for Foreign Literature elected him honorary member in 1830. Some of his periodical articles were noticed, not only by Goethe – Müllner quoted from his 'German Playwrights' (*Foreign Review*, 1829) in his newspaper, the *Mitternachtsblatt*. Eckermann translated Carlyle's eulogy 'Death of Goethe', which appeared in the *New Monthly Magazine* in June 1832.

Goethe took Carlyle's remarks about the general ignorance of Germany in England so literally that he wrote of the first volume of the *Foreign Quarterly Review* in 1827:

In diesem gleich vom Anfang solid und würdig erscheinenden Werke finde ich mehrere Aufsätze über deutsche Literatur: *Ernst Schulze, Hoffmann* und unser *Theater*; ich glaube darin den Edinburger Freund zu erkennen, denn es wäre doch wunderbar, wenn das alte Britannien ein paar Menächmen hervorgebracht haben sollte.

I find in this solid and always worthy periodical several essays on German literature: Ernst Schulze, Hoffmann, and our drama: I think I detect the hand of our Edinburgh friend [i.e. Carlyle] in these, for it would indeed be wonderful if old Britain were to have produced a pair of twins.[47]

The three articles in question were by George Moir, Sir Walter Scott, and Gillies, as Carlyle admitted in his reply. Nevertheless,

Goethe adhered to his image of Carlyle as the lonely mediator of German culture, and the idea took root in Germany. Bismarck wrote to congratulate him on his eightieth birthday in 1875, expressing his gratitude for the *Life of Schiller* and the *Life of Frederick the Great*.[48]

It may seem strange that, in spite of invitations from Goethe and an occasional sketchy plan by Carlyle to go to Germany – in 1821 he exclaimed, 'I would travel *above* fifty miles on foot to see Goethe'[49] – the two men never met. Carlyle's poverty in the late 1820s helps to explain this, though he did manage to finance his brother Jack's visit to Germany in 1827. It is likely that Carlyle did not want to meet Goethe, lest the ideal collapse into the reality of the Weimar 'Bürger', a debasement Carlyle did not wish to see. The old man's impartial diplomacy (or, as Carlyle saw it, his ability to suffer fools gladly) puzzled Carlyle, who wondered how it was that 'the Author of *Faust* and *Meister*' could '*tryste* himself with such characters as "Herr Heavyside" (the simplest and stupidest man of his day. . .) whom he mentions in his last epistle'. In a letter to Sterling in 1836 he admitted that, on reading Eckermann's newly published *Gespräche mit Goethe* (*Conversations with Goethe*), he found it 'very curious to see the *Welt-Dichter* conditioned down into the Weimar Burgher and *Staats-rath*', adding that 'in place and work, he and I part wider every day'.[50] All Carlyle's heroes, Luther, Rousseau, Burns, Goethe, Schiller, Jean Paul, Frederick the Great, belonged either to the past or in the distance. His bitterness towards Coleridge, due chiefly to their different opinions about the functions of the established Church, was undoubtedly caused partly by Carlyle's inevitable disappointment with the man in the flesh.

Carlyle did not visit Germany until 1852, and only then because he needed materials for his book on Frederick. The visit included some time in Weimar, but gave Carlyle little pleasure. Inevitably, he was disappointed with the people he met. George Eliot heard two years later of the mutual dislike between Carlyle and Varnhagen von Ense, whose correspondence about Goethe had been so cordial.[51] Varnhagen had written warmly to Carlyle in 1837, addressing him as the friend of Goethe and of German literature ('als der Freund Goethe's und der deutschen Litteratur').[52] But when they met in 1852, Carlyle thought Varnhagen a dandy and Varnhagen entered *his* disappointment in his diary. Carlyle, he wrote, did nothing but complain.[53] Carlyle wrote to James Marshall of his impressions of

Berlin: 'I met with hardly any man worth going ten yards to see.'[54] No doubt it was as well that Carlyle and Goethe never met. Nevertheless, Carlyle became known in England and Germany as Goethe's advocate. Sterling reviewed his essays in 1839, adopting an imitation of Carlyle's own way of writing: 'Grasshoppers had before chirped for and against the rumoured foreign singer; and these are often pleasant verdant animals. But now it was no grasshopper; the creature is of a different race. *Bos locutus est.* It was the roaring of a bull, which the mountains needs must hear and reply to.'[55] Lewes dedicated his *Life of Goethe* 'to Thomas Carlyle, who first taught England to appreciate Goethe'.

If Carlyle preferred heroes to real men, the 'universal man' he so much admired had different tastes. Lewes, in his 1843 article on Goethe, noticed that Goethe's protagonists, from Werther to Faust, are not heroic. He suggested that this was because Goethe knew the nature of men too well to depict heroes, and that he was in general more interested in the real than the ideal.[56] It seems strange that Carlyle found in Goethe the answers to the aesthetic, philosophical, and spiritual problems that troubled him. In fact, his early comments on Goethe reflect doubts little different from those of Coleridge when he wondered if it would be prudent to translate *Faust*.

While Coleridge was corresponding with Boosey in 1820 about writing the text to Retzsch's illustrations to *Faust*, Carlyle had just begun to learn German, taught by an Edinburgh friend, Robert Jardine. He used his knowledge of the language first to contribute articles on German studies in magnetism and mineralogy to Brewster's *Edinburgh Philosophical Journal* in 1820, but he was also reading Lessing, Klopstock, and Goethe.[57] He tended to absorb new impressions from his reading and dispose them according to his needs, and in 1820 what he most needed was consolation for his unhappiness in teaching, his feeling that he had not found where his vocation lay, and his growing religious doubts. Thus when he read *Faust* his response was on the whole one of delight at finding Goethe dealing with the very problems which exercised him. He wrote to Edward Irving:

With respect to Goethe's Faust – if I were at your side you should hear of nothing else for many hours; and sorry am I that your brows will suddenly contract – if I give free scope to my notions even by this imperfect vehicle. I wish Goethe were my countryman, I wish – O, how I wish – he were my friend. It is not for his masterly conception of human nature –

from the heroes of classical story down to the blackguards of a Leipsic alehouse – that I admire him above all others; his profound sentiment of beauty, his most brilliant delineations of all its varieties – his gayety of head and melancholy of heart, open all the floodgates of my sympathy. Faust is a wonderful tragedy. I doubt if even Shakespeare with all his powers had sadness enough in his nature to understand the arid and withered feelings of a passionate spirit, worn out by excessive studies and the want of all enjoyment; to delineate the chaos of his thoughts when the secrets of nature are bared before him; to depict his terrible volition and the bitter mockery of the demon gives scope to that volition. All this and much more is done by Goethe; and but for his *speaking* cats and a good deal besides of a like stamp, I should be an unexcepting admirer of the execution. Upon the whole, I advise you strongly to persist in German. These people have some muscle in their frames.[58]

When he wrote his review of *Faust* in 1822 – his first article on German literature, and, he felt, a poor one, 'being written on a subject which I have never expressed myself about before, and hence with no small difficulty'[59] – his remarks were less favourable. He was probably aware of *Faust*'s reputation for bad taste and immorality, and may have directed his attention to its faults partly for that reason. He thought the riotous Walpurgisnacht, which Shelley, with unerring nonconformity, had translated along with the Prologue in Heaven (though even he omitted Mephistopheles' more smutty jokes), offensive, but was eager to find a moral outcome of the shocking episodes, particularly Faust's seduction of Gretchen and her subsequent murder of her child: 'Faust mingles in this satanic revelry more than we could wish; yet he soon grows tired of it; and we can almost pardon him for having snatched a few moments of enjoyment, or at least forgetfulness, from a source however mean, when we reflect that they are the last allotted to him.'[60] This timid apology for Faust fails to take into account Goethe's control over the witches' scene, which makes its own moral point dramatically. It is placed after Faust has seduced Gretchen and killed her brother, and before he learns of her crime and imprisonment. The nudity, rudeness, and mad dancing of the witches both attract and offend Faust; such is his bargain with Mephistopheles that in the very fulfilment of his lusts he suffers from a fitful awareness of his guilt and a self-loathing which God had clearly predicted in the Prologue in Heaven:

> Ein guter Mensch in seinem dunklen Drange
> Ist sich des rechten Weges wohl bewusst.

A good man is well aware of the right path
even in the midst of his dark struggle.

Like all the other early critics of the play, Carlyle seems not to have
noticed that its apparent episodic structure conceals an artistic
control which implicitly counters what seems like moral licence.

In spite of these doubts about Goethe, Carlyle went on reading
him, and began to translate *Wilhelm Meisters Lehrjahre* in 1823.
The task of rendering into English this work, with its combination of
the symbolic and the mundane,[61] was not a completely happy one.
He undertook it with much the same feelings as those expressed by
Thomas Lovell Beddoes (at that time living in Germany), a 'double
feeling of contempt of & delight in him'.[62] Carlyle's letters and notebooks of 1823 and 1824 are full of complaints about the 'insipidity'
and prosaic nature of the work (of which Novalis had also accused
it, setting out to correct its 'coldness' and 'utilitarianism' in his
fragment of a novel, *Heinrich von Ofterdingen*, 1802).[63] Carlyle
commented:

Meanwhile I go on with Goethe's Wilhelm Meister; a book which I love
not, which I am sure will never sell, but which I am determined to print
and finish. There are touches of the very highest most etherial genius in it;
but diluted with floods of insipidity, which even *I* would not have written
for the world.

There is poetry in the book, and prose, prose forever...The Book is to be
printed in winter or spring. No mortal will ever buy a copy of it...

Goethe is the gre[atest ge]niu[s that has] lived for a century, and the greatest
ass that [has I]ived for th[ree. I] could sometimes fall down and worship
him; at other times I could kick him out of the room...[64]

No doubt the lack of conventional plot disconcerted Carlyle; as
George Eliot and Lewes later pointed out, Goethe moves at a
leisurely pace, allowing ample time for Wilhelm to make his mistakes and for the awareness of them to dawn on him slowly. Goethe
frequently suspends the narrative to make room for long discussions
– the most famous example being the players' and Wilhelm's
analysis of *Hamlet*. He includes a circumstantial memoir, 'Bekennt-
nisse einer schönen Seele' ('Confessions of a Beautiful Soul', translated by Carlyle as 'Confessions of a Fair Saint', which both
Coleridge and Crabb Robinson commented on as a mistranslation[65]),
which has limited relevance to Wilhelm's education. Above all, the
reader needs to be patient; new characters appear suddenly, un-

announced and, as in life but less often in novels, unaccompanied by a helpful curriculum vitae supplied by the narrator, so that assessing them is at first impossible. Like Wilhelm, the reader does not know which characters to trust, he must amass clues, often contradictory, and not be too hasty with either his approval or his dismissal. For example, Jarno, a member of the mysterious society of moral guardians who oversee Wilhelm's affairs, appears first as a treacherous cynic whom we, with Wilhelm, are disinclined to trust.

In his preface to the translation, Carlyle warns his readers that many of them will find it 'beyond endurance weary, flat, stale and unprofitable'.[66] They will have particular difficulty with the first few books, in which Goethe concentrates on Wilhelm's first friends, the travelling actors, and all the petty quarrelling in the theatre which he knew so well from his own attempts as theatre director in Weimar. Here Carlyle touched on a real problem: not everyone is as interested in the details of the theatrical life as Goethe. Schiller had made the same objection when he read the novel in manuscript in 1795.[67] Carlyle also admitted frankly that 'the hero is a milksop, whom, with all his gifts, it takes an effort to avoid despising'. Goethe himself called Wilhelm 'ein armer Hund' ('a poor dog'), but explained that just such unformed, passive characters best illustrate life in all its facets:

Nur an solchem lässt sich das Wechselspiel des Lebens und die tausend verschiedenen Lebensaufgaben recht deutlich zeigen, nicht an schon abgeschlossenen festen Charakteren.

Only with such a character can one show really clearly the vicissitudes and the thousand different tasks of life, not with characters which are already rounded and fixed.[68]

Indeed, Goethe successfully balances irony at Wilhelm's expense – especially early on where Wilhelm discourses pompously and at length on subjects he yet knows little about – with sympathy for his being victimised and cheated by the others. Wilhelm's great patience, though closely allied to the passivity of his conscience, wins him respect in the end.

Carlyle's main embarrassment concerned the actions, and sometimes the language, of the selfish, greedy, promiscuous players and their bored aristocratic exploiters. He explained simply in the preface:

In many points, both literary and moral, I could have wished devoutly that he had not written as he has done; but to alter anything was not in my commission. The literary and moral persuasions of a man like Goethe are objects of a rational curiosity; and the duty of a translator is simple and distinct. Accordingly, except a few phrases and sentences, not in all amounting to a page, which I have dropped as evidently unfit for the English taste, I have studied to present the work exactly as it stands in German.[69]

Even with his occasional tempering of language, Carlyle could not prevent British critics from complaining of vulgarity. Not only Jeffrey, but even De Quincey reviewed the translation from the righteous point of view of impeccable English taste. 'No other of Goethe's works', he wrote, 'is likely to be more revolting to English good sense: the whole *prestige* of his name must now totter.'[70] Although English critics felt superior in dealing with *Wilhelm Meister*, the novel had met with similar complaints from some German critics on its publication twenty years before. They, too, had objected to the bad company Wilhelm keeps and Goethe's seeming lack of disapproval of it.[71] Goethe was rightly annoyed by such criticism. He told Eckermann in 1825:

Es gibt wunderliche Kritiker...An diesem Roman tadelten sie, dass der Held sich zu viel in schlechter Gesellschaft befinde. Dadurch aber, dass ich die sogenannte schlechte Gesellschaft als Gefäss betrachtete, um das, was ich von der guten zu sagen hatte, darin niederzulegen, gewann ich einen poetischen Körper und einen mannigfaltigen dazu.

There are strange critics...They complained about this novel that the hero finds himself too often in bad company. But precisely by regarding the so-called bad company as a vessel into which to put what I had to say about good company, I gained a poetical form and a comprehensive one too.[72]

Henry James, reviewing an American republication of Carlyle's translation of *Wilhelm Meister* in 1865, clearly saw what Goethe was doing:

He introduces us to the shabbiest company, in order to enrich us with knowledge; he leads us to the fairest goals by the longest and roughest roads. It is to this fact, doubtless, that the work owes its reputation of tediousness; but it justifies the reputation only when, behind the offensive detail, the patient reader fails to discover, not a glittering, but a steadily shining generality.[73]

Carlyle's double feeling about Goethe's art stemmed mainly from the same source as his surprise at Goethe's polite, aloof tolerance of all sorts of people in his life of literary lion in Weimar. Goethe's way of holding back from direct moral comment saddened him. In his preface he was non-committal, saying merely:

> The author himself, far from "doing it in a passion," wears a face of the most still indifference throughout the whole affair; often it is even wrinkled by a slight sardonic grin. For the friends of the sublime, then, for those who cannot do without heroical sentiments, and "moving accidents by flood and field," there is nothing here that can be of any service.[74]

But elsewhere he was more open. In 1832 he wrote, 'in Goethe's Writings. . .we all know, the moral lesson is seldom so easily educed as one would wish'.[75] It was the 'sardonic grin', Goethe's cool ability to make Wilhelm boring – he sends his mistress to sleep in the opening chapters of the work with his naive narrative of his childhood delight in puppet theatres – without fearing to lose his reader's interest in Wilhelm, which Carlyle rendered least well in his translation. In Wilhelm's description of his severe father (doubtless modelled on Goethe's own), there is a light bitterness which Carlyle failed to catch:

> Der Vater hatte seinem Freunde das alles zu veranstalten erlaubt, er selbst schien nur durch die Finger zu sehen, nach dem Grundsatze, man müsse den Kindern nicht merken lassen, wie lieb man sie habe, sie griffen immer zu weit um sich; er meinte, man müsse bei ihren Freuden ernst scheinen und sie ihnen manchmal verderben, damit ihre Zufriedenheit sie nicht übermässig und übermütig mache.

> My father had allowed his friend to arrange it all [i.e. amateur theatricals], while he himself seemed not to notice, on the principle that one ought not to let children see how much one loves them, lest they come to expect too much; he thought one ought to look serious at their fun and occasionally spoil it, so that their satisfaction might not make them excessive and presumptuous.

Carlyle softens this in several particulars. His translation runs:

> My father had allowed his friend to arrange all this; himself, in the mean time, seeming only to look at the transaction, as it were, through his fingers; for his maxim was, that children should not be allowed to see the kindness which is felt towards them, lest their pretensions come to extend too far. He was of opinion, that, in the enjoyments of the young, one should assume a serious air; often interrupting the course of their festivities, to prevent their satisfaction from degenerating into excess and presumption.[76]

On the whole, Carlyle translates accurately, and if he does not always convey Goethe's lighter ironies, he manages the more comic aspects well. For example, there is Wilhelm's pompous 'know-all' attitude when he is at the very beginning of his 'apprenticeship' for life. Melina, an experienced actor, tells Wilhelm that he will never return to the stage, but will take up a good useful trade instead. Wilhelm does not ask the reason for this drastic decision, but immediately takes it upon himself to advise Melina, whereupon the latter cuts him down to size:

Das ist ein sonderbarer Entschluss, den ich nicht billigen kann; denn ohne besondere Ursache ist es niemals ratsam, die Lebensart, die man ergriffen hat, zu verändern, und überdies wüsste ich keinen Stand, der so viel Annehmlichkeiten, so veil reizende Aussichten darböte, als den eines Schauspielers.

Man sieht, dass Sie keiner gewesen sind, versetzte jener.

Carlyle translates well:

"This is a strange resolution, which I cannot give my approbation to. Without especial reasons, it can never be advisable to change the mode of life we have begun with; and, besides, I know of no condition that presents so much allurement, so many charming prospects, as the condition of an actor."

"It is easy to see that you have never been one," said the other.[77]

Carlyle manages the songs from *Wilhelm Meister* less well. His version of Mignon's song 'Kennst du das Land' ('Know'st thou the land') is less rhythmical than Coleridge's.[78]

Like Coleridge before him, he toyed with the idea of translating *Faust*, 'for which', as he wrote to Goethe in 1830, 'the English world is getting more and more prepared'.[79] Fortunately he gave up after attempting Faust's curse at the end of the second study scene. This unrhythmical and strained fragment appeared in the *Athenaeum* in 1832. A sample of it indicates Carlyle's ineptitude:

> Verflucht, was uns in Träumen heuchelt,
> Des Ruhms, der Namensdauer Trug!
> Verflucht, was als Besitz uns schmeichelt,
> Als Weib und Kind, als Knecht und Pflug!
>
> A curse on all, one seed that scatters
> Of hope from death our Name to save;
> On all as earthly Good that flatters,
> As Wife or Child, as Plough or Slave.[80]

It is amusing to compare Jane's rather good efforts at translating Goethe and Schiller poems in 1822 under the guidance of Carlyle, who offered wayward corrections as 'Variations by Hypercriticus'.[81] As Richard Holt Hutton wrote, Carlyle's verse was 'like the heavy rumble of a van without springs'.[82] Carlyle himself admitted to Sterling in 1839 that he had failed to get hold of Goethe's 'tune'.[83]

In spite of these shortcomings, the translation was good enough to attract many readers to Goethe, and Carlyle's hints in the preface about the work's special quality are intelligent, particularly where he stresses the importance of re-reading and keeping an open mind. Many 'apparent blemishes', he says, will turn out to be none and may even be seen as beauties.[84] Henry James made the same point in his review: 'few other books. . .so steadily and gradually *dawn* upon the intelligence'.[85] Carlyle reminded those who wrote to him about Goethe that much in *Wilhelm Meister* might be distasteful, even distressing, but that they would find 'real truth even in what you hate' and a 'mirror in which other minds may see their own likeness, find some interpretation of themselves'.[86] It is greatly to his credit that as early as 1824, he recognised, in spite of his 'very mixed sentiment' about it, that in *Wilhelm Meister* 'lay more insight into the elements of human nature, and a more poetically perfect combining of these, than in all the other fictitious literature of our generation'.[87] He himself had believed in Goethe's general wisdom from the beginning, though he often had doubts about particular passages. In 1823, when he was translating Goethe, he was at his lowest physically and emotionally. It looked as though Jane did not love him, he was often ill, and was discontented with his work. His notebook in December 1823 even carries the thought of suicide. But it also notes Goethe's advice to 'do the task that lies nearest us' and not dwell hopelessly on the mistakes of the past.[88] Thus translating *Wilhelm Meister* was an activity which he felt to be beneficial to him as a whole, though it threatened to defeat or upset him from time to time. He never forgot his gratitude for the practical wisdom he found in the book; in 1827 he wrote to Goethe:

You are kind enough to inquire about my bygone life. With what readiness could I speak to you of it, how often have I longed to pour out the whole history before you! As it is, your works have been a mirror to me; unasked and unhoped for, your wisdom has counselled me; and so peace and health of soul have visited me from afar. For I was once an Unbeliever, not in Religion only, but in all the Mercy and Beauty of which it is the symbol; storm-tossed in my own imaginations; a man divided from men; exasperated, wretched, driven almost to despair; so that Faust's wild *curse* seemed the only fit greeting for human life, and his passionate *Fluch von allen der Geduld*! [sic] was spoken from my very inmost heart. But now, thank Heaven, all this is altered: without change of external circumstances, solely by the new light which rose upon me, I attained to new thoughts, and a composure which I should once have considered as impossible.[89]

An almost inevitable result of Carlyle's investing so much feeling about his personal history in his view of Goethe was that that view erred on the idealistic side. Goethe became 'our Teacher', 'our Greatest' (in an essay on Goethe in 1832), 'the Wisest of our Time' (in *Sartor*), and Carlyle concentrated on the deep lessons to be learnt from Goethe. Not surprisingly, he enjoyed reading and translating the more symbolic, doctrinal *Wilhelm Meisters Wanderjahre* (*Wilhelm Meister's Travels*, published in *German Romance* in 1827) more than the *Lehrjahre*. As an old man he recommended it as 'the Book of Books on Education of the young soul in these broken distracted times of ours'.[90] Here was overt moral education (the subtitle was 'Die Entsagenden', 'The Renunciants') in place of the easily misunderstood animal gaiety of the earlier work. In his essays on Goethe, Carlyle wrote resonantly though vaguely about Goethe's wisdom. He wrote a brief rhapsodic sketch of Goethe in *Fraser's Magazine*'s 'Gallery of Literary Characters', in which he summed up his, and the world's, debt to Goethe in a style which was out of step with the other facetious 'portraits' in the series:

Reader! within that head the whole world lies mirrored, in such clear ethereal harmony as it has done in none since Shakspeare left us; even *this* rag-fair of a world, wherein thou painfully strugglest, and (as is like) stumblest, – all lies transfigured here, and revealed authentically to be still holy, still divine. What alchemy was that: to find a mad universe full of scepticism, discord, desperation; and *transmute* it into a wise universe of belief, and melody, and reverence! Was not *there* an *opus magnum*, if one ever was? This, then, is he who, heroically doing and enduring, has accomplished it.[91]

He saw that Goethe had trodden the path from scepticism to belief in the later works, and used him increasingly as an example to an age too liable to scepticism:

To our minds, in these soft, melodious imaginations of his, there is embodied the Wisdom which is proper to this time; the beautiful, the religious Wisdom, which may still, with something of its old impressiveness, speak to the whole soul; still, in these hard, unbelieving utilitarian days, reveal to us glimpses of the Unseen but not unreal World, that so the Actual and the Ideal may again meet together, and clear Knowledge be again wedded to Religion, in the life and business of men.[92]

As always with Carlyle, the core of this assessment is correct, but the mode of stating it distances us from Goethe rather than bringing us closer to him.

Carlyle identified his own life with Goethe's, seeing in it a mirror of his difficulties in the early 1820s, when he had questioned his previous religious and philosophical assumptions. But Goethe and Carlyle expressed themselves in very different ways. Carlyle's experiences are reflected in *Sartor*, in the episode of the 'Rue Saint-Thomas de l'Enfer', where Teufelsdröckh closely resembles Carlyle in Edinburgh. The hero goes through a period of scepticism, when 'Doubt had darkened into Unbelief'. A defiant indifference follows the Everlasting No, until, by a process of Self-Annihilation, he reaches a position of faith and devotion to Duty.[93] The 'Sorrows of Teufelsdröckh' are scarcely distinguishable from those of Carlyle in 1823. *Die Leiden des jungen Werthers*, on the other hand, contained echoes from Goethe's experience: in representing the one-sided love affair between Werther and Charlotte, and the hero's painful situation in the household of Charlotte and her husband, Goethe had to some extent been ridding himself of a 'sickness'.[94] But the novel was more than a painful experience recollected in tranquillity; it was a considered work of art. Werther represents more than a melancholy lovesick boy; his malaise is social and representative as well as personal.

Carlyle thought he owed his rigorous notion of 'self denial' to Goethe's doctrine of Entsagung (renunciation), when in fact it was as much a product of his Calvinism, supplemented by his reading not only of Goethe but of Fichte and Novalis.[95] The concept was for Carlyle a social and religious one, whereas Goethe's 'Entsagung' belongs also to an aesthetic context, and is to be understood as the individual's ordering of experience towards personal culture and serenity. It includes social duties – for instance, Wilhelm Meister earns his full 'citizenship' when he has acted as a father to the boy Friedrich without knowing that he is his own son – but Goethe also allows duty and inclination to coincide. When Wilhelm 'renounces' Therese, it is only partly because he realises another man's prior claim to her, and partly because he has realised that he really loves Natalie, not Therese.[96] Carlyle's descriptions of Goethe for the

education of British readers are too strenuous to be accurate: 'in
Goethe there lay Force to educe reconcilement out of such contra-
diction as man is now born into, [which] marks him as the Strong
One of his time'.[97] Even if Goethe's later works, the second part of
Faust, Wilhelm Meisters Wanderjahre, the late poems in *West-
Östlicher Divan*, provide a moral symbolism to satisfy Carlyle, he is
not quite right to attribute 'religion' in an unqualified sense to
Goethe, even if we understand 'religion' in Carlyle's peculiar sense,
as embracing all facets of daily life, especially the 'sacredness' of
daily work.[98] Carlyle saw Goethe as one of the 'prophetic' and
'religious' phenomena of modern Europe (the other being the
French Revolution), thus forcing upon him a representativeness
which other readers could not accept. Matthew Arnold, for one,
criticised Carlyle's 'infatuation' with Goethe. 'On looking back at
Carlyle', he wrote in 1877, 'one sees how much of *engouement* there
was in his criticism of Goethe, and how little of it will stand. That
is the thing – to write what will *stand*.'[99]

Mill also objected to Carlyle's vagueness and the rhapsodic tone
he adopted in discussing Goethe. He felt that the essays did not carry
their own evidence.[100] This was particularly true of Carlyle's short
essay on Goethe's death, which Hayward had asked him to write for
the *New Monthly Magazine*. The Goethe whose death Carlyle
lamented was a creature spiritualised by Carlyle's imagination:

Beautiful rose our summer sun, gorgeous in the red fervid east, scattering
the spectres and sickly damps (of both of which there were enough to
scatter); strong, benignant in his noonday clearness, walking triumphant
through the upper realms; and now, mark also how he sets! *'So stirbt ein
Held; anbetungsvoll,* So dies a hero; sight to be worshipped!'[101]

Most of those who came to Goethe first through Carlyle's articles
– including Sterling, Mill, and Lewes – realised sooner or later that
Carlyle was to some extent a falsifying medium. Crabb Robinson
thought him 'idolatrous' of Goethe, and Holt Hutton noted his
'undiscriminating, strained, and lashed-up furor of adoration'.[102]
But all gave him credit for boldly praising an unpopular German
author, about whom there were more prejudices in England than
about any other except Kant, and forcing his countrymen to interest
themselves in Goethe.[103] His articles and translations did, in fact,
bring about a greater interest in the author of *Faust*. Most of the
periodicals in the first few years of the 1830s noticed at least some

of the volumes of posthumous works, and the many collections of reminiscences, correspondence, and memoirs which appeared after Goethe's death. A more balanced view followed Carlyle's exaggerations. Lewes, for example, insisted on the organic necessity in *Faust* of the Prologue in Heaven, defended *Wilhelm Meister* against charges of immorality by suggesting that Goethe's intention was to 'paint scenes of life, *without comment*', and stressed the importance of an aesthetic approach to Goethe.[104] It was Lewes, with his *Life of Goethe*, who did for Goethe what Carlyle had done for Schiller with the *Life of Schiller* thirty years before. He not only gave the British the first comprehensive view of Goethe, but succeeded, like Carlyle, in attracting the praise of the Germans.[105] Appropriately, Lewes dedicated the *Life* to Carlyle. He also summed up Carlyle's achievement for Goethe, simultaneously pointing to his shortcomings:

Carlyle's fervent and eloquent Essays...give no definite image of the man, they are exquisite exhortations to study, rather than information of what the student will find, or how to seek it. They did immense good in their time; they crushed the flippant tone of those Edinburgh reviewers, who thought Göthe 'wanted taste', and was 'not a gentleman'; and they prepared the way for his reception amongst us.[106]

Carlyle and German philosophy (1824–34)

The *Life of Schiller*, based on articles first published in the *London Magazine* in 1823 and 1824, was the first of Carlyle's attempts at biography, a genre to which he attached great importance. History was the biography of Great Men,[107] and poets were more congenial to him when he could point to their lives as heroic. Schiller fitted this need better than Goethe, and the *Life* was a largely undistorting work. He wrote sympathetically of the poet's struggle against external circumstances. Men like Schiller, Otway, Cowper, Collins, and Chatterton, he wrote, are 'the vanguard in the march of mind; the intellectual Backwoodsmen, reclaiming from the idle wilderness new territories for the thought and the activity of their happier brethren'.[108] Schiller's moral and political idealism, his notion of the moral function of art, his questionings in the *Philosophische Briefe* and the other essays of the 1780s and 1790s, as well as his poverty and ill-health were topics to which Carlyle easily warmed. Schiller had characterised himself as the type of the modern, 'reflective' poet, who expressed self-awareness problematically in his works.

From the *Räuber* (1781) and *Don Carlos* (1787) to *Wallenstein* (1798–9) the 'problem', of personal or political liberty, social order, allegiance, responsibility, is stated in dramatic terms and followed through several stages to some kind of moral solution. Schiller saw the stage as a moral institution, 'der gemeinschaftliche Kanal, in welchen von dem denkenden bessern Teile des Volks das Licht herunterströmt und von da aus in milderen Strahlen durch den ganzen Staat sich verbreitet' ('the common channel, into which the light of wisdom streams down from the better, thinking part of the nation, and from there spreads out through the whole land in milder rays').[109] Besides being a poet and dramatist, he was professor of history at Jena, and the author of a history of the Fall of the Netherlands (1788) and of the Thirty Years War (1791). With his moralist view of literature, his lofty idealism, his philosophic sense of history, Schiller was a writer to suit Carlyle.[110] It was characteristic of Carlyle's taste for the heroic and comparative lack of interest in aesthetic and dramatic qualities that his favourite works of Schiller were the two dramatically weakest, *Die Jungfrau von Orleans* (*The Maid of Orleans*, 1801) and *Wilhelm Tell* (1804).[111] In spite of some weaknesses of judgment, the *Life of Schiller* is a landmark in Anglo-German relations, being the first English biography of a great German writer. It has many positive distinctions – clarity, comprehensiveness, sympathy – and is plentiful in quotations and translated extracts.

Carlyle's main difficulty in dealing with Schiller's life came when he had to follow Schiller in his philosophical studies, particularly his engagement with Kant. Carlyle's knowledge of Kant was slight. He probably did not get beyond the 150th page of the *Kritik der reinen Vernunft*, though he had at that early stage hopes of 'instructing my benighted countrymen on the true merits of this sublime system'.[112] It is not surprising that he had difficulties with this part of the *Kritik* ('Transzendentale Deduktion der reinen Verstandesbegriffe', 'Transcendental Deduction of the Concepts of Pure Understanding'), leading to the difficult deduction of the categories. Coleridge, who did persevere beyond this point, found this section obscure.[113] But if Carlyle gave up at this early point, he could not be in a position competently to discuss the *Kritik* as a whole. He admitted in his journal in 1823 that he did not understand Kant: 'I wish I understood the philosophy of Kant. Is it a chapter in the history of human folly or the brightest in the history of h. wisdom? Or of both mixed?

And in what degree?'[114] When he came to discuss Kant's influence on Schiller, he had not been able to answer these questions, and contented himself with a rhetorically vague passage:

The air of mysticism was attractive to the German mind, with which the vague and the vast are always pleasing qualities; the dreadful array of first principles, a forest huge of terminology and definitions, where the panting intellect of weaker men wanders as in pathless thickets, and at length sinks powerless to the earth, oppressed with fatigue, and suffocated with scholastic miasma – seemed sublime rather than appalling to the Germans; men who shrink not at toil, and to whom a certain degree of darkness appears a native element, essential for giving play to that deep meditative enthusiasm which forms so important a feature in their character.[115]

It is clear from the journals that Carlyle was unhappy with his work on Schiller, probably because of his lack of grasp of Kant's influence. 'Schiller', he confided in November 1823, 'is in the wrong vein. Laborious, partly affected, meagre, bombastic: too often it strives by lofty words to hide littleness of thought.'[116] Yet he could not leave it at that. In the *Life of Schiller* he felt compelled to admit his 'only very limited acquaintance with the subject'. His remarks are un-certain, but he makes a case, presumably based on his reading of the beginning of the *Kritik*, where Kant discusses the 'transcendental ideality' of Time and Space, for the transcendental philosophy as an antidote to the materialism of the eighteenth century and the new Utilitarian creed. He seems to be saying that Kant may not be worth much, but at least his system is preferable to Benthamism:

The Philosophy of Kant is probably combined with errors to its very core; but perhaps also, this ponderous unmanageable dross may bear in it the everlasting gold of truth! Mighty spirits have already laboured in refining it: is it wise in us to take up with base pewter of Utility, and renounce such projects altogether? We trust, not.[117]

It was at this point that Carlyle, in his difficulty, made his appeal for help to Coleridge, whom he publicly acknowledged as the chief critic of the materialist philosophy, though he felt a personal and ideo-logical antipathy to the man whom he described privately, as we have seen, in terms of spices and dunghills.

By 1831 Carlyle was far enough from the Kantian 'problem' to be able to venture the confident assertion that:

...the Transcendental Philosophy, which arose in Schiller's busiest era, could not remain without influence on him: he had carefully studied Kant's

System, and appears to have not only admitted but zealously appropri-ated its fundamental doctrines; remoulding them, however, into his own peculiar forms, so that they seem no longer borrowed, but permanently acquired, not less Schiller's than Kant's.[118]

This assertion is so vague that one would doubt Carlyle's qualifica-tion to assess the details of Schiller's debt to Kant even without the evidence of the notebooks. Carlyle, like De Quincey, was content to remain in a state of half-knowledge about Kant. By 1840 Carlyle had forgotten that he had ever had problems, and could write to Geraldine Jewsbury and Francis Espinasse that Kant had given him 'deliverance from the fatal incubus of Scotch or French philosophy, with its mechanisms and Atheisms'.[119] Carlyle's appreciation of Schiller, sound in many respects, remained in this as limited as it had been when he was first preparing the articles on Schiller for the *London Magazine* in 1823, despite the acquisition of a more authoritative tone.

Although Carlyle showed a lack of stamina with regard to Kant, his confident public announcements and what was understood to be his thoroughgoing 'Germanism' brought him celebrity as a philo-sophical thinker. Though George Eliot shrewdly placed him as more artist than philosopher,[120] Francis Espinasse, Thomas Spedding, Leigh Hunt, and initially Emerson thought of him as a philosopher, and a more recent critic thought he had 'transfused' the Kantian philosophy 'into the substance of his *Sartor Resartus*, and in a thousand ways presented significant ideas from that philosophy throughout his works'.[121] The confusion stems from Carlyle himself. There are discrepancies in his utterances, public and private, on Kant. He wanted to find idealism in Kant, or 'the Kantists'. His small direct knowledge of Kant did not allow him to be sure on this point, but he recognised the closeness of German Romantic aesthetics to Kant's system, and he felt obliged to introduce it to British readers, especially in the 'State of German Literature' article.[122] There he admitted, 'we are still inquirers at the mere outskirts of the matter', and apologised to the 'Kantians' for speaking in such a 'loose and popular manner' of Kant and the Germans generally. Having given this precautionary apology, he launched into a partial misinterpretation of German philosophy. He defined the terms Reason and Understanding as he understood Kant to mean them:

To most of our readers this may seem a distinction without a difference: nevertheless, to the Kantists it is by no means such. They believe that both

Understanding and Reason are organs, or rather, we should say, modes of operation, by which the mind discovers truth; but they think that their manner of proceeding is essentially different; that their provinces are separable and distinguishable, nay, that it is of the last importance to separate and distinguish them. Reason, the Kantists say, is of a higher nature than Understanding; it works by more subtle methods, on higher objects, and requires a far finer culture for its development, indeed in many men it is never developed at all: but its results are no less certain, nay, rather, they are much more so; for Reason discerns Truth itself, the absolutely and primitively *True*; while Understanding discerns only *relations*, and cannot decide without *if*. The proper province of Understanding is all, strictly speaking, *real* practical and material knowledge, Mathematics, Physics, Political Economy, the adaptation of means to ends in the whole business of life. In this province it is the strength and universal implement of the mind: an indispensable servant, without which, indeed, existence itself would be impossible. Let it not step beyond this province however; not usurp the province of Reason, which it is appointed to obey, and cannot rule over without ruin to the whole spiritual man. Should Understanding attempt to prove the existence of God, it ends, if thoroughgoing and consistent with itself, in Atheism, or a faint possible Theism, which scarcely differs from this: should it speculate of Virtue, it ends in *Utility*, making Prudence and a sufficiently cunning love of Self the highest good.[123]

Here are Reason and Understanding as defined by Coleridge in *Aids to Reflection*, mingled with what little Carlyle picked up directly from his reading of Kant (for example, the Understanding discerning relations) and made more vehement with Carlyle's own particular worries about the social and ethical implications of Utilitarianism.

Perhaps the clearest single example of Carlyle's proceedings with regard to German philosophy is his article on Novalis in the *Foreign Review* in 1829. Carlyle felt that he had here a German poet of some distinction, who had not yet been noticed in England. It was therefore his duty to introduce him. Moreover, he found Novalis useful for furnishing him with ready quotations for *Sartor*: Teufelsdröckh's 'Self-Annihilation' owed something to the German poet's notion of 'Selbsttödtung',[124] and Novalis's shadowy dream world of fairy-tale allegory and nature mysticism (as in *Die Lehrlinge zu Sais*, 1797–8) appealed both to the Calvinist and to the rhapsodist in Carlyle. Novalis shared Carlyle's hero-worship; there was, for example, his idea of the king's function as an ideal father.[125] But Novalis had studied Fichte, and Carlyle was less at ease with the philosophers than with the poets. He realised that 'mysticism' was a phrase used indiscriminately of the Germans by English critics, usually in a derogatory sense. Now that he was to deal with a real 'German mystic', he had to come to terms with the subject.

His method was to discuss Novalis with a view to communicating, as he claims at the end to have done, 'some views not of what is vulgarly called, but of what *is* a German Mystic'. The beginning of the article shows Carlyle in a dilemma: he is about to introduce these difficult writings in a country in which Coleridge's *Friend* and *Biographia Literaria* have been roundly declared unintelligible, yet his own understanding of these works is fragmentary.[126] He begins by giving generalised praise of Novalis:

> . . .a man of the most indisputable talent, poetical and philosophical; whose opinions, extraordinary, nay, altogether wild and baseless as they often appear, are not without a strict coherence in his own mind, and will lead any other mind, that examines them faithfully, into endless considerations; opening the strangest inquiries, new truths, or new possibilities of truth, a whole unexpected world of thought, where, whether for belief or denial, the deepest questions await us.[127]

Suggesting that 'if his editors, Friedrich Schlegel and Ludwig Tieck, declined commenting on these Writings, we may well be excused for declining to do so', he takes refuge in the congenial and comparatively easy task of sketching the poet's life.

Having warmed to this part, he seems to gather confidence, so that he can broach the topic of philosophy and mysticism again, this time in greater detail:

> He much loved, and had assiduously studied, Jacob Böhme and other mystical writers; and was, openly enough, in good part a Mystic himself. Not indeed what we English, in common speech call a Mystic; which means only a man whom we do not understand, and, in self-defence, reckon or would fain reckon a Dunce.[128]

At this point we recognise the Carlyle of the *Edinburgh Review* articles. British readers have got the wrong idea about German 'mysticism', and Carlyle will instruct them. Having begun by protesting his inability to comment on the works, he has now gathered enough confidence to attempt an interpretation. Novalis's metaphysical creed, he hazards, 'appears everywhere in its essential lineaments synonymous with what little we understand of Fichte's, and might indeed, safely enough for our present purpose, be classed under the head of Kantism, or German metaphysics generally'.[129] Carlyle is certainly right about Novalis's close study of Fichte: his 'Philosophische Studien' of 1795-7 show a concern with identity, consciousness, and the 'Ich' with its 'Nicht-Ich' as a necessary external boundary imposed by the 'Ich' on itself in order to provide objects on which to exercise its restless activity.[130] But he is not 'safe' in classing such ideas 'under the head of Kantism', since it was on the very problem of consciousness that Kant and Fichte disagreed, Fichte rejecting the unknowable 'Dinge an sich' which are the basis of Kant's epistemological system.

Disregarding details – there is no need, he says, to 'enter into the intricacies of German Philosophy' – he firmly sketches Idealism, Transcendentalism, the Ich and Nicht-Ich, and Kant's theory of Time and Space. He commences an impressive misinterpretation of Kant as an idealist whose theory of Time and Space he takes to mean that these two 'conditions' of experience have no real existence, a conclusion which Kant explicitly denies,[131] and that therefore the only realities are Eternity and Infinity, with God omnipresent and alone not subject to the laws of time and space: 'Nay, to the Transcendentalist, clearly enough, the whole question of the origin and existence of Nature must be greatly simplified: the old hostility of Matter is at an end, for Matter is itself annihilated; and the black Spectre, Atheism, 'with all its sickly dews', melts into nothingness for ever.'[132] When he goes on from here to talk of the 'majesty of Reason' and 'its vassal, Understanding', he is far from Kant's *Kritik* and unconsciously much closer to Coleridge.

Like Coleridge in his excited letter to Poole of 1801, Carlyle thought Kant and his successors in Germany had provided him with the desired refutation of empiricism, that 'sick, impotent Scepticism' which he had accepted intellectually as a student at the 'Rational University' of Edinburgh.[133] His notebooks in 1829 and 1830 show him increasingly concerned with his 'Sartor' material – Utilitarianism as the most dangerous heir of the eighteenth-century empiricism and the major threat to spirituality:

I have now almost done with the Germans. Having seized their opinions, I must turn me to inquire *how* true are they?...I think I have got rid of Materialism: Matter no longer seems to me so ancient, so unsubduable, so *certain* and palpable as Mind. I am Mind: whether matter or not I know not – and care not.[134]

97

Sartor itself was full of this eclectic, patched 'philosophy', which was, as Crabb Robinson noticed, 'essentially that of Coleridge'.[135] Frothingham, the first historian of the American transcendentalists (whose philosophy was itself very different from Kant's transcendentalism, largely because it was mediated to the Americans, including Emerson, by Coleridge and Carlyle[136]), observed, '[Carlyle's] Transcendentalism seems to have been a thing of sentiment rather than conviction'.[137] The passion of the anti-Utilitarian rhetoric in *Sartor* bears this out. Carlyle was not a systematic thinker; he was, said Herbert Spencer, 'almost incapable of consecutive thinking – if he could not reach by intuition he could not reach at all'.[138] As Mill, whom Carlyle mistakenly took for a 'new Mystic' when they met in London in 1831, wrote:

I have already mentioned Carlyle's earlier writings as one of the channels through which I received the influences which enlarged my early narrow creed; but I do not think that those writings, by themselves, would ever have had any effect on my opinions. What truths they contained, though of the very kind which I was already receiving from other quarters, were presented in a form and vesture less suited than any other to give them access to a mind trained as mine had been. They seemed a haze of poetry and German metaphysics, in which almost the only clear thing was a strong animosity to most of the opinions which were the basis of my mode of thought; religious scepticism, utilitarianism, the doctrine of circumstances, and the attaching any importance to democracy, logic or political economy.[139]

Yet Mill testifies also that Carlyle's 'wonderful power' made a deep impression on him. Indeed, it was Carlyle's bold intuitive assertions which so impressed his contemporaries generally, making them think him their most reliable guide in difficult times. One of the many letters he received about *Sartor* was from a Boston woman, Lydia Maria Childs, who responded, as did most of his readers, to the 'philosophy' rather than to the humour of the work: 'Last summer, when I was alone in a remote country-town, struggling with worldly discouragements, craving sympathy and spiritual food, which none had to bestow – a friend sent me your Sartor Resartus; which thenceforth was to my soul as sunshine, flowers, and the pure, strengthening breeze'.[140] In his comprehensive articles, where he aimed to share with his readers the new fund of knowledge, art, and spirituality he had found in the German Romantics, he may have misrepresented and mistaken much, but his 'passionate power'[141] interested a larger section of readers than ever before in German literature and thought.

Sartor Resartus, *a beginning and an end* (*1830–4*)

Carlyle had scarcely begun to enjoy his fame as the chief Germanist of his age when he began to move away from the study of literature, German or otherwise, towards a lifelong concern for the social condition of England. He took ideas and aphorisms from Goethe (Entsagung, Renunciation), Novalis (Selbsttödtung, Self-annihilation, and the body as a temple), Kant (Time and Space 'annihilated'), Schiller (the moral function of art, 'Ernst ist das Leben', 'Life is earnest'), and others. He appropriated them to his purposes, his mind acting like a 'magnet', extracting and isolating phrases.[142] Thus his works, as well as his letters and conversation, abound in quotations, misquotations, and half-quotations from German sources. 'Ohne Hast, aber ohne Rast' ('Without haste, but without rest') was his favourite maxim from Goethe, and at his suggestion it was used as the motto on the birthday seal sent by a group of Englishmen to Goethe in 1831. (Goethe himself attached less importance to the phrase than Carlyle did, expressing surprise at the choice of it for the seal and assuming that they must have liked it because it expressed their own way of doing things.[143]) Other favourites of Carlyle's were Goethe's 'Mein Acker ist die Zeit' ('Time is my fair seedfield' as Carlyle translated it), and Jean Paul on dreams. Long after his period of lively interest in German literature was over, he still followed the custom of heading his works and rounding off articles with German phrases which had attracted him in the past.

Where he had first found Goethe and Schiller useful in helping him out of his personal doubts, he now employed them in the cause which was uppermost in his mind even when he began 'Germanising' the public in 1827. The English philosophical tradition was still, as Bulwer Lytton pointed out in his *England and the English* (1833), characteristically materialist, 'and this is the more remarkable, because, both in Scotland and in Germany, the light of the Material Schools has already waxed dim and faint, and Philosophy directs her gaze to more lofty stars, out of the reach of this earth's attraction'.[144] Carlyle was only too aware of this; hence his appeal to Coleridge in the *Life of Schiller* and his unconscious manipulation of Kant's views to attack atheism in the Novalis article of 1829. There is even a brief reference in the 'State of German Literature' essay to the horrors of 'utility', and his very next article for the *Edinburgh Review* was the un-German socio-political 'Signs of the Times'. We have seen that Carlyle invoked Goethe's 'religious Wisdom' as an antidote to 'these hard, unbelieving, utilitarian days', and even in his posthumous tribute to Goethe, his thoughts strayed more and more away from Goethe's works to the state of England, the Reform Bill, the 'prosaic age', and Benthamism. He held up Schiller, too, as a noble contrast to the typical modern man whose 'only god' was Utility.[145] The consciousness that his 'mission' was to combat the evils of industrial and materialist society is apparent.

A related reason for the change of interest was Carlyle's desire to write in a more original and memorable way than he had scope for in translating and reviewing. He had been flattered by Goethe's description of the translator as a prophet, but he wanted to earn the reputation by creative efforts, by 'spread[ing] abroad Reverence over the hearts of men', and he felt that this was a 'higher task' than mere translating.[146] As for the 'craft of reviewing', like Coleridge he thought that a 'despicable business', to be dispensed with as soon as possible. Each year his journal records his frustration at the lack of achievement, not counting his German translations and reviews as useful work.[147] He wanted as early as 1828 to 'give *work* for reviewing' by others. The physical move in 1834 from the seclusion of Craigenputtoch to the 'huge, tumultuous, never-resting Babel' of London brought to a climax the change of direction he had been feeling for several years.[148]

Carlyle's interest in, and debts to, German authors culminated in the serialisation of *Sartor* in *Fraser's Magazine* in 1833-4. Goethe appears as 'the Wisest of our Time', and the reading of his works signals the shift in Teufelsdröckh's moral crisis from the Centre of Indifference to the Everlasting Yea; Jean Paul is invoked for his 'World-Mahlstrom of Humour'; there, too, are Novalis's idea of Nature as the hieroglyphic expression of God and Fichte's view of history as alternating periods of faith and scepticism.[149] From Kant he took what he thought was a proof of the ideality of time and space, which allowed him to voice his dualism rhapsodically:

Think well, thou too wilt find that Space is but a mode of our human Sense, so likewise Time; there *is* no Space and no Time: WE are – we know not what; – light-sparkles in the aether of Deity!

So that this so solid-seeming World, after all, were but an air-image, our ME the only reality: and Nature, with its thousandfold production and destruction, but the reflex of our own inward Force, the "phantasy of our Dream"...[150]

Man is not a mere 'forked radish', not just matter, but spirit, a 'mystery'.[151] Instead of materialism, utility, and atheism, Eternity and Infinity are the true realities, and the phenomena of Nature merely symbols of them. Here are Kant's noumena, except that they are accessible to some men, according to Carlyle. Symbols have a double nature; they both conceal and reveal. Vision is all-important. He who judges by appearances only falls into the error of 'logic-chopping' materialism, but he who penetrates the outward symbol to the hidden reality is the true seer or prophet: 'The man who cannot wonder, who does not habitually wonder (and worship), were he President of innumerable Royal Societies, and carried the whole *Mécanique Céleste*, and *Hegel's Philosophy*, and the epitome of all Laboratories and Observatories with their results, in his single head, – is but a Pair of Spectacles behind which there is no Eye.'[152]

In all this, Carlyle speaks through Teufelsdröckh. Yet he uses the ironic device of a doubting editor who constantly undermines the rhapsodist, so that finally it is difficult for the reader to assess Teufelsdröckh's 'philosophy' – is it mere ranting, folly, or is it a bright chapter in the history of human wisdom (to echo Carlyle's notebook question about Kant)? Certainly his readers were unsure how to respond,[153] and on the whole opted to concentrate on the moral and social message, which they could recognise as Carlyle's own view. But the irony was a necessary defence against the hostility to 'German mysticism' which Carlyle knew from his own experience and from Coleridge's. No doubt he used the editor to represent the views of common-sense British critics like Jeffrey when confronted by a 'typically' German work – obscure, idealistic, formless, chaotic. It was a useful rhetorical bracket to put round subversive material (a device well known to Carlyle from Swift's *Tale of a Tub*). More than that, Carlyle could here give vent to his own doubts. For all his debts to German authors, he, like Coleridge, shared some of his countrymen's worries, as we have seen, about *Faust* and *Wilhelm Meister*, Kant and Novalis. In his role as translator and mediator of German culture he could not well include his difficulties and differences (except unconsciously, as in the Novalis article of 1829). But in his own creative work he was free to range through several shades of opinion; he was free, finally, to retain a thorough two-facedness about what Jeffrey inconveniently called his 'idols'. In his essay 'Characteristics' (1831) he gave his readers a general, un-ironic view of 'the Germans':

In France or England, since the days of Diderot and Hume, though all thought has been of a sceptico-metaphysical texture, so far as there was any Thought, we have seen no Metaphysics; but only more or less ineffectual questionings whether such could be. In the Pyrrhonism of Hume and the Materialism of Diderot, Logic had, as it were, overshot itself, overset itself. Now, though the athlete, to use our old figure, cannot, by much lifting, lift up his own body, he may shift it out of a laming posture, and get to stand in a free one. Such a service have German Metaphysics done for man's mind.[154]

In a complementary passage in *Sartor*, he made the same gesture, but allowed irony to deny complete acceptance of the view:

But here, as in so many cases, Germany, learned, indefatigable, deep-thinking Germany comes to our aid. It is, after all, a blessing that, in these revolutionary times, there should be one country where abstract Thought can still take shelter; that while the din and frenzy of Catholic Emancipations, and Rotten Boroughs, and Revolts of Paris, deafen every French and every English ear, the German can stand peaceful on his scientific watch-tower; and, to the raging, struggling multitude here and elsewhere, solemnly, from hour to hour, with preparatory blast of cowhorn, emit his *Höret ihr Herren und lasset's Euch sagen*; in other words, tell the Universe, which so often forgets that fact, what o'clock it really is.[155]

Carlyle is here released from the responsibility of endorsing and can use the editorial framework to express a little incredulity with impunity. Undoubtedly Carlyle was proud to be the kind of bridge-builder he describes with humorous exaggeration in *Sartor*:

Never perhaps since our first Bridge-builders, Sin and Death, built that stupendous Arch from Hell-gate to the Earth, did any Pontifex, or Pontiff, undertake such a task as the present Editor. For in this Arch too, leading, as we humbly presume, far otherwards than that grand primeval one, the materials are to be fished-up from the weltering deep, and down from the simmering air, here one mass, there another, and cunningly cemented, while the elements boil beneath: nor is there any supernatural force to do it with; but simply the Diligence and feeble thinking Faculty of an English Editor, endeavouring to evolve printed Creation out of a German printed and written Chaos, wherein, as he shoots to and fro in it, gathering, clutching, piercing the Why to the far-distant Wherefore, his whole Faculty and Self are like to be swallowed up.[156]

But we know from the journals and letters that he wished to be more than this. The *Sartor* passage continues:

What is the use of health, or of life, if not to do some work therewith? And what work nobler than transplanting foreign Thought into the barren domestic soil; except indeed planting Thought of your own, which the fewest are privileged to do?

Sartor Resartus, Carlyle's first original work, contains thus the expression of his desire to be free from the secondary work of explaining the Germans and is the first fruit of that desire.

Carlyle's friends thought the work too mystifying. Mill doubted whether 'that mode of writing between sarcasm or irony and earnest' was likely to be effective. Carlyle in his reply refers to his isolation and unsureness of critical response, as well as to his inner tensions:

Irony is a sharp instrument; but ill to handle without cutting *yourself*. I cannot justify, yet can too well explain what sets me so often on it of late: it is my singularly anomalous position to the world, – and, if you will, my own singularly unreasonable temper. I never know or can even guess what or who my audience is, or whether I have any audience: thus too naturally I adjust myself on the Devil-may-care principle. Besides I have under all my gloom a genuine feeling of the ludicrous; and could have been the merriest of men, *had I not* been the sickest and saddest.[157]

Sterling, too, objected to the strangeness of the style: 'there is not a sufficient basis of the common to justify the amount of peculiarity in the work'.[158] Crabb Robinson referred to it initially as 'some crazy articles' in *Fraser's Magazine*, but on re-reading it in book form in 1838 observed that 'even for its style [it] delights me – perhaps but few besides, for one must be German to relish it'.[159] In fact, many who were not 'German' relished it. The Americans were first, led by Emerson, who arranged its publication in Boston in 1836 (two years before a publisher in England took it on) and directed readers in his introduction to its merits as 'a Criticism upon the Spirit of the Age'. Like the woman who wrote to Carlyle from Boston, most readers took away an impression less of its bewildering humour than of its moral earnestness and reinstatement of spirituality. Young men looked to its author rather vaguely for help. Espinasse recounted his view of *Sartor* as the *Pilgrim's Progress* of the nineteenth century; James Hutchison Stirling, later one of the chief Hegelians in Britain, wrote to Carlyle in 1840 asking advice on literary matters, and he too later remembered the impression *Sartor* and Carlyle's other writings made on him: 'Carlyle lived when Dickens and Thackeray, when Tennyson and Browning, lived, but there can be no doubt that of them all it was he that excited the intensest and most general interest. He was every literary young man's idol, almost the god he prayed to.'[160]

Similarly, Richard Hengist Horne, a friend of Lewes's, wrote to Carlyle in 1839, bewailing his difficulties as a struggling writer and professing his eagerness to begin, with Carlyle as his guide, a 'search through the broad depths of German literature for an Answer to the cry within'.[161] Geraldine Jewsbury also wrote to Carlyle for guidance, and he replied, referring exclusively to the serious aspect of *Sartor*:

In an English book called *Sartor Resartus*, of my writing, G. E. J. will see shadowed forth under strange emblems a spiritual conflict not unlike her own, even in minute particulars; and discern what wild convulsions others before her have had, which nevertheless ended in victory. It is in this way that *teaching* of man by man becomes possible.

He wrote to her also of his double feeling towards Goethe, 'the wretchedest of materialists', whose writings held 'much to repel you', yet who was in the end a teacher of spiritual wisdom.[162] With *Sartor* Carlyle's public advocacy of German literature ended. He wrote to Eckermann in 1834:

My Goethe and all that belongs to him stands out ever the grander, the more genuine, as I myself increase; yet stands out, I might say, as an object *finished*, to which there will be no *continuation* made; like a granite Promontary...With him and his, however, it seems as if my labours in the German field might profitably terminate, at least make pause. As respects our own England again, my task in that direction, so far as it was my task, may be considered amply done: witness only this one fact, that within the last twelvemonths we have had no fewer than three new Translations of *Faust*...In fact, the fire is kindled, and there is smoke enough and to spare.[163]

It was fitting that he should see the introduction of Goethe as both the beginning and the end of his German 'mission'. He was right to feel proud of his achievement. Most of the increasing number of interested readers of German literature and philosophy declared their interest to have begun by reading Carlyle's works, though Coleridge, too, partly through what was Coleridgean in Carlyle, had his share of influence on the awareness of the Victorians of German culture.

3

G. H. Lewes

Lewes: one of Carlyle's 'young men' (1835-9)

It was through Carlyle that Lewes, on his first trip to Germany in 1838, made the acquaintance of Varnhagen von Ense, whom he described in the *Life and Works of Goethe* (1855) as 'my oldest German friend'.[1] He handed over a copy of *Sartor* and was warmly received as an ambassador from Carlyle, hitherto the chief interpreter of Goethe in England. Lewes wrote in an article of 1841: 'We went to Berlin, carrying a letter of introduction to him from Thomas Carlyle, which was, of course, a patent for cordial reception... bearing a book (the *Sartor Resartus*) and tidings from one whom all respect, and to whose exertions Germany owes so much of her spiritual recognition in England.'[2] On that visit Varnhagen presented Lewes with his own copy of Hegel's *Aesthetik*, on which Lewes wrote an important introductory article in 1841-2,[3] and when Lewes returned to Germany briefly in 1845 and again (with George Eliot) in 1854-5, Varnhagen lent him books, introduced him to important literary people in Berlin, and helped him greatly with materials for the *Life of Goethe*, the work which was to make Lewes's reputation and which established him as Carlyle's successor in the interpretation of Goethe in England.

Lewes began in the mid-1830s as one of Carlyle's many 'young men',[4] attracted to German literature by Carlyle's articles and by *Sartor*, the most 'German' of works, which, as we have seen, was at the same time Carlyle's last sustained word on the subject. After *Sartor* came the important *French Revolution* (1837), and from then on Carlyle did as J. S. Blackie, translator of *Faust* in 1834, described him in 1840: 'Thomas Carlyle, the great apostle of the Teutonic gospel, can now afford to leave the serving of tables to deacons, and expound leisurely to admiring assemblies the mysteries of cosmopolitan hero-worship from Odin to Mirabeau.'[5] These 'deacons' included Blackie himself and the numerous other translators from

German,[6] as well as John Sterling, Mill, Emerson, and Lewes. This new generation shared a culture which, largely thanks to Coleridge and Carlyle, was almost as much German in its origins as it was English. The three 'magic' names for these writers, and for George Eliot, Matthew Arnold, Leslie Stephen, Pater, Froude, and many other Victorians were Coleridge, Carlyle, and Goethe. Mill's lucid if generalised statement of his own 'education' is well known. In the *Autobiography* he described his awakening in the 1820s to new streams of thought, despite the efforts of Bentham and James Mill:

The influences of European, that is to say, Continental, thought, and especially those of the reaction of the nineteenth century against the eighteenth, were now streaming in upon me. They came from various quarters: from the writings of Coleridge, which I had begun to read with interest even before the change in my opinions; from the Coleridgians with whom I was in personal intercourse [i.e. particularly Sterling and Maurice]; from what I had read of Goethe; from Carlyle's early articles in the Edinburgh and Foreign Reviews, though for a long time I saw nothing in these (as my father saw nothing in them to the last) but insane rhapsody.[7]

There are several such accounts. It was agreed that Carlyle's chief importance was his striking way of putting Goethe before his readers as the wisest man of his age. Arnold in his lecture on Emerson in 1883 announced roundly that 'the greatest voice of the century came to us in those youthful years through Carlyle: the voice of Goethe'.[8] Sterling, reviewing Carlyle's collection of *Critical and Miscellaneous Essays* in the *London and Westminster Review* in 1839, declared it to be

the most important series of papers that any one man has contributed to the present race of Reviews and Magazines – nay, as incomparably the most so. About two-thirds of the whole relate to German literature...It is not too much to say, that to these and other labours of the same hand is due almost all the just appreciation of Goethe now existing in England.[9]

It is clear from Sterling's correspondence with Carlyle in the 1830s that he first read Goethe under Carlyle's influence, though he soon came to see Carlyle's views on Goethe as idiosyncratic and excessive.[10] The pattern repeats itself with Mill, whose diary in 1854 records his dissent from Carlyle over Goethe's representativeness of modern man, and Arnold, who found Carlyle too shrill in his assessment of Goethe.[11] Lewes praised Carlyle's essays on Goethe for 'crushing' the flippant tone of the *Edinburgh* Reviewers, but criticised them for giving 'no definite image of the man'.[12] And

Leslie Stephen sketched Carlyle's place in the history of the 'importation of German', finding, like the others, that Carlyle's Goethe was 'something quite different from the Goethe of other people, and, indeed, of historical fact'.[13]

If Carlyle influenced the younger men mainly through his promotion of Goethe and his own mixture of the Goethean idea of education with his perception of the ills of society in England and his prescription – sincerity, earnestness, and duty – in *Sartor*, they agreed in naming Coleridge as a second influence, also 'German'. The lessons they drew from Coleridge were, for reasons which should by now be clear, less immediate and direct. Through his conversations, lectures, and diffusely through works like *The Friend* and *Aids to Reflection*, the 'Coleridgian leaven' worked in 'many directions' in 'later fermentations'.[14] We have seen that Sterling felt he owed his introduction to Goethe and German literature to Carlyle. To Coleridge he said he owed 'education': 'He taught me to believe that an empirical philosophy is none, that Faith is the highest Reason, that all criticism, whether of literature, laws, or manners, is blind, without the power of discerning the organic unity of the object.'[15] Sterling knew that much of what he read in Coleridge was of German origin. In his simplified parable of Coleridge's intellectual and moral life, written for his son in 1844, he regretted Coleridge's many 'repetitions omissions mistakes & thefts from German authors', but ranged opposite those the positive importance of Coleridge's German studies:

In the full strength of his powers as a grown man he went to Germany & became aware of that new & boundless World of Thought contained in its modern literature. . .He came back bringing from this source innumerable new Thoughts many of them most precious & such as no one else in England then nor till long after ever heard of except from him. . .To those who knew nothing of Germany many of these Ideas seemed nothing less than a direct Revelation out of the Morning Sun or wherever is nearest to the One Fountain of Light.[16]

Already in 1828 Sterling spoke up for Coleridge, defending him in the *Athenaeum* from the familiar taunts of critics that his works were 'mystical, obscure, metaphysical, theoretical, unintelligible, and so forth'.[17] He and his fellow Coleridgian, F. D. Maurice, published a series of aphorisms in the *Athenaeum* in 1829, called 'The Museum of Thoughts' and including scraps of criticism by Goethe, Fichte, Novalis, and A. W. Schlegel. And Sterling's tutor and later his editor, Julius Charles Hare, published in 1827 two volumes of *Guesses at Truth* with his brother Augustus. This was a collection of idealistic, amateur philosophical remarks, owing a great deal to Coleridge and through him to the German post-Kantian philosophers. Its form as well as its content owes something to that of Coleridge's *Friend* and *Aids to Reflection*.

Lewes, like the rest of his generation, read these works of Coleridge during the late 1830s and early 1840s. His copy of *The Friend* (the 1837 edition, published by Henry Nelson Coleridge) is full of marginalia which show how Coleridge stimulated him, though the free-thinking Lewes dissented from his intolerance of empiricism[18] and his attempt to identify morality with religion. He borrows Carlyle's argument (and his tone) in objecting to Coleridge's statement that 'in fine, religion, true or false, is and ever has been the moral centre of gravity in Christendom, to which all other things must and will accommodate themselves'. Lewes adds:

In fine Religion false & never true, is & ever has been the *immoral* centre of gravity in Christendom; to which all the bickerings, heart-burnings, intolerances & oppressions are greatly if not wholly to be referred; Religion has become a Profession since its first Origin & no Apostles have we now, but some quite other Apostles in Bishopguise; Power is the end of their Endeavours. Now all these evils have their cause precisely in the one fatal Error which the Friend so poorly defends viz the identifying Religion and Morality.[19]

Coleridge might not impress Lewes in matters of religion, but he did impress him as a critic and a thinker with detailed knowledge of German philosophy. Even before he went to Germany in July 1838, Lewes was writing precocious criticism in minor periodicals. His short-lived series 'The Student' in the equally short-lived *National Magazine and Monthly Critic* (two volumes, 1837–8) is an ambitious account of conversations with the learned Herbert, a thinker who, like Carlyle's Dalbrook, is a semi-humorously conceived Coleridge figure:

Herbert was a metaphysician. We were almost daily together, and I used often to write down, when I reached home, as much of our conversation as I could remember. I present these fragments to the reader: they are poor copies, and bear about the same resemblance to the original as the Table Talk of Coleridge does to his inexhaustible incomparable *monologues*.

Herbert ranges from comments on the nervous system to quotations from Jean Paul Richter and Spinoza. He echoes Coleridge (and

Schelling) in his theory of life:[20] 'Look through nature, and you find one imperishable and progressive system of organism – one universal life! Strip off the *outer integuments* – the mere vehicle of the soul – and there is no such thing as death in the creation.' And he gives a flamboyant 'exposition' of Kant, quoting Kant (in Tissot's French translation of 1835–6, not in the original, which Lewes did not know in 1837) on Sensibility, Understanding, and Reason. The knowledge of Kant displayed is sketchy and obviously second-hand; the terminology is more that of eighteenth-century empirical philosophy than Kant's own; and Lewes–Herbert joins the ranks of those who thought Kant an idealist – '*Pure reason* is the faculty which gives principles by whose aid we know something absolutely, *a priori*.'[21] Yet in spite of the half-joking approach to the metaphysics of Coleridge and in spite of Lewes's imperfect knowledge of Kant, these articles (along with a contribution to Leigh Hunt's *Monthly Repository* at about the same time[22]) do show Lewes early on catching at the importance of Kant and of Coleridge's German studies. Already showing 'a mind peculiarly sensitive to the *Zeitgeist*',[23] he went off to Germany to acquaint himself with its culture.

He met several leading literary men in Berlin, as he reported to Leigh Hunt:

Tell Carlyle that I have delivered his parcel. Varnhagen is one of the first literary men here and the only elegant man I have met with – that is, elegant according to our notions. . .We had a long chat upon English Literature and the Spanish poets, and have interchanged the loan of Books together. . .Besides him I have made several literary and scientific acquaintances, among the rest the great Boeckh, who is a perfect bit of amiability and philosophy. . .I may also mention a Mr. Gleim, a relation of the poet Gleim, and Madame Beer the grand daughter of Moses Mendelssohn, Niece of Schlegel, Cousin of Meyerbeer, and Felix Mendelssohn, and friend of Weber.[24]

In the company of such people he became aware of a different and, he thought, superior, approach to literature:

My days are spent in study – my evenings in society – at concerts or theatre. Touching the former I am reading "Faust" in the original – no easy task – & translating Goethe's "Torquato Tasso". . .I am ever working at Shelley,[25] and am more than ever delighted at having come to Germany were it only on this account, for my views have been much altered & developed. I have *felt* the necessity for a deep & aesthetical exposition of his poems & philosophy, which I am endeavouring to accomplish & in which if I fail there will at least be the seeds for one better capable to develope. Criticism here is a very different thing from criticism in England & believing it also to be immeasurably superior I shall not shun it.[26]

Accordingly, on his return in 1839 he set about writing serious critical essays, pleading, like Carlyle in the 'State of German Literature' article, for an adoption of criticism as a 'science', of that German spirit which regarded art not as a 'branch of *trade*', as it was viewed in England, but as 'something far transcending any commerce yet invented'.[27]

Following Coleridge and Carlyle, Lewes found in Germany a literature of 'Ideas', something which seemed so lacking in England. Thus his first novel *Ranthorpe*, written in 1842 and published in 1847, is a novel of education loosely following *Wilhelm Meister* in its broad-minded study of the seemingly haphazard experiences of the potential artist. Ranthorpe shares with Wilhelm, Goethe, and Lewes himself a passion for the theatre which has been soured by unscrupulous or ungenerous theatre managers, squabbling and inept actors, and unresponsive audiences.[28] Like Wilhelm, Ranthorpe becomes involved with a set of people who hold up his progress, though for a time he thinks himself in his proper element with them. Ranthorpe enters an expensive and corrupt society on the strength of one literary success; Lewes points up the parallel with *Wilhelm Meister* by quoting from it:

Er erinnerte sich der Zeit, in der sein Geist durch ein unbedingtes hoffnungsreiches Streben empor gehoben wurde, wo er in dem lebhaftesten Genusse aller Art, wie in einem Elemente schwamm. Es ward ihm deutlich, wie er jetzt in ein unbestimmtes Schlendern gerathen war!

He remembered the time in which his spirit was upraised by an unlimited hopeful effort, when he bathed in lively enjoyments of all kinds as in an element. It became clear to him that he had now got into a vague jog-trot.[29]

Again as in *Wilhelm Meister* Ranthorpe's love – sometimes denied and hidden from himself – of the right woman brings him through temporary renunciation to permanent happiness. His life, Lewes tells us at the end, 'is now one of activity and happiness: the true ideal of an author's life. . .He has won his spurs. . .He has felt, and he has thought: he has dreamed, and he has suffered. He is now to "preach from the text of his own errors" – to make his experience incarnate in song'.[30] Early on, Lewes quotes Goethe's saying, using

Carlyle's translation of the *Lehrjahre*, about the misery of not finding a profession to which one feels an inward calling,[31] and he has
his despairing hero saved from suicide by a wise man, whose very
wisdom is first signified by the mere statement that he 'had lived at
Weimar, and had known Göthe, of whom he loved to speak'. The
wise man convinces Ranthorpe that 'Göthe wrote 'Werther,' but
he did not *act* it!'

Take him as a model; see how he lived and worked. From a wild youth
growing into a great man, and till his eighty-third year preserving an
unexampled intellect amidst almost unexampled activity. That is the man
you authors should venerate and imitate! He understood the divine significance of a man's destiny which is work.[32]

There are echoes here of Carlyle in *Sartor*, both in the emphatic
use of syntax and in the gospel of work.

In 1850 Lewes published several chapters of a story called 'The
Apprenticeship of Life' in *The Leader*, the newspaper which he
founded and edited with Thornton Hunt. This unfinished fragment
again recalls Goethe, not merely in its title, but in its indulgence
towards the hero's amorous exploits and in the programmatic advice
offered to him to choose a career either as a Thinker, an Artist, or
an Industrialist.[33]

Like Carlyle, Lewes saw the ridiculous side of 'German' wisdom,
so that even while he eagerly took up Goethe, Hegel, A. W. Schlegel,
and praised their grasp of critical theory, he echoed Teufelsdröckh's
'editor' on the excesses of German literary scholarship. He published
some early pieces of raillery, the 'Prospectus of an intended course
of lectures on the philosophy of humbug. By Professor Wolfgang
von Bibundtücker', and the same professor's solemn interpretation
of 'Where are you going to, my pretty maid?' in terms of its significant 'symbols of the infinite'. Lewes adds a 'Note by the Translator': 'I have thought it right to give the public the remains of this
great man uncorrupted; but I cannot let this pass without observing,
that he seems to me to be here truly German, with his Aesthetic
spectacles to see "more than is set down in the book".'[34] But, again
like Carlyle, he was excited by the depth and energy of the German
authors he read, and was as keen as Carlyle had been to introduce
worthy examples to Britain.

Lewes and German aesthetics (1840–5)

It was in this pioneering spirit that Lewes endeavoured to introduce Hegel's lectures on aesthetics (delivered throughout the 1820s and edited posthumously for publication in three volumes in 1835) to a philosophically still ignorant reading public. In his article, written in 1841 and published in the *British and Foreign Review* in 1842, he benefited from Carlyle's example, taking his reader by storm:

Art may not with us be a "revelation of the Infinite," but it is a very positive branch of *trade*, and subject to all the fluctuations of market and fashion, in common with every other produce of refined civilization. . .How far this commercial theory may be true we know not; at the same time we are happy in the knowledge that such is not the universal belief, that other nations regard Art as something far transcending any commerce yet invented, and that many even here in Britain share the same opinion; to these then we address ourselves in the hope of calling their attention to the aesthetical systems of German philosophers, and so let an examination and comparison of them with their own take place, which may not be fruitless in disseminating truer notions amongst our artists.

If German literature itself no longer needed introducing to Britain, its aesthetics, that is 'the philosophy of Art', did:

The immense influx of German literature has brought with it an importation of its aesthetics – unfortunately only in fragments and imperfect insights – nowhere as a complete system; and the great diffusion of the works of the two Schlegels, already translated, is an evidence that the subject itself is not uncongenial. But to attain some more complete insight into Art, to produce something higher than acute fragmentary criticism, we must go back to Germany and obtain some idea of it as a science. It is to facilitate this purpose that we propose introducing to our readers the works we have placed at the head of this article.[35]

The works alluded to here are Hegel's *Vorlesungen über die Aesthetik*, Solger's work of the same title (1829), Jean Paul's *Vorschule der Aesthetik* (in an edition of 1826), Quatremère de Quincey, *Essai sur l'Idéal dans ses applications pratiques aux arts du Dessein* (1837), and De Quincey, *Essay on the Nature, the End, and the Means of Imitation in the Fine Arts* (1827). The list misleads somewhat, since the article deals chiefly with Hegel. Mill had suggested that Lewes add the other titles, 'as you are so long in coming to Hegel', and also in order to make the article more attractive to Napier, the editor of the *Edinburgh Review*, in which Lewes originally hoped to publish it. Mill rightly thought it too 'German' and too polemical for the *Edinburgh*:

I do not know how the Edinburgh will like such severe diatribes against English criticism, which will fall heavier on the Ed. itself than on anything else, but if it were my own case & I were sending such matter to the editor of the Edinburgh I should feel as if I were civilly giving him a thump on the face. In revising, it might be well to make it look as little German as possible...[36]

Lewes may have taken Mill's advice, but the revised article was nevertheless rejected by Napier. Lewes wrote explaining why he had thought it suitable – 'my reason for supposing the *Edinburgh* would print such a paper was solely that it had printed more *unusual* things of Carlyle's – tho' to be sure, *his* writing compensates for its excentricity'. What Jeffrey had tolerated from Carlyle, Napier did not accept from Lewes, but Kemble, 'innovating and German!', of the *British and Foreign Review*, was willing to publish the Hegel article.[37] Mill, who had recommended Lewes to Napier, also introduced him to Kemble, as 'a young friend of mine' who 'is rather a good writer, has ideas (even in the Coleridgian sense) & much reading, & altogether I think he is a contributor worth having'.[38]

The final article is a long, ambitious essay. Mill's observation that Lewes takes a long time getting to Hegel is correct: indeed it is a pity Lewes allowed his enthusiasm for the views of so many critics of varying degrees of importance to obscure the real aim of introducing the difficult Hegel.[39] For the first eighteen pages Hegel shares Lewes's attention – Lewes having asked the ambitious question which even Coleridge had raised and avoided answering: 'What is poetry?'[40] – with a large number of critics. Lewes adopts Wordsworth's and Coleridge's view that the language of poetry is opposed, not to prose, but to science, and adds the Shelleian definition of 'a philosophical critic' in the *Monthly Repository* of 1833 (Mill's article 'What is Poetry?') that 'eloquence is *heard*, poetry is *overheard*'. But as if these contentions were not problematic enough,[41] he further complicates the subject by quoting widely from Professor Wilson (of *Blackwood's*), George Sand, Sir Walter Scott, his unknown friend Richard Hengist Horne, Jouffroy, Carlyle, as well as the critics heading the list at the beginning of the article.[42] Hegel's notion of poetry in its abstract and concrete definitions does underpin the whole discussion, but the reader to whom Lewes is introducing Hegel is left in doubt about this as Lewes changes some of the terminology and presents much of Hegel's view as his own.[43] Lewes complains of the confusion existing in aesthetics: 'The dispute as to whether "prose can be poetry," is one of the most astounding instances of the want of clear notions on art which could well be selected...', yet his very desire for inclusiveness (and to show off his wide reading) militates against his succeeding in clarifying the subject. One wishes he had kept to his stated aim to take us to the source of the philosophy of art in Hegel and his predecessors in German philosophy and criticism, Kant, Schiller, and Schelling (to whom Hegel himself pays homage in the long introduction to the first volume[44]). He would have done in 1842 what still remains to be done – placed Hegel's work 'in the context of aesthetic discussions by his contemporaries and immediate seniors'.[45] In 1842 Lewes was probably not yet equipped to study Hegel in his full German context; and his permanent change of opinion away from the *a priori* philosophical approach (documented in the *Biographical History of Philosophy* in 1845–6 and already apparent in articles of 1843[46]) meant that by the time he had the requisite knowledge he lacked the sympathy towards Hegel's approach which he shows here in the 1842 article.

Even if Lewes had opted to concentrate solely on Hegel, confusion might not have been avoided. Although Hegel, as Lewes saw,[47] always gives his reader a sense of his serene mastery and logical control over a massive range of matter – no less than the entire history of all the fine arts from their beginning to Hegel's day, brought under systematic headings and seen in their phases of manifestation of the absolute, the Idea – the reader himself may feel understandably bewildered. As Mill tersely put it, 'conversancy with [Hegel] tends to deprave one's intellect',[48] by its audacity and yet strict chain of impeccable logic. In the *Aesthetik* Hegel built on the work already done by Kant, Schiller, and Schelling, in applying philosophy to art. His aim was to complete their efforts in bridging the objective and subjective realms by means of art and to show

dass das Kunstschöne als eine der Mitten erkannt worden ist, welche jenen Gegensatz und Widerspruch des in sich abstrakt beruhenden Geistes und der Natur – sowohl der äusserlich erscheinenden, als auch der innerlichen des subjektiven Gefühls und Gemüths – auflösen und zur Einheit zurückführen.

that the beautiful in art has been recognised as one of the means which reconcile and unify that opposition and contradiction between abstract Spirit and Nature – Nature both as outward appearance and as inner subjective feeling and mood.[49]

While giving Kant full credit for beginning to form this view of art, Hegel found him incomplete in his conception of 'das Kunstschöne' (the beautiful in art) and undertook painstakingly to account for art as the supreme means of uniting necessity with freedom, the particular with the universal, the sensuous with reason.[50] The scope of Hegel's aim is breathtaking. He sees no contradiction in presenting a history of the arts which is at the same time a theoretical treatise on the Ideal in art. As in his works on logic and the philosophy of history, the clue lies in the reconciliation of the Ideal with the Actual. The key notion, or Idea, is ideal and constant, but by manifesting itself in the spirit of each age, it is constantly adapting and changing, 'becoming' itself. The abstract becomes concrete, the Absolute is itself a relation, all contradiction is erased, as Lewes saw:

...the *Idee* is the totality of the universe both of mind and matter, in its unique conception; and this *Idee*, this Absolute, conceived under the form of thought, is truth; when conceived under the form of nature or of external phaenomena, is Beauty. Thus Beauty is spirit contemplating the spiritual in an object. Art is the Absolute incarnate in the beautiful.[51]

Thus for Hegel there is no inconsistency in holding the views that Art is a bridge between the finite and the infinite, a representation of a timeless Idea, and that the present age (that is the early nineteenth century) is a predominantly critical one which can produce no art worthy of the name of Art:

In dieser ihrer Freiheit nun ist die schöne Kunst erst wahrhafte Kunst,... wenn sie sich in den gemeinschaftlichen Kreis mit der Religion und Philosophie gestellt hat, und nur eine Art und Weise ist, das Göttliche, die tiefsten Interessen des Menschen, die umfassendsten Wahrheiten des Geistes zum Bewusstseyn zu bringen und auszusprechen...Es ist die Tiefe einer übersinnlichen Welt, in welche der Gedanke dringt, und sie zunächst als ein Jenseits dem unmittelbaren Bewusstseyn und der gegenwärtigen Empfindung gegenüber aufstellt; es ist die Freiheit denkender Erkenntnis, welche sich dem Diesseits, das sinnliche Wirklichkeit und Endlichkeit heisst, enthebt. Diesen Bruch aber, zu welchem der Geist fortgeht, weiss er ebenso zu heilen; er erzeugt aus sich selbst die Werke der schönen Kunst als das erste versöhnende Mittelglied zwischen dem bloss Aeusserlichen, Sinnlichen und Vergänglichen und zwischen dem reinen Gedanken, zwischen der Natur und endlichen Wirklichkeit und der unendlichen Freiheit des befreienden Denkens.

Art first becomes true Art in this freedom it has, when it has placed itself in the same sphere as Religion and Philosophy, and becomes merely another way of making conscious and expressing the godlike, the deepest interests of man, and the most comprehensive truths of the Spirit...It is the depth of a super-sensuous world into which thought penetrates and which it sets up at first as a Beyond in contrast with immediate consciousness and present feeling; it is the freedom of the intellectual recognition which escapes from the Here and Now, called sensuous reality and finitude. But this breach to which the Spirit proceeds it knows also how to heal; it produces from within itself the works of fine art as the first reconciling means between the merely outward, sensuous, and transient and pure thought, between nature and finite reality and the infinite freedom of conceptual thought.[52]

Yet a few pages further on Hegel writes:

In allen diesen Beziehungen ist und bleibt die Kunst nach der Seite ihrer höchsten Bestimmung für uns ein Vergangenes. Damit hat sie für uns auch die ächte Wahrheit und Lebendigkeit verloren, und ist mehr in unsere Vorstellung verlegt, als dass sie in der Wirklichkeit ihre frühere Notwendigkeit behauptete, und ihren höheren Platz einnähme.

In all these respects Art is and remains, in its highest vocation, a thing of the past. Thus it has lost for us real truth and life, and is more a matter of ideas for us rather than reality, as it was in its erstwhile necessity when it occupied a higher place.[53]

Lewes, in annotating his copy prior to writing the article, protested against this seeming lack of logic,[54] but since the key for Hegel is reconciliation, he is able in the *Aesthetik* as elsewhere to pursue simultaneously two contradictory methods. Thus the lectures on aesthetics can use both an inductive and a deductive method, drawing conclusions from an abundant source of examples from the Greeks and the Egyptians to Goethe and Schiller, and at the same time imposing a rigorous system of ideal 'epochs' on art.[55] Hegel can be both descriptive and prescriptive, his perspective can be both historical and a-historical with impunity. Lewes soon became impatient with this boldness. In the *Biographical History* he wrote amusedly of Hegel's perfect consistency and ingenuity of argument which leads finally to nothing but 'clouds of mysticism' and 'bogs of absurdity'.[56] But in 1841–2 he was greatly impressed, as his marginalia and his reliance on Hegel's doctrine in attempting one of his own in the *British and Foreign Review* article show. Hegel offered a 'theory of the inner life and *essence* of Art' which could answer 'the oft-mooted question – *What is poetry?*' on which even Coleridge, the most philosophical of English critics, was 'everywhere vague and unsatisfactory'.[57] Moreover, his theory allowed for both a serious moral view of art as instructive, akin to religion and philosophy, and a view (dear to Lewes, as to Shelley and Mill) of art as the expression of emotion and as appealing primarily to the emotions.[58] Thus Lewes explains his two definitions (based closely on Hegel) of poetry:

1. Its *abstract* nature, *i.e.* Art as Art – the "spirit which informs" architecture, sculpture, painting, music and poetry, considered in its abstract existence.
2. Its *concrete* nature, *i.e.* poetry as an individual art, and as such distinguished from the others, and from all forms of thought whatever. These definitions we offer as
1. *Poetry is the beautiful phasis of a religious Idea.*
2. *Poetry is the metrical utterance of emotion.* [This either expressive of emotion in itself, or calculated to raise emotion in the minds of others.] These two definitions, united into one general definition, may therefore stand thus: – the metrical utterance of emotion, having beauty for its result, and pervaded by a religious Idea which it thereby symbolizes.[59]

He rejoices in Hegel's insistence on the necessary form or condition of art as being 'eine sinnliche Hülle' (a sensuous form) and, following Mill's advice in one of his letters about the article,[60] is careful to explain 'religious Idea' as '*more Germanico*', 'every Idea as partaking essentially of the religious character, which is the formula of any truth leading to new contemplations of the infinite, or to new forms in our social relations'.[61] This is Lewes's not altogether clear way of paraphrasing Hegel's notion of the spirit of each individual age as the temporary manifestation of the timeless Ideal.

Lewes does not succeed fully in giving a clear idea of Hegel to his readers, both because of his lack of a full sense of Hegel's German context and because of his unfortunate secondary aim to include as many critics as possible in his survey. For example, his endorsement of Mill's definition of poetry as overheard, 'confessing itself to itself in moments of solitude', does not sit well with his insistence on the conscious principles of art:

An artist has a certain aim; to attain this he must use certain means: is he to be ignorant of them for the better employment of them? He must not only ascertain correctly the nature, power and limits of these means, but must apply them to his own wants. Now rules in poetry are nothing more than conclusions arrived at by critics for the best means of attaining this end.[62]

Hegel's breadth of view and his terminology allow for both the unconscious and the conscious view of art (since that which is unconscious constantly strives to become conscious), but where Lewes abandons Hegel for the individual aperçus of Mill and others, he spreads rather than dispels the confusion. Soon he rejected Hegel for his *a priori*, ontological approach to philosophy and for the absurd lengths to which he carried his absolute idealism, but here he tried to give a sympathetic account of a difficult work which is still little known except to scholars of German philosophy and criticism.[63] When, three-quarters of the way through the article, he drops the others and faces Hegel squarely, offering a brief biography and résumé of his works, he shows admirable honesty:

We candidly admit that we neither *understand* every part of Hegel's 'Aesthetik,' nor do we agree generally with German philosophy; but that, nevertheless, Hegel is the most delightful, thought-inciting and instructive work on the subject we have yet met with, and that four years' constant study of it has only served the more to impress us with its depth and usefulness. This is said to encourage those whom it may at first repel; for, unlike the other works, it may be read without any agreement with its first principles; its detached remarks and criticisms, its scientific and elaborate arrangement of the subject, and its treatment of details, may all be received.

He offers a brief glimpse of Hegel's 'fundamental principle',

that the Idea (*i.e.* the absolute – the *ens*) determines or manifests itself subjectively (or in the mind of man), as Reason – objectively (or externally), as the universe – the *non ego*. There are three epochs in the evolution of the Idea. I. It determines itself as quality, quantity, objectivity, etc. *i.e.* Logic. II. It determines itself as the universe, and developes itself in nature. III. It determines itself as mind, cognizant of its prior states.

Then he remembers how difficult Hegel is and how unprepared the British reader, and takes refuge in a vague admonition reminiscent of Carlyle:

We do not conceal from the reader that he will meet with many obstructions; difficulties of language (this work, however, is generally written in an intelligible, sometimes eloquent style) and of thought; differences of philosophy, and a tendency to what the English call "mysticism" (because they persist in not translating it into their forms of thought); but these obstructions are unimportant, and with courage are soon conquered. If a "light work" be required, if "pleasant critical chat" be wished for, let no one open Hegel; but if an earnest inquiring spirit wishes for the light of a vast and penetrative mind, and does not grudge a little patient study, then we would say – read Hegel. Let none touch it who are not in earnest; it is a sealed book to them, and they will only rise from its non-perusal to gabble about its "German mysticism."[64]

He offers two pieces of criticism by Hegel (on Dutch painters and the embodiment of passion in character) and deems his task, 'of introducing Hegel and German aesthetics to our readers', performed.[65] Lewes alone of his contemporaries attempted an exposition of Hegel's aesthetics, and his achievement demands our attention for that reason.[66]

Lewes soon became disenchanted with German aesthetics. In 1843 he was beginning to suspect the 'affectation of philosophic depth' in the celebrated criticism of A. W. Schlegel:

Freely admitting that his influence in England has not been on the whole without good result, we are firmly convinced that it has been in many things pernicious...Whatever benefit it was in his power to confer has already been reaped; and now it is important that his errors should be exposed. We beg the reader therefore to understand this article as polemical rather than critical: not as an estimate of Schlegel's works, but as a protest against his method, and examination of his leading principles.[67]

He gives Schlegel his due as 'one of the first who taught us to regard Shakspeare as the reverse of a "wild, irregular genius"', briefly digressing to prove that Coleridge plagiarised from Schlegel on *Romeo and Juliet* and in comparing Greek drama to Shakespeare.[68] His argument is that Schlegel's 'synthetic' method of criticism (which had impressed him during his stay in Germany as just what was needed in place of carping English criticism[69]) is 'injurious' because 'it dignifies itself with lofty names, and wishes to pass off easy theorizing for philosophic judgment':

We owe the jargon of modern criticism, which styles itself 'philosophic,' principally to Schlegel...Every body knows that the criticism of the last century was bad, but at any rate it was positive; it was intelligible; it treated of the matter in hand, and measured it according to standards which were appreciable, if limited. Bad as it was, it was more satisfactory, more instructive than much of what passes as philosophic in the present day. Ridiculous though it be to talk of the 'elegance and sublimity' of Homer, or the 'irregularity' of Shakspeare, we prefer it to the rhapsodies of Schlegel on Calderon, wherein he defends the glittering nonsense of his favourite upon the ground that it is 'a sense of the mutual attraction of created things to one another on account of their common origin, and this is a refulgence of the eternal love which embraces the universe.' If there is better criticism in the present day than in the last century, it is because knowledge of art is greater and taste more catholic; not because 'analysis' has given place to 'synthesis,' as many people maintain.[70]

Lewes's chief objection to Schlegel is the vagueness of his terms. He intelligently draws attention to Schlegel's inconsistency in his application of the vexed term 'romantic':

Let us also add that Schlegel who uses the words 'romantic spirit' as if they contained the key to all the problems of modern art, utterly fails in applying his classification. To call the Greeks classic was easy enough, but the Italians puzzled him: he felt that they belonged to the same class, and felt also that in spite of Christianity they were not romantic. In one place he reproaches the Italian drama "with a total absence of the romantic spirit;" but he does not say that Italy was not Christian; how then, if Christianity is the source of the 'romantic Spirit,' are Christian poets not romantic? This dilemma he seems never to have felt. Dilemmas and contradictions never trouble his 'synthetic mind.' Yet would a true philosopher have seen, in this case, either that the notion of Christianity being the cause of the 'romantic spirit' was erroneous; or else he would have investigated the causes of the apparent contradiction.[71]

In pursuing this argument, Lewes makes an important point about Greek tragedy, one which Nietzsche, also in irritated response to Schlegel and his uncritical admirers, made polemically in his *Geburt der Tragödie* (*Birth of Tragedy*, 1872):

A very strong example of the rashness of Schlegel's 'synthesis,' and its defiance of due analysis is what he says of the Greeks: "The whole of their art and poetry is expressive of the consciousness of the harmony of all their faculties. *They have invented the poetry of gladness.*"...Where is this gladness which the Greeks invented? Nowhere but in the *Anacreontica*: and they are but a collection of songs composed for festivals...Schlegel's idea is founded upon an *a priori* view of the consequences of such a religion as polytheism, not upon an examination of the facts. He thinks the Greeks were conscious of no wants, and aspired at no higher perfection than that which they could actually attain by the exercise of their faculties. We, however, are taught by a superior wisdom that man through a high offence forfeited the place for which he was originally destined: consequently that the Christian is more dissatisfied with his life, than the pagan is, and hence the poetry of desire. We reject this reasoning. It seems to us that if religion had the effect on art which he asserts, then would polytheism more than Christianity be the religion of sadness. The Christian dies but to be born into a higher life. This hope compensates for much of this life's ills; and makes him look on death as a subject of rejoicing, not of grief. The polytheist has not such a hope. Achilles – the haughty Achilles, declares that he would rather be a tiller of the earth, than a king in the regions of Erebus. The Christian weeping o'er the vanity of earthly wishes, has a consolation in the life to come. The polytheist can only weep. Thus is Schlegel's notion contradicted by the facts; and we believe unsupported by his reasoning.[72]

Finally, according to Lewes, Schlegel's method leads him to write eloquent 'highflown panegyric' on Shakespeare, 'a masterly pane-gyric, which many years ago was of beneficial influence'. But though Schlegel talks of Shakespeare's profound art, he 'gives no example of it', he 'spins phrases; he says fine things *about* Shakspeare; and too much 'about,' not enough to the purpose'.[73] It was a fault Coleridge and Bulwer Lytton, among others, had noticed. Coleridge annotated his copy of the *Athenäum* (1798–1800) by the brothers Schlegel, objecting at one point to their vagueness in an essay they wrote jointly on Greek elegy as

the plague of the Germans. Why not say at once what the word Elegy means, then what it was made to mean, i.e. (what it comprehended)/ then, to what it became more especially appropriated; and lastly, find out, if you can, some one character distinctive of the Elegy in all its various kinds – or if not, say so – and *propose* to confine the word to a determined [? form].[74]

Bulwer wrote to Hayward in 1832, saying he was unable to meet Schlegel, who was in London – 'a Pseudo Philosopher is like what Johnson said of the Hebrides "worth seeing, but not worth going to see" '.[75] Certainly, Schlegel's lectures on Shakespeare are written in the form of enthusiastic paraphrases, with little attention to textual details, but they are intuitively critical, and are rich in suggestive insights, for which he became justly famous and some of which Coleridge borrowed from him. There is, for example, his comparison between Shakespeare and the Greeks in terms of architecture, his defence of Shakespeare's judgment, his view of Shakespeare's Protean ability to become all things in imagination, and his descrip-tion of young, southern love in *Romeo and Juliet*.[76]

From 1843 on, Lewes ranged himself on the side of analysis, not synthesis, in criticism, just as he stood for empiricism rather than apriorism in philosophy.[77] His remarks on Schlegel were consistently hostile, and in 1850 he made a strong but fair statement in a review of another German work on Shakespeare, by Gervinus:

> Although we think German criticism has, on the whole, as much darkened and confused this subject as it has enlightened and simplified it, we cannot withhold the praise of painstaking investigation, and serious thought. Vicious metaphysics, and, as a consequence, vicious aesthetics, combined with an inordinate love of rhetoric, have *displaced* the real subject, and given us ambitious verbiage where we needed calm inquiry and keen perception of poetic truth, nevertheless the reverence felt for Shakspeare has been so deep, and the patience with which his works have been studied so steady, that, with all deductions, we must admit the inquiries have not been without valuable results. . .The *a priori* method is no less vain in criticism than in science.[78]

In his *Life of Goethe*, where he sustains an empirical approach to both Goethe's life and his art, Lewes expresses his preference in a now famous anecdote:

> A Frenchman, an Englishman, and a German, were commissioned, it is said, to give the world the benefit of their views on that interesting animal the Camel. Away goes the Frenchman to the *Jardin des Plantes*, spends an hour there in rapid investigation, returns, and writes a *feuilleton*, in which there is no phrase the Academy can blame, but also no phrase which adds to the general knowledge. He is perfectly satisfied, however, and says, *Le voilà, le chameau!* The Englishman packs up his tea-caddy and a magazine of comforts; pitches his tent in the East; remains there two years studying the Camel in its habits; and returns with a thick volume of facts, arranged without order, expounded without philosophy, but serving as valuable materials for all who come after him. The German, despising the frivolity of the Frenchman, and the unphilosophic matter-of-factness of the Englishman, retires to his study, there *to construct the Idea of a Camel from out of the depths of his Moral Consciousness.* And he is still at it.

> With this myth the reader is introduced into the very heart of that species of criticism which, flourishing in Germany, is also admired in some English circles, under the guise of Philosophical Criticism, and which has been exercised upon *Wilhelm Meister* almost as mercilessly as upon *Faust*, but which reaches the depths of absurdity when it treats of Shakspeare. There are many excellent critics in Germany, and I should be sorry if laughter at pretenders and pedants were supposed to extend to writers really philosophical; but in the name of Art and common-sense, I protest against the fundamental error, and the extravagant fruits, of a school which claims to be profound, and is profoundly absurd. The fundamental error is that of translating Art *into* Philosophy, and calling it the Philosophy of Art; a work is before the critic, and instead of judging this work he endeavours to get *behind* it, beneath it, into the *depths* of the soul which

produced it. He is not satisfied with what the artist has *given*, he wants to know what he *meant*. He guesses at the meaning; the more remote the meaning lies on the wandering tracks of thought, the better pleased is he with the discovery, and sturdily rejects every simple explanation in favour of this exegetical Idea. Thus the phantom of Philosophy hovers mistily before Art, concealing Art from our eyes. It is true the Idea said to underlie the work was never conceived by anyone before, least of all by the Artist; but *that* is the glory of the critic: he is proud of having plunged into the *depths.* Of all horrors to the German of this school there is no horror like that of the *surface* – it is more terrible to him than cold water.[79]

By contrast with Schlegel, Lessing was for Lewes (as previously for Coleridge and De Quincey) a refreshingly untypical German critic. He was the common-sense critic, and unlike Hegel he was suitable for discussion – even in the *Edinburgh Review*. Lewes offered Napier an article on Lessing, being careful to stress both Lessing's and his own freedom from rhetorical enthusiasm and mannerism:

This reminds me of a project of writing a...paper on Lessing, the father of German Literature, which as I should require some months to execute I now venture to ask you, whether you would like to have such an article in some future number, should you like the manner in which it was written. I propose to give a picture of the man in a biographical sketch; & an introduction to the study of his works; with a view of their influence on the literature of his country & the criticism of this. Mr. Macaulay when I had the pleasure of talking with him upon Lessing said he thought him the greatest of modern critics. I also propose to insist on the admirable style and lucid masterly exposition of Lessing in which qualities his countrymen are so lamentably deficient, & in which our countrymen do not shine now adays.[80]

The article itself drew praise from Jeffrey.[81] It lacks the 'Carlylism' of Lewes's earliest articles,[82] and is obviously less ambitious than those on Hegel and Schlegel. Lewes follows the well trodden *Edinburgh* route of sketching his subject's life and remarking on the works in that context. There is no frantic rhetoric of praise or blame, but a steady sympathy with Lessing, whose mind Lewes designates as 'of a quality eminently British. Of all the Germans, he is the least German; yet he created German literature.'[83] Lewes is clearly on his best behaviour here for the *Edinburgh*; indeed Napier himself tampered with the article to keep its tone sober. Lewes wrote deferentially to him, 'though I have not yet seen the Lessing & do not therefore know what alterations you have made, I am well assured that they were improvements', though his private opinion, recorded in a marginal comment to his own copy of the article, was less polite: 'This closing paragraph is by the editor who first cuts out all the fact and argument wherewith I established my view, and then apologises for the boldness of the article!'[84]

In spite of this enforced tameness, the article does reflect the direction Lewes's critical sympathy was taking. He wrote to Bulwer Lytton from Berlin in 1845, drawing his attention to the forthcoming Lessing article and saying, 'I am a very great admirer.'[85] When James Sully set about appraising Lewes after the latter's death (*New Quarterly Magazine*, October 1879), which he did under the careful scrutiny of George Eliot, he singled out Lewes's 'characteristic' mode of answering 'Schlegel's unverified assertions' on Greek drama by 'a simple reference to the facts', and linked Lewes with Lessing in this:

His philosophical studies, moveover, and his habits of reflection, supplied him with a luminous perception of principles, his references to which – like those of Lessing, of whom he so often reminds one – are never dragged in in a pedantic fashion, but seem to arise naturally out of reflection on the particular work under discussion. His critical temper is a warm one, but the warmth is duly controlled by a judicial fairness.[86]

The comparison pleased George Eliot, and would have pleased Lewes. As an example of this critical temper at work on Lessing, we may quote his brief but valuable remarks on the *Laokoon*:

Perhaps the characteristics of Lessing's mind are nowhere more distinctly visible than in his treatise on the *Laokoon*. The clearness and the directness of the style, are qualities so rare in such works, that one is apt to think lightly of its ideas; a journey, so easily performed, does not seem difficult; ideas, so easily grasped, seem obvious. But, on closing the book, if you compare the state of your opinions on art with those entertained previous to the perusal you will be able to estimate its value.[87]

It is hardly surprising that with his opposition to 'synthetic' criticism and the 'vicious' metaphysics from which it sprang Lewes found Schiller little to his taste. He wrote no sustained piece on Schiller,[88] but his remarks in scattered essays, and particularly in the *Life of Goethe*, are mainly adverse. Already in his first uneven essay on Goethe in the *British and Foreign Review* in 1843, Lewes put himself on the side of the 'objective' intellect, of which Goethe was his chief example, against the 'subjective' class, which included Schiller:

There are two distinct tendencies manifested by two classes of intellects. The first is the *objective* tendency, whereby the mind is impelled to attach an almost exclusive attention to *things*. The second is the *subjective* tendency, whereby it is impelled to attach an almost exclusive attention to *ideas*. The one works from without inwards, and the other from within outwards. . .The dominant tendency of Göthe's mind, as of all the *greatest* poets – Homer, Sophocles, Dante and Shakspeare – was the objective. . . The subjective repeats itself – all its works are but variations of one theme, instead of being separate melodies.[89]

Lewes's remarks on Goethe and Schiller were the occasion of Bulwer Lytton's opening a long and friendly correspondence with him, in which they argued at length about the respective merits of Goethe and Schiller, of objectivity and subjectivity, of realism and idealism. Bulwer wrote praising the Goethe article, but objecting that 'you underrate Schiller's mind, when you antithetically call it narrow. – It might be narrow compared with the measureless Goethe – but it is surely monstrous wide compared with most others. It is wide – for it embraces the Great – wide for it covers Humanity.'[90] He wrote again, asking for Lewes's help in interpreting one of Schiller's philosophical poems, 'Das Ideal und das Leben', which he was translating for a volume of Schiller's poems and ballads, to be published in 1844. He needed the benefit of Lewes's 'German Scholarship' for verses ten and eleven, which he believed to express 'some exaggeration from Kant, but I know not eno' of Kant to be much wiser from that belief.'[91] Lewes replied: 'I do not wonder at your being puzzled over Schiller; the transparent clearness necessary for philosophical poetry was not in his power; and if, as Göthe says: "Alles Lyrische muss im Ganzen sehr vernünftig, im Einzelnen ein Bischen unvernunftig seyn" I can only say that Schiller seems to have availed himself freely of the latter condition.' He gave an explanation of the verses in terms of the 'gap between the Ideal & the Realization which no mortal did o'erleap, which no mortal ever can', and though he finds the last four verses difficult, even obscure, he recognises the introduction of the Kantian idea of the Categorical Imperative – 'the Ideal of Virtue & Truth'.[92] Lewes felt that Schiller could best be judged by comparison with Goethe:

I cannot place him on the same level with Göthe. He is a great Intelligence; but surely not a great Poet. A great Rhetorician – in the best sense – utters manly sentiments, sometimes wise thoughts – but rarely uttering those exquisite & indefinable thoughts & expressions which distinguish

Poetry. . .He has often good Ideas; but seldom that exquisite Form, which not only gives endurance to Ideas, but which constitutes poetry *as an art*. L'art n'est qu'une forme as George Sand profoundly says.[93]

Lewes and German philosophy

By this time Lewes was coming to terms with the German philosophers in order to include them in his *Biographical History of Philosophy* (1845–6). This was a simplified study of the main directions of philosophy from Bacon (whose great achievement, according to Lewes, was the introduction of a scientific Method) to his modern counterpart, Comte. Lewes made clear his allegiance to empiricism, and hailed Comte as 'the Bacon of the nineteenth century', who 'fully sees the causes of our intellectual anarchy, and also sees the cure'.[94] His chief desire was to win over public attention and approval for Comte, whose scientific method seemed to him the most promising and exciting step in modern philosophy. He felt, like Mill, that there was now too much attention given to the German philosophers – in 1849 he went so far as to deplore 'the prevailing mania for German philosophy'.[95] Thus his attitude to the Germans in the *Biographical History*, particularly to Hegel, was a negative one. The work was confessedly an introductory guide for the layman, and was very successful as such.[96] More surprisingly, Herbert Spencer testified to its importance in his philosophical education:

I doubt not that the reading of Lewes's book, while it made me acquainted with the general course of philosophical thought, and with the doctrines which throughout the ages have been the subjects of dispute, gave me an increased interest in psychology, and an interest, not before manifest, in philosophy at large; at the same time that it served, probably, to give more coherence to my own thoughts, previously but loose.[97]

Frederic Harrison wrote of it as having 'acted on the mind of this generation almost more than any single book except Mr. Mill's *Logic*'.[98] Certainly it is a lucid and lively book, though on the Germans Lewes is, not surprisingly in view of his aim, brief and largely dismissive. Before coming to the Germans, he deals with Spinoza.

Lewes first wrote on Spinoza in the *Westminster Review* in 1843; as with Hegel, he was the first of his generation to draw the attention of his readers to a neglected author.[99] His remarks on Spinoza in the *Biographical History* are mainly a repetition of that article. Lewes could not accept Spinoza's philosophy, because it was an ontological one, referring everything to a first principle, or substance, which was God. He was nevertheless attracted to Spinoza's doctrine (as were Goethe and Coleridge) for its tendency to unification rather than dualism: God is the only substance; thought and extension are attributes; all that exists exists in and by God.[100] He admired Spinoza's logic, his remarkable clarity, and made it clear that if he could ever agree with a non-empirical method, it would be with Spinoza's: 'no believer in Ontology, as a *possible* science, can escape the all-embracing dialectic of Spinoza'.[101] 'Spinoza', he wrote in the *Biographical History*, 'stands out from the dim past like a tall beacon whose shadow is thrown athwart the sea, and whose light will serve to warn the wanderers from the shoals and rocks on which hundreds of their brethren have perished.'[102] The *Westminster* article was published as a pamphlet, and sold out immediately, as Lewes told William Hickson, editor of the *Westminster*, in September 1843.[103] Lewes made some notes and translations for a planned edition of extracts from Spinoza's works with his own introduction and comments, and during the stay in Germany in 1855–6 George Eliot took over from him and translated almost the whole of the *Ethics*.[104] Neither of them published a translation of Spinoza, though Lewes thought he had secured an agreement with Bohn.[105] He even promised an edition of Spinoza in a footnote to the *Life of Goethe*, 'edited by the writer of these lines'.[106] In the same work, he rightly stressed the importance for Goethe of his discovery of Spinoza: 'Although he did not study the system of Spinoza with any view of adopting it as a system, he studied it to draw therefrom food which his own mind could assimilate and work into new forms. Spinoza was to him what Kant was to Schiller...' He also struck a rare personal note: 'It was the casual citation of a passage from Spinoza which made my youth restless, and to this day I remember the aspect of the page where it appeared, and the revolution in thought which it effected!'[107] When he wrote again on Spinoza, in the *Fortnightly Review* in 1866, he added little in substance to what he had written in 1843, but he was again unusually autobiographical. He recalled a club to which he had belonged in the mid 1830s, where a watchmaker called Cohn had introduced the group to Spinoza: 'at that time no account of Spinoza was accessible to the English reader; nothing but vague denunciation or absurd misrepresentation'.[108]

Lewes also stressed Spinoza's wide influence on Germans from Lessing, Herder, and Goethe to Kant and the post-Kantian philosophers. He did not, however, extend the warmth he felt towards Spinoza to these successors, with their 'curious subtleties and cobwebs so indefatigably produced by the arachnae philosophers of Germany'.[109] His attitude to Kant in the *Biographical History*, for example, is mainly hostile. He does begin by defending Kant against the notion of him in England as 'a sort of Mystic': 'The "dreams of the Kantian philosophy," and "transcendental nonsense," are phrases which, once popular, now less so, are still occasionally to be met with in quarters where one little expects to find them.' On the contrary, says Lewes, Kant's system 'for rigour, clearness, and, above all, intelligibility, surpasses, by many degrees, systems. . ., hitherto considered easy enough of comprehension'. Lewes gives a brief but accurate notion of Kant's procedure in the *Kritik der reinen Vernunft*, his aim to criticise the operations of the mind, and his mediating between scepticism and dogmatism.[110] But he sees Kant as finally doing no more than furnishing 'a scientific basis for Scepticism', and gives only minimal attention to Kant's system of morality and 'his splendid vindication of the great idea of duty' in the *Kritik der praktischen Vernunft*.[111] The chapter in which he claims to assess Kant's contribution reverts stubbornly to the pre-Kantian opposition of empiricism and rationalism, and, as if Lewes knows he is doing Kant less than justice, he takes refuge in a rebuttal, not of Kant's system directly, but of Dr Whewell's version of it in his recent *Philosophy of the Inductive Sciences* (1840). His conclusion, 'that inasmuch as [Kant's] stronghold – the existence of *à priori* ideas – cannot sustain attack, the entrance of the enemy Scepticism is inevitable. Kant was not a sceptic; but he deceived himself in supposing that his system was any safeguard from Scepticism',[112] may be correct, but it has not been proved by Lewes in a direct confrontation of Kant's views.

His chapters on Fichte and Schelling are brisk and 'necessarily brief', but he pays more attention to Hegel, chiefly because Hegel, like Bacon and Comte, can be credited with 'the invention of a new Method'. This method works by means of the identity of contraries which for Hegel is the condition of all existence. Lewes finds himself admiring Hegel's 'perverse ingenuity' and his ability to be 'consistent to audacity, to absurdity':

Hegel especially impresses you with a sense of his wonderful power. We who trace these lines, in which respect for common sense, no less therefore sound logic forces a condemnation of the system of Hegel – we are amongst his warm admirers. His works we have always found very suggestive; his ideas, if repugnant to what we regard as the truth, are yet so coherent, so systematically developed, and the whole matter so obviously coming from matured meditation, that we have always risen from the perusal with a sense of the author's greatness, and of having had new lights thrown on the subject. . .But the system itself we may leave to all readers to decide, whether it be worthy of any attention, except as an illustration of the devious errors of speculation. A system which begins with assuming that Being and Non-Being are the same, because Being in the abstract is the Unconditioned, and so also is Non-Being; therefore both, as unconditioned, are the same; a system which proceeds upon the identity of contraries as the method of Philosophy; a system in which Thought is the same as the Thing, and the Thing is the same as the Thought; a system in which the only real positive existence is that of simple Relation, the two terms of which are Mind and Matter; this system were it wholly true, leaves all the questions, for which science is useful as a light, just as much in the dark as ever; and is, therefore, unworthy the attention of earnest men working for the benefit of mankind.[113]

In a notebook he remarks that 'Hegel always keeps you on the alert always inspires you with a conviction that there is something marvellously deep in what he says; and so there is, but the deepest thing in him is the art by which he inspires that conviction'.[114] Small wonder that he had succumbed to Hegel's power when studying the *Aesthetik* a few years earlier. What he now rejected in Hegel was the ontological approach,[115] the absolute idealism, and most significantly the lack of practical use to which his system might be put. He wrote in *The Leader* in 1850:

By the way, how completely the realities of life have crushed out of men's minds the ghostly phantoms with which SCHELLING and HEGEL endeavoured to direct them! The singular incompetence of German Metaphysics to grapple with any of the social problems imperatively demanding a solution. . .must have opened many eyes to its intrinsic futility, and may save some thousands from the idle theorizing upon assumed data, which has hitherto enervated German thought. . .We agree with the French wit that the Germans have *l'habitude de l'Infini*; and the force of this habit may be difficult to break, but let us hope it is not impossible.[116]

These remarks perhaps provide us with a clue for Lewes's (and George Eliot's and Mill's) otherwise inexplicable embracing of the system of Comte, which, after all, was not so very different from

Hegel's with its far-fetched division of history into epochs, its classification of the sciences as evolving one into another, its balancing of order and progress as the two contrary but complementary bases of society.[117] Comte called his positive system a 'scientific' one, and he was concerned chiefly to study social forces as the most complex of modern subjects for study, and make a new science – sociology – evolved from the other known sciences. He shared with Hegel the attraction of a comprehensive and ordered system, but his aim was practical, human, social, not idea-spinning.[118] Yet it is odd that Lewes could see the illusiveness of Hegel's idea of history, for example, where he was blind to that of Comte's:

Such is the art with which Hegel clothes his ideas in the garb of philosophy, that though aware that he is writing fiction, not history, and giving us perversions of notorious facts as the laws of historical developement, – telling us that the Spirit of the World manifests himself under such and such phases, when it is apparent to all that, granting the theory of this World-spirit's developement, the phases were *not* such as Hegel declares them to have been – although aware of all this, yet is the book so ingenious and amusing, that it seems almost unfair to reduce it to such a *caput mortuum* as our analysis.[119]

As Benjamin Jowett later commented of Lewes, it seemed 'a poor thing to have studied all philosophies and to end in adopting that of Auguste Comte'.[120]

Lewes went on reading and re-reading both Kant and Hegel, especially in the 1870s during his preparation for the *Problems of Life and Mind*, and he corresponded with the leading teachers of philosophy in Britain and Germany.[121] He remained an empiricist, antagonistic to the *a priori* method, but in his last works he tried to introduce an empirical metaphysics and coined a new middle term – 'metempirical' – for the unknowable and unacceptable element, to be distinguished from both 'empirical' and 'metaphysical':

If then the *Empirical* designates the province we include within the range of Science, the province we exclude may fitly be styled the *Metempirical* ...since this term is the exact correlative of Empirical, and designates whatever lies beyond the limits of possible Experience, it characterises inquiries which one class [i.e. positive thinkers] regards as vain and futile, another [i.e. metaphysicians] as exalted above mere scientific procedure. Nor is this the only advantage of the term; it also detaches from Metaphysics a vast range of insoluble problems, leaving behind it only such as are soluble.[122]

His use of the term seems not to have been consistent; he sometimes allowed the metempirical to have access to real knowledge and sometimes not.[123] Sully, Professor of Logic at University College London, gave a lukewarm appraisal of Lewes's late work in his obituary article, but he was by contrast warm about Lewes's early achievements in criticism. He saw as 'the crowning achievement of his general literary activity' *The Life of Goethe*.[124] He was not alone in this judgment. Indeed Lewes first became celebrated as a serious author on the publication of this work and was for most of his life known primarily as the author of the *Life*.[125]

Lewes and Goethe (*1843–55*)

The Goethe article of 1843, though it drew praise from Bulwer Lytton and Mill, and was, according to Lewes, translated into French and German,[126] is rather rambling and inconclusive. It begins dramatically with the two opposite types of reviewer, one (Jeffrey) seeing Goethe as a 'charlatan', the other (Carlyle) worshipping him as a 'Weimarian Jove'. Lewes intends to take a middle way. Mill criticised the 'considerable Carlylism in the opening pages',[127] and Kemble must have chided Lewes too, for the latter wrote a long defence of his method in the article:

I always consider an essay a work of Art. I draw out a programm of my intentions, dispose the parts, then work off a careful *cartoon* & then finally set to work at the picture. Error there may be, & shortcoming but not carelessness. Whenever particularly dull as Swift says there is some design in it, whenever flippant there is some serious intention. I therefore always, as a matter of Art, begin an article with either a joke, a paradox, or a startling proposition, and I have always found it succeed. It provokes the readers [sic] attention, and he will allow you to 'nod' occasionally provided you do not begin with a 'yawn.' Knock a man down – especially on a subject like that of Göthe which has been so much talked about with so little really said, that people are not naturally disposed to listen to more prosing, & how prima facie are they to know that the present article is not prosing at more or less length, and not an attempt at something new?[128]

His boast is not fully justified, as the article does not proceed calmly and impartially, but shows Lewes not yet sure of the attitude he should adopt towards the controversial Goethe.

In taking note of Goethe's life and character he writes in a breathlessly dramatic tone:

His son is dead, his only son. What does Göthe? Why, stifling the sorrow in his breast, he renews his literary labours with intense ardour, completely absorbing himself in them. In a fortnight he finishes the last volume of his *'Dichtung und Wahrheit.'* But nature is not thus to be bent by man's will; a violent hemorrhage caused by these suppressed emotions nearly puts an end to his life.[129]

He confesses to being puzzled by the contradictions in Goethe's character, and tries to explain them in terms of Goethe's devotion to the artistic life. Still under the spell of Hegel's idea that art is but a step from religion and philosophy, he sets out as if to prove Goethe's artistic concern one-sided, but, unsure of this, he veers off into a defence of Goethe's artistic self-culture:

Göthe was essentially an artist. From long devotion to this idea he had at last come to merge all moral points into aesthetical questions, and to consider truth and right as only tantamount to, if not convertible with, beauty and grace. The τὸ ἀγαθὸν was to him no more than the τὸ καλὸν; ethics became subordinate in fact to aesthetics. Art was the end of life. In the highest region of speculation this is unquestionably true; but its truth remains vital only in that region, and is chilled and withered, and rendered impracticable, if not false, directly it descends into the region of practical life. It is as a star in the intellectual heaven, to which the mind may yearn; not a sun, which keeps the foot from stumbling over the darkened paths of life. It may be true that our tumultuous existence will finally seek its culmination and repose in the Beautiful; it may be the destination of humanity; we know not – cannot know. But in the meanwhile the course through which we must pass in the various stages of development, this demands, – this forces our attention. What are the great demands of this life of ours? Are they to be summed up into a desire for art? – or are there other wants, passions and objects which must also be satisfied, even if they eventually merge themselves in art? Are not religion and philosophy equally demands of the intellectual life? Must they not too be consummated? Assuredly. Whatever be the destination of man, this threefold form of his intellectual life (religion, philosophy, art,) must be consummated ere it can be attained. At present they are separate – distinct; each cultivated independent of the other two; the individual cultivator sees vital importance only in his department. With Göthe we have seen a subversion of ethical in favour of aesthetical judgment; and this devotion to his idea entitles him to the name of *Der Künstler,* for it is not every one who cultivates an art who also devotes himself to it. Alas, no! in these days of ours we see too much of the contrary; we see too much cultivation of art, and devotion to – money! or else to vulgar applause and "moving in the first circles," and hence the utter want of art in any but a mercantile sense! Devotion to an idea in these days is rather a matter of ridicule than admiration. Yet it must be comprehended as a fact in human history before any great men can be understood, and therefore before the reader can get much insight into the interior of Göthe's nature.[130]

As we have seen, he characterises Goethe's mind, by contrast with Schiller's, as predominantly objective and analytical. His interest in this quality in Goethe bore fruit in his discussion of Goethe as a man of science. This was an area of Goethe studies which few had discussed, and for which Lewes was, as George Eliot proudly wrote in her otherwise deliberately impartial notice of the *Life of Goethe*, uniquely equipped by his own interests to evaluate. Having begun her *Leader* review, 'For reasons which will be easily divined, we have received an injunction to deliver no judgment on this work, but simply to make the reader acquainted with its general character and purpose', she kept her word, only stopping to single out the chapter on science, describing it as 'a full account, intelligible even to unscientific persons, of what Goethe really achieved in Botany and Comparative Anatomy and of what he *failed* to achieve in Optics'.[131] The chapter referred to is based on an article Lewes wrote in the *Westminster Review* in 1852, called 'Goethe as a Man of Science'. He researched the subject carefully, probably already intending it to be included in the *Life*, on which he had been working since 1846.[132] He combined his own scientific work (for *Sea-Side Studies*, 1858, and *The Physiology of Common Life*, 1860) with that on Goethe. He wrote to Sir Richard Owen, probably in 1852:

Could you spare me twenty minutes of your most valuable time, any afternoon at the College? I want to propound an anatomical discovery of no great importance it is true, but as Touchstone says of Audrey "An ill-favored thing, your honor, but *my own*." And I also want to ask you one or two questions about Goethe's position in the history of comp. anat.[133]

In both the article and the *Life*, Lewes shows great sympathy with Goethe, whose work was ridiculed or ignored by scientists.[134] He could not get a fair hearing from the experts because they believed a poet could be nothing but an amateur dabbler in science.[135] By the help of experts like Owen, and from his own reading, Lewes was able to give Goethe full credit for his discoveries in anatomy (finding that man has an intermaxillary bone in common with animals) and in botany (offering a morphological theory in *Die Metamorphose der Pflanzen*).[136]

For the *Life of Goethe* Lewes got help not only from leading scientists, but also from German friends and acquaintances of Goethe. The famous flight to Weimar with George Eliot in July 1854 had as part of its object the final researching of the *Life*. Lewes made and renewed several useful acquaintances in Weimar and then in Berlin,[137] where Varnhagen was again helpful. Varnhagen's diary records visits from Lewes during which they discussed Goethe, and Lewes borrowed books from him. And George Eliot reported in her diary that 'Varnhagen was a real treasure to G. for his library supplied all the deficiencies of the public one where to ask for books was generally like "sinking buckets into empty wells".'[138] Lewes also wrote, just before completing the book, to the grand old man of German letters in England, Henry Crabb Robinson:

I trust the purpose of this note is sufficient apology; for although accident has hitherto prevented my desire to make your personal acquaintance, I am sure the name of Goethe is enough to recommend your interest at once. It is of Goethe I would speak.

For many years I have been employed writing his Biography. Many of his personal friends in Germany have kindly assisted me. You, also, I believe had some personal acquaintance with him in his later years, and I should esteem it a great favor if your inclination & leisure would permit you to furnish me with any personal details.[139]

The book was published in November 1855. Its success was immediate and well deserved. On the whole, Lewes's avowedly analytical method makes for fairness and clarity on both the man and his work. As George Eliot pointed out in her review (holding back from praise or blame not only because of her closeness to Lewes, but also because she had a hand in the writing, having translated several passages Lewes quoted from the German[140]):

Some acquaintance with Goethe is felt to be indispensable in these days. Those who are unable to study him directly, find him mentioned by great authorities as the intellectual father, or grandfather of this age, which is said to be living chiefly on the ideas it has inherited from him...They read translations of *Wahrheit und Dichtung* [sic], *Wilhelm Meister*, and the *Wahlverwandtschaften*, and while they find some wisdom and beauty which they understand and appreciate, they perhaps find much more which seems to them not at all wisdom or beauty, and they have generally a sense that a *clue* is wanted. For readers thus baffled, few books can be more interesting than one which will give them such a history of Goethe the Man as will throw light on Goethe the Writer – such a descriptive and analytical account of his works as will enable them to conceive the artistic merits which have won him the supreme place among modern poets, such a *natural history* of his various productions as will show how they were the outgrowth of his mind at different stages of its culture.[141]

Certainly the method works excellently. Lewes finds out and highlights the most important of Goethe's pursuits at each stage in his life. His interest in history, in art, in science, in theatre management – each has its appropriate chapter. Lewes is particularly good where he relates Goethe to the modern tradition by contrasting his dramatic handling of *Iphigenie* with that of Euripides. He shows how Goethe has adopted a Greek story, Greek singleness of plot, and Greek serenity, but has produced a play in which the sentiment and the morality are of the eighteenth century and German: 'It is a German play. It substitutes profound moral and psychological struggles, for the passionate struggles of the old legend. It is not Greek in ideas nor in sentiments.' Goethe's characters, unlike Euripides', abhor treachery, refusing to take advantage of their host Thoas. Thoas himself is not the fierce, barbaric foreigner he is in Euripides: 'Thoas, in Goethe, is a *moral*, not a *dramatic* figure.'[142] In Goethe the *deus ex machina* is a psychological insight into the symbolic meaning of the oracle of Apollo (about bringing the 'sister' back to Greece to end the curse on the family) rather than a dramatic fulfilment of its surface meaning:

I will merely allude to the characteristic difference between Ancient and Modern Art: the Furies in Euripides are terrible Apparitions, real beings personated by actors; in Goethe they are Phantasms moving across the stage of an unhappy soul, but visible only to the inward eye; in like manner, the Greek dénouement is the work of the actual interference of the Goddess in person, whereas the German dénouement is a loosening of the knot by deeper insight into the meaning of the oracle.[143]

Trollope wrote to Lewes on the publication of the second edition of the *Life* (1863), 'there never was better criticism than that on Greek tragic art in the first two pages of your chapter – called Iphigenia and I make you my compliments'.[144]

Lewes makes meaningful his description of Goethe's mind as 'concrete' when he says Goethe in his plays and poems 'embalms his own experience' and yet writes not solely from self but also reflects, with a clarity which shows passion to be controlled, the temper of his age:

Götz is the greatest product of the *Sturm und Drang* movement. As we before hinted, this period is not simply one of Titanic hopes and mediaeval retrospections, it is also one of unhealthy sentimentalism. Goethe, the great representative poet of his day – the secretary of his Age – gives us master-pieces which characterize both these tendencies. Beside the insurgent Götz stands the dreamy Werther. And yet, accurately as these two works repre-sent two active tendencies of that time, they are both far removed above the perishing extravagances of that time; they are both *ideal* expressions of the age, and as free from the disease which corrupted it as Goethe himself was free from the weakness of his contemporaries. Wilkes used to say that he had never been a Wilkite. Goethe was never a Werther.[145]

This is an expansion of the remarks he had put into the mouth of his wise man in *Ranthorpe*.

Lewes coolly approaches the *Wahlverwandtschaften* (*Elective Affinities*), from which William Taylor, himself something of a free-thinker, had been too timid to quote or paraphrase forty years before.[146] He shows how Goethe adopts neither a moral nor an 'immoral' attitude on the subject of his protagonists' desired and imagined adultery, being 'an Artist, not an Advocate'. Indeed he comes close to seeing that Goethe takes all the heat and possible sensationalism out of the crisis by his slow, deliberate, digressive narrative. There is much weighty discussion of the best method of landscaping the estate, of improving views and restoring the chapel, as well as many scattered pieces of general wisdom. Lewes finds these tedious, but makes a point for which he was probably in-debted to George Eliot:

A dear friend of mine, whose criticism is always worthy of attention [this is strengthened in the third edition – i.e. after George Eliot had become famous as a novelist – to 'a great writer, and one very dear to me'], thinks that the long episodes which interrupt the progress of the story during the interval of Eduard's absence and return, are artistic devices for impressing the reader with a sense of the slow movement of life; and, in truth, it is only in fiction that the dénouement usually lies close to the exposition.[147]

Of *Wilhelm Meisters Lehrjahre* he contends, similarly, that for Goethe ethics is subordinate to aesthetics, yet he has to admit that though the first five books, dealing with Wilhelm's adventures with the actors, are presented in lively fashion, without moral comment, the last three are heavily moralistic, treating seriously of religion, morality, education, and the guiding forces for good in the universe. Knowing that Goethe recast the book from an earlier, more theatre-oriented version, 'Wilhelm Meisters Theatralische Sendung' ('Wil-helm Meister's Theatrical Mission', written in 1775–85, but not published until 1911), Lewes thinks Goethe's later addition of a moral is a weakness:

After a lapse of ten years he resumes the novel; and having in that period lived through the experience of a false tendency – having seen the vanity of cultivating an imperfect talent – he *alters* the plan of his novel, makes it symbolical of the erroneous striving of youth towards culture; invents the cumbrous machinery of a Mysterious Family whose watchful love has guided all his steps, and who have encouraged him in error that they might lead him through error into truth.[148]

Here he does Goethe less than justice. The humour and levity surrounding the actress Philina and others in the earlier part *do* continue even into the later, more sober, episodes. For example, Goethe allows the silly, immature, but good-natured boy Friedrich to be the direct means of bringing together Wilhelm and his true bride Natalie – 'Natalie ist dein! ich bin der Zauberer, der diesen Schatz gehoben hat' ('Natalie is yours! I am the magician who has raised this treasure'). Friedrich has heard Natalie admit that she loves Wilhelm when eavesdropping at her door. The wise Abbot, otherwise the chief organiser of others' lives, is left to admit humorously to Friedrich, 'ich komme, so scheint es, heute nicht mehr zum Wort' ('it seems as though I'm not getting a look in today'[149]).

Equally, the moral guardians who govern affairs in their Tower at the end have made several enigmatic and at the time unassessable appearances during Wilhelm's apparently aimless wanderings. Their part in guiding his life only becomes clear in retrospect once he has come to accept his responsibilities. The point about Wilhelm's education is that, though he has to listen to some heavy generalising maxims at his transition from apprentice to Meister (at the end of Book 7), these are seen to be true only when applied to the chaotic incidents Wilhelm has already lived through:

Jene allgemeine Sprüche sind nicht aus der Luft gegriffen; freilich scheinen sie demjenigen leer und dunkel, der sich keiner Erfahrung dabei erinnert.

Those general maxims are not just out of the blue, though to the person who does not remember his past experiences when hearing them they of course seem empty and obscure.[150]

The moral point Goethe is making about experience and learning is precisely matched by the narrative form. The shift in tone from the mysterious, ambiguous, or incomplete to the slow, sober, patient exposition of the last books signals Wilhelm's journey towards and arrival in his proper element. Lewes's view that Goethe superadded the moral symbolism in order to 'flatter the German tendency' to look for deep meanings, that bad habit of 'philosophical criticism', is over-simple.[151] But Lewes does make some good points about *Wilhelm Meister*, particularly where he applies the definition, given in the 1843 article, of Goethe's mind as objective and analytical:

If we look through the works with critical attention, we shall observe the *concrete* tendency determining – first, his choice of subjects; secondly, his handling of characters; and, thirdly, his style. We shall see the operation of that law of his mind, *which made the creative impulses move only in alliance with emotions he himself had experienced*...Hence we see why he was led to pourtray Men and Women, instead of Demigods and Angels: no Posas and Theklas [characters in plays by Schiller], but Egmonts and Clärchens. Hence also his portraitures carry their moral *with* them, *in* them, but have no "moral" superimposed – no accompanying verdict as from some outstanding judge. Further, – and this is a point to be insisted on, – his style, both in poetry and prose, is subject to the same law. It is vivid with images, but it has scarcely any "imagery." Most poets describe objects by metaphors or comparisons; Goethe seldom tells you what an object is *like*, he tells you what it *is*.[152]

In the chapter dealing with *Wilhelm Meister*, Lewes applies this remark aptly to the novel:

I have only to refer to the marvellous art with which the characters unfold themselves. We see them, and see through them. They are never described, they exhibit themselves. Philina, for example, one of the most bewitching and original creations in fiction, whom we know as well as if she had flirted with us and jilted us, is never once described. Even her person is made present to us through the impression it makes on others, not by any direct information. We are not told that she was a strange mixture of carelessness, generosity, caprice, wilfulness, affectionateness, and gaiety; a lively girl, of French disposition, with the smallest possible regard for decorum, but with a true decorum of her own; snapping her fingers at the world, disliking conventions, tediousness, and pedantry; without any ideal aspirations, yet also without any affectations; coquetting with all the men, disliked by all the women, turning everyone round her finger, yet ready to oblige and befriend even those who had injured her.[153]

With these remarks Lewes gives the reader a tool by which he can turn his puzzlement or annoyance about the 'carelessness' with which Goethe introduces and moves Philina into admiration of Goethe's art. For it is the very volatility of Philina, with Goethe's refusal to blame her for it, which forces us into open-mindedness about her merits, so that when we find her acting relatively nobly towards Wilhelm when others fail him, we are pleasantly surprised (though on reflection not shocked) into approving of a character we were tempted to dismiss as worthless.[154]

When Lewes deals with *Faust*, his method of common-sense analysis rather lets him down. Firstly, he made the understandable mistake of using old material for his chapter on *Faust*, part one. He incorporated almost bodily an article, written for the *British and Foreign Review* in 1844, on *Faust*, Marlowe's *Doctor Faustus*, and Calderón's *El mágico prodigioso*.[155] Thus the perspective shifts temporarily away from Goethe's works in relation to his life and to his age, and the long passages on Calderón seem out of place.[156] Secondly, neither *Faust*, part one, nor *Faust*, part two, yields its essence by the attempt to summarise its plot and movement. Lewes restates his method in this chapter, perhaps aware that it is less successful here: 'A poem is before me, and I dissect it, take up one piece of the organism after the other, show its position, and try to indicate its function. If the reader object to such criticism, this is a warning to skip the present chapter.'[157] Lewes properly defends the infamous Prologue in Heaven against the charges of blasphemy, and draws attention to the significance of the two prologues – that in the theatre and that in Heaven – in indicating the scope of Goethe's concerns:

The reason of this I take to lie in the twofold nature of the poem, in the two leading subjects to be worked out. The world and the world's ways are to be depicted, the individual soul and its struggles are to be pourtrayed. For the former we have the theatre-prologue, because "All the world's a stage, and all the men and women merely players." For the latter we have the prologue in heaven, because heaven is the centre and the goal of all struggles, doubts and reverence. . .[158]

Unfortunately, in his method of summarising and briefly analysing the episodic scenes of *Faust*, Lewes is less able to convey a sense of the play's special nature. He mentions Coleridge's lack of enthusiasm, quoting his remark (in *Table Talk*) on the scenes being 'mere magic-lantern pictures' and the work as a whole 'very flat'. Lewes argues: 'The successive scenes of a magic-lantern have no connexion with a general plan; have no dependence one upon the other. In the analysis just submitted to the reader, both the general plan and the inter-dependence of the scenes have, it is hoped, been made manifest.'

Ironically, the reader's experience is that precisely in the scene-by-scene analysis Lewes has failed to convey the plan, but where he makes general defining remarks about *Faust*, he is most useful in offering hints for understanding. For example, he says *Faust* is not an ordinary drama, its purpose is not to unfold the evolutions of an episode of life, to keep our attention through a story. It is rather 'a grand legendary spectacle, in which all phases of life are represented'.[159] He might have noticed here the stress in the Prologue in Heaven on mankind as a whole. While Mephistopheles talks persistently about winning over one soul – Faust's – from God, God equally persistently treats Faust as but a representative of mankind, for whom He plans a benevolent providence. A tension of the confused here-and-now versus the harmonious after-life is set up here:

> So lang er auf der Erde lebt,
> So lang sei dirs nicht verboten:
> Es irrt der Mensch, solang er strebt.

While he lives on earth, you are not forbidden [i.e. from trying to win him]. As long as they struggle, men are in error.

This is the tension which persists through the apparently unconnected scenes of the play. If Lewes had followed up his promising beginning, and related individual scenes to his perspective, he would have provided a better introduction for his readers.

Of part two, Lewes knows that he is unequipped to clarify it by means of his chosen method:

In the presence of this poem, I feel more embarrassment than with any other of Goethe's works. . .I have tried to understand the work; tried to place myself at the right point of view for perfect enjoyment; but repeated trials, instead of clearing up obscurities and deepening enjoyment, as with the other works, have more and more confirmed my first impressions.

One may well agree with his conclusion that part two is a failure, because it has taken refuge in hieroglyphics.[160] On the other hand, it might have been possible to make something of it by abandoning all attempts to paraphrase and to set it in its biographical context in favour of a bold literary interpretation in terms of Goethe's desire to unite all cultures in symbolic form.

Nevertheless, the *Life of Goethe* stands out in nineteenth-century biography for its candour, clarity, and critical insights. Lewes's translations are always accurate; he even shows agility in translating

Goethe's fluent verse. There is his rendering of one of the Roman Elegies (1788–90), which, despite the hexameters, more awkward in English than in German, runs relatively smoothly. Goethe's verse is as follows:

> Lass dich, Geliebte, nicht reu'n, dass du mir so schnell
>   dich ergeben!
> Glaub' es, ich denke nicht frech, denke nicht niedrig von dir.
> Vielfach wirken die Pfeile des Amor: einige ritzen
> Und vom schleichenden Gift kranket auf Jahre das Herz.
> Aber mächtig befiedert, mit frisch geschliffener schärfe [sic],
> Dringen die andern ins Mark, zünden behende das Blut.
> *In der heroischen Zeit, da Götter und Göttinnen liebten,*
> *Folgte Begierde dem Blick, folgte Genuss der Begier.*
> Glaubst du, es habe sich lange die Göttin der Liebe
>   besonnen,
> Als in Idäischen Hain einst ihr Anchises gefiel?
> *Hätte Luna gesäumt, den schönen Schläfer zu küssen,*
> *O, so hätt' ihn geschwind, neidend, Aurora geweckt.*

Then comes Lewes's translation, for which he apologises, describing it as a 'rough plaster-cast':

> Let not my Loved One repent that she so quickly surrendered!
> Trust me, I think thee not *bold*, – think naught unworthy
>   of thee.
> Amor has manifold shafts with manifold workings: some
>   scratch,
> And with insidious steel poison the bosom for years.
> Others are mightily wing'd, and, keen in new-polished
>   sharpness,
> Pierce to the innermost depths, kindling the blood into flame.
> In the Heroical Age, when the gods with goddesses wantoned,
> Passion was born in a glance, fruition followed desire.
> Think'st thou the goddess of love "demanded time to
>   consider,"
> When in Idalian groves she gazed on Anchises with joy?
> Luna delaying one moment to kiss the beautiful Sleeper,
> Soon had seen him awake 'neath the kiss of eager Aurora.[161]

The most controversial aspect of the *Life*, and inevitably that which preoccupied critics, was Lewes's explicit handling of Goethe's notorious affairs with women. Lewes drew no veil of vague conjecture, nor did he pronounce anathema on Goethe's abandoning of his early love, Friederike,[162] and his liaisons with Frau von Stein and the woman he later married, Christiane. He was aware of the problem of dealing honestly, yet delicately, particularly with Frau von Stein. It had been thought by most observers, at least in England, that Goethe's relationship with the mature, intellectual Frau von Stein was spiritual, not physical. Goethe had testified in his poems and letters to her influence on his work. But Lewes found, on examining the records and consulting people in Weimar, that the affair had been consummated. He wrote to Blackie: 'Yes, the liaison with the Frau von Stein *did* become more than platonic, as you will see I quietly indicate in one passage; but I was forced to keep that part in a subdued light because the British public would have gone into fits at the open avowal. His letters leave *no* doubt of the fact.'[163] Indeed, Lewes in his short chapter on Frau von Stein leaves the reader to draw his own conclusions from a selection of Goethe's passionate letters to her. But when he comes to deal with Christiane Vulpius, the girl of less glittering social standing with whom Goethe lived and who bore him a son many years before he decided to marry her, he is more open: 'It has already been intimated that Weimar was loud in disapprobation of this new liaison; although it had uttered no word against the liaison with the Frau von Stein. The great offence seems to have been his choosing one beneath him in rank.'[164]

Some reviewers of the *Life* objected to Lewes's tolerant attitude. In the *Edinburgh Review* Sarah Austin, who had translated several German works in the 1830s, including *Characteristics of Goethe* (1833)[165] and who had encouraged both Mill and Sterling in their German reading, took a high moral line. She recounted the Friederike episode in detail, being 'not satisfied with Mr. Lewes's reflections on this passage in the life of his hero', and she accused Lewes of speaking 'with something of a sneer of the accusation of 'moral laxity' so frequently brought against Goethe'.[166] But she was careful to separate her assessment of the *Life*'s treatment of Goethe's life and its critical comments on his works. A reviewer in the *Athenaeum* also found fault with Lewes's 'placid manner' of treating the affair with Frau von Stein.[167] Crabb Robinson, reading it in November and December 1855, noted in his diary that he was enjoying it – 'it is a book that fully appreciates the magnitude and superiority of Goethe' – but felt that Lewes's 'moral tone is low'.[168] But it had its share of praise from discerning critics. Richard Holt Hutton dissented mildly from Lewes's stance on Goethe's morality, but praised his candour and his clear critical sense.[169] In 1857 Matthew Arnold mentioned Lewes's 'delightful *Life of Goethe*', and in 1878 he described the *Life* as 'a work in many respects of brilliant cleverness'.[170]

Carlyle, to whom Lewes dedicated the book, wrote kindly, though with vaguely suggested reservations:

Furthermore I got the *Goethe* the other night, almost at the same time with your Note. Every night since, in my reading hours, I am dashing athwart it in every direction; *truanting*; for I w^t wait a time to read the work with such deliberation as I well see it deserves. My conviction is, we have here got an excellent Biography, – altogether transcendently so, as Biographies are done in this country. Candid, well-informed, clear, free-flowing, it will certainly throw a large flood of light over Goethe's life, with many German things which multitudes in England have been curious about, to little purpose, for a long while. It ought to have a large circulation, if one can predict or anticipate in regard to such matters. On the whole, I say *Euge*, and that heartily, – tho' dissenting here and there.[171]

Carlyle was right about the circulation. When Blackie, whose *Faust* translation Lewes had used in the *Life*, praising it as the best of the verse translations, wrote to congratulate him, Lewes replied: 'The book has met with far more success than I ventured to hope – 900 copies have been sold in six weeks. But sale is only one kind of test. The approbation of men like yourself is far more valuable. Your good word will have great influence in Edinburgh.'[172] In January 1857 Lewes noted in his journal that the past year had been 'a happy & successful one, & will be memorable to me...as the year in which my greatest literary success – *The Life of Goethe* was assured'.[173]

In Germany, the response was mixed. Everyone took notice of this, the first full biography of Goethe, which had shamed German critics and scholars by being written by an Englishman. There was some hypercritical reviewing by those who felt insulted by Lewes's nationality and by his light, cool tone. For example, Adolf Schöll in the *Weimarer Sonntags-Blatt* (13 December 1857), quarrelled at length over minor details of Goethe's life, and objected to the 'knabenhafte Zungenkeckheit des englischen Zeitungschreibers' ('schoolboyish cheek of the English journalist') and the 'Abwechslung von Moralität und Empfindsamkeit mit Philister-bonsens und frivolem Humor' ('alternation of morality and sensitivity with sops to the philistines and frivolous humour').[174] H. Siegfried wrote *An*

Lewes, eine Epistel (1858), a pamphlet in the form of a letter to Lewes which contained an impassioned defence of Bettina von Arnim, the neurotic woman who had exaggerated her relationship with Goethe in *Goethes Briefwechsel mit einem Kinde* (1835) and whom Lewes had dismissed with amusement. The worshippers of Goethe, including Varnhagen, could forgive no comment of Lewes's which was less than adoring. Varnhagen even wished to believe that Goethe, in his unfortunate attempt to outdo Newton in optics, might have been right and Newton wrong.[175] One Karl Biltz took Lewes to task for a derogatory remark about the appearance of the people of Weimar. Lewes had referred to the provincialism of Weimar, calling the inhabitants 'a slow, heavy, ungraceful, ignorant, but good-natured, happy, honest race, feeding on black bread and sausages; the stupidest people I have ever lived among, and perhaps the ugliest, but a people of whom that is the *worst* to be said'. George Eliot, too, in her article 'Three Months in Weimar' (1855), referred to the Weimarians as having 'more than the usual heaviness of Germanity' and a 'somewhat stupid *bien-être*'.[176] Biltz took these casual aspersions and answered them at great length and with great seriousness.

Apart from these extreme responses, the work was a success in Germany, and went through several editions in the translation of Frese (who also translated *Adam Bede*). Lewes could say in his preface to the second edition (1863): 'The sale of thirteen thousand copies in England and Germany, and the sympathy generously expressed, not unmingled, it is true, with adverse and even angry criticism, are assurances that my labours were not wholly misdirected, however far they may have fallen short of their aim.' When Sully sent the proof of his article on Lewes to George Eliot for approval, she picked out his assessment of the reception of the *Life of Goethe* for comment: 'Perhaps you a little underrate the (original) effect of his 'Life of Goethe' in Germany. It was received with enthusiasm, and an immense number of copies, in both the English and German form, have been sold in Germany since its appearance in 1854 [i.e. 1855].'[177] Some of the adverse criticism in Germany seems to have been caused by Lewes's German translator, Frese, who exaggerated the originality of Lewes's achievement by leaving out some of Lewes's generous references to German works from which he had benefited in his study. Adolf Schöll, reviewing the German *Life of Goethe* adversely in 1857, takes exception particularly to Frese's remarks about Viehoff, Rosenkranz, and other German commentators on Goethe.[178] Lewes wrote to his German publisher Duncker saying that the omission of such references had been 'very painful to my feelings, & I cannot in the least conceive why it was done'. He had been scrupulous in naming his sources, and felt that 'much ill-feeling would have been spared in Germany, if the authors had seen their works acknowledged'. Lewes wanted to make sure that any errors and omissions were corrected for the next edition, and he asked Duncker to send him all the German reviews of the work, particularly the unfavourable ones, so that he might benefit from them.[179]

Meanwhile, when he and George Eliot went to Germany again in 1858, they found themselves fêted: 'the author of the 'Life of Goethe' is naturally an object of interest & attention to all cultivated Germans.'[180] Lewes's work on physiology was greatly helped by the access he gained to the laboratories of Liebig and other celebrated scientists in Munich. He recorded in his journal:

...in came [Martius] the celebrated traveller & botanist...He spoke very flatteringly of the Life of Goethe, & asked us to come & see him & his family which we agreed to do tomorrow evening...Dressed & went to a small party at Oldenburgs. He had invited *Liebig, Heyse, Geibel,* & *Carrière* to meet us, and a most brilliant evening it was. With Liebig we were greatly charmed...He – indeed they all – spoke of the Life of Goethe in high terms. The book is evidently making a sensation.[181]

Although Lewes would have preferred in later life to be celebrated for his work in physiology and psychology, he remained for others the author of the *Life of Goethe*. In 1876 the Belgian King asked to meet him and opened the conversation with a remark about the *Life*.[182] The work has lasted well. Modern scholars of German still praise it.[183] Richard Holt Hutton first pointed to the qualities which Lewes showed in it – a thorough knowledge and understanding of the German context and an English candour and ability to wear his learning lightly:

Mr. Lewes's volumes give us a very able and interesting biography, – a book, indeed, of permanent value; the incidents illustrating character, though not quite exhausting his materials, are disposed with skill, and the artistic criticism, while thoroughly appreciating Goethe's transcendent poetical genius, is independent, sensible, and English...He gives his readers the elements for forming their own moral judgments, and he has shaken off from his feet the ponderous rubbish of the German scholiasts.[184]

145

Or, as his friend and admirer Robert Lytton chose to express it, 'you alone combine the depth & accuracy of German & English thinking with the charming grace & crystalline lucidity of French writing'.[185] Many contemporaries noticed the 'French' wit, charm, even naughtiness, of Lewes's writings and more particularly his conversation. Not all observers approved of it.[186] But his serious interest in German literature and philosophy offended no one. Among his varied literary activities, the contribution to the introduction and understanding of the best German authors stands out in its importance. He impressed Carlyle, Mill, the not easily impressible Herbert Spencer,[187] Hutton, and many others with his German knowledge. And his relationship with George Eliot was closely related to their joint interest in German literature. They had that interest in common when they met. They fled together to Weimar, where they knew their liaison would be accepted socially, where they could work together on Goethe, and from where they could send articles on German subjects to British magazines. Lewes's great achievement in the history of German studies in England was the *Life of Goethe*, and his articles on Spinoza, Hegel, and Goethe as a man of science were, despite some faults, innovative in their time.

4

George Eliot

When George Eliot began learning German early in 1840 – like Coleridge and Carlyle, she seems to have begun the study of German literature with Schiller[1] – there no longer prevailed an atmosphere of hostility towards German literature. She was of the generation which had benefited from the efforts of Coleridge, Carlyle, the translators and reviewers, to make works of German literature known and judged without prejudice. Even in her earlier days of strict Evangelical piety she felt it no sin to read and enjoy German texts, as well as that most 'German' of English texts, *Sartor Resartus*, though she did warn a friend to whom she recommended it that it was not 'orthodox'.[2] Almost inevitably her mental shift from Evangelicalism to free-thinking was closely connected with her German reading. The great movement of German historical criticism of the Bible with which Coleridge had been intimate since his student days in Göttingen surfaced again in England in the 1830s and 1840s, largely through the works of the Brays and Hennells with whom George Eliot lived and studied.[3] Where the literature of Germany had become generally accepted (though naturally there was dissent in particular cases), the philosophy and historical criticism caused a fresh outcry from orthodox British critics. As Baden Powell, reviewing theological works in 1847, wrote:

While German literature has become of late much more familiar to us – though not yet quite naturalised – German theology, one of its most important branches, has never had justice done to it. . .For, whether Strauss's *Life of Jesus* be presented to us as the triumphant exercitation of a scholar, bent on what can be made by sufficient learning out of the most hopeless hypothesis, or as a grave philosophical dissertation set down in sad and sober earnest, we are satisfied, that, in either case, it lies as far beyond the visible diurnal sphere of English comprehension as the philosophy of Hegel.[4]

This reference to Strauss's *Leben Jesu* in George Eliot's translation of 1846 was as near as the *Edinburgh Review* came to reviewing that dangerous work. The burden of suspicion of the Germans
had moved away from the 'immoral' plays and novels translated
and reviewed in the 1820s to the controversial German critiques of
Biblical texts. As Goethe had been chosen to stand for the general
tendency of German literature to corrupt, so Strauss represented for
the British the (long established) study by Germans of Biblical history in its most 'dangerous' conclusions. Archdeacon Hare wrote
forcefully of Sterling's 'unfortunate' study of Strauss in 1839:
'About the same time he read Strauss's *Life of Jesus*, a book which
a person can hardly read without being more or less hurt by it. If
we walk through mire, some of it will stick to us, even when we have
no other aim than to make our way through it, much more when
we dabble about in it and sift it.' After 'some painful controversial
letters on the subject of Strauss' Hare's friendship with Sterling
cooled.[5] Sterling himself took a more hopeful view of Britain's
present readiness to absorb German Biblical criticism. He recalled
in 1841–2 the older hostility towards German literature, thinking he
lived in better times:

...in my boyhood, twenty years ago, I well remember that, with quite
significant exceptions, all the active and daring minds which would not
take for granted the Thirty-Nine Articles and the Quarterly Review took
refuge with teachers like Mackintosh and Jeffrey, or at highest Madame de
Staël. Wordsworth and Coleridge were mystagogues lurking in caverns, and
German literature was thought of with a good deal less favour than we are
now disposed to show towards that of China.

Thought is leaking into this country, – even Strauss sells.[6]

Thus George Eliot, by undertaking to translate Strauss's work,
took her place in the introduction of German thought to England.[7]
She took over the task from Rufa Hennell (née Brabant, and first
called Rufa by Coleridge) in January 1844. Her friend Sara Hennell
advised and proof-read, acting also as a spur to George Eliot to keep
going when, as frequently happened, she became 'Strauss-sick'.[8]
Some of her many complaints probably refer only to the length of
the original and the linguistic difficulties in translating it, but
occasionally George Eliot indicates partial dissent from Strauss's
method or conclusions: 'I am never pained when I think Strauss
right – but in many cases I think him wrong, as every man must be

in working out into detail an idea which has general truth, but is only one element in a perfect theory, not a perfect theory in itself.'[9] The strict logic which she praised in Strauss – she thought John Sibree, translator of Hegel's *Philosophy of History* in 1849 and friend of the Hennells, ought to benefit from reading Strauss because of his own lack of that quality – was also a cause of boredom to her: 'The last 100 pages have certainly been totally uninteresting to me, considered as matter for translation. Strauss has inevitably anticipated in the earlier part of his work all the principles and many of the details of his criticism, and he seems fagged himself.'[10] The comment is comparatively mild, considering that Strauss's method, admirable in its consistency, was to take each separate account of every event in the life of Jesus and subject it to the same minute analysis. As Strauss said, the task of protestantism in the 1830s was to carry the rationalist movement of the eighteenth century (Reimarus, Lessing, Eichhorn) one step further:

It is not by any means that the whole history of Jesus is to be represented as mythical, but only that every part of it is to be subjected to a critical examination, to ascertain whether it have not some admixture of the mythical. The exegesis of the ancient church set out from the double presupposition: first, that the gospels contained a history, and secondly, that this history was a supernatural one. Rationalism rejected the latter of these presuppositions, but only to cling the more tenaciously to the former, maintaining that these books present unadulterated, though only natural, history. Science cannot rest satisfied with this half-measure: the other presupposition also must be relinquished, and the inquiry must first be made whether in fact, and to what extent, the ground on which we stand in the gospels is historical.[11]

Strauss takes each event in the life and gives first, an account and criticism of the supernatural explanations of it offered by orthodox theologians; second, a scrutiny of the 'natural' (historical) explanations of the rationalists;[12] and finally his own mythical interpretation. As his first example he takes the story of the annunciation to Zacharias of the forthcoming birth of John the Baptist. Zacharias is incredulous because of his wife's age; the angel strikes him dumb. Strauss points out that this punishment is excessively severe; it had not happened to Abraham, and it did not happen to Mary when she doubted the annunciation of Christ's birth. He concludes that such a punishment accords with the Jewish view of a strict deity. He takes the natural explanation, that Zacharias mistakes a man for an

angel, or that he dreams or imagines the occurrence: the dumbness
is then the result of a shock, a fit, or guilt at his imaginings. But, says
Strauss, how is it that he is struck *only* by dumbness? And further,
how is it that the prediction is fulfilled, if it was no true prediction
but a mere fancy? Strauss's explanation is mythical: long barrenness
in a couple is a common theme in Hebrew poetry, and the story of
the annunciation is borrowed from the history of another late-born
child, Samson:

So that we stand here upon purely mythical-poetical ground; the only
historical reality which we can hold fast as positive matter of fact being
this: – the impression made by John the Baptist, by virtue of his ministry
and his relation to Jesus, was so powerful as to lead to subsequent glorifi-
cation of his birth in connection with the birth of the Messiah in the
Christian legend.[13]

The same detailed pattern of criticism is followed in every chapter.
While George Eliot obviously approved of Strauss's undertaking,
she undoubtedly found his dry, relentless pursuit of the method
trying.[14] She told Sara Hennell that she thought the middle section
on the miracles of Christ unconvincing – 'I shall send you a muddy
draught and bolus of miracles by [i.e. via] Mr. Bray. This part of the
work pleases me the least and is the weakest.'[15] In this she agreed
with Matthew Arnold, who years later maintained that 'simple,
flexible common-sense is what we most want' in approaching the
New Testament accounts of miracles:

It is easy to be too systematic. Strauss had the idea, acute and ingenious, of
explaining the miracles of the New Testament as a reiteration of the
miracles of the Old. Of some miracles this supplies a good explanation. It
plausibly explains the story of the Transfiguration, for instance. The story
of the illumined face of Jesus, – Jesus the prophet like unto Moses, whom
Moses foretold, – might naturally owe its origin to the illumined face of
Moses himself. But of other miracles Strauss's idea affords no admissible
explanation whatever. To employ it for these cases can only show the
imperturbable resolution of a German professor in making all the facts suit
a theory which he has once adopted.[16]

That George Eliot felt something like this about German philosophy
generally – and here she agreed with Lewes – is clear from her
article in *The Leader* in 1855, 'The Future of German Philosophy':

'The age of systems is passed...System is the childhood of philosophy; the
manhood of philosophy is investigation.' So says Professor Gruppe in the

work of which we have given the title above [*Gegenwart und Zukunft der Philosophie in Deutschland*, 1855, *Present and Future of Philosophy in Germany*], and we quote this dictum at the outset in order to propitiate those readers who might otherwise turn away with disgust from the mention of German philosophy, having registered a vow to trouble themselves no more with those spinners of elaborate cocoons – German system-mongers.[17]

Like Lewes, she could not accept any *a priori* system of philosophy:

The chief argument in favour of *à priori* ideas, as insisted on by Leibnitz and Kant is, that they can never be arrived at by induction; that induction may lead to the *general* but never to the *universal*, and that, nevertheless, this idea of universality is found in speech and in thought with the mark of necessity. But this argument will not bear a rigid examination. The language of all peoples soon attains to the expressions *all, universal, necessary*, but these expressions have their origin purely in the observations of the senses; they are simply a practical expedient, and are valued only under certain well-known and presupposed conditions. To isolate such expressions, to operate with them apart from experience, to exalt their relative value into an absolute value, to deduce knowledge from them alone, and to make them a standing point higher than all experience – this, which is what Parmenides and all speculative philosophers since him have done, is an attempt to poise the universe on one's head, and no wonder if dizziness and delusion are the consequence.[18]

We may assume from some of her comments on *Das Leben Jesu* that she was aware of the philosophical tradition to which Strauss belonged. His way of criticising the work of his predecessors and by means of that criticism arriving at his own conclusion obviously follows Kant's great critical method. The very title, *Das Leben Jesu, kritisch bearbeitet*, is suggestive of this. George Eliot wrote to Sara, 'I should like if possible to throw the emphasis on *critically* in the title-page. Strauss means it to be so.'[19] Her rather indirect comment to Sara on the Schlussabhandlung (Concluding Dissertation) suggests that she disagreed with its argument: 'It is the only part on which I have bestowed much pains, for the difficulty was *piquing*, not *piquant*.'[20] The objection here may well have been to its sophistry, for she probably noticed the similarity between its relationship to the rest of the work and that of Kant's *Kritik der praktischen Vernunft* to his *Kritik der reinen Vernunft*. Strauss prepares for the conclusion early on: 'The author is aware that the essence of the Christian faith is perfectly independent of his criticism. The supernatural birth of Christ, his miracles, his resurrection and ascension, remain eternal truths, whatever doubts may be cast on their reality as historical facts.'[21] Unlike Feuerbach, who acted on this hint to develop his theory of the essence of Christianity as the essence of human feeling and imagination, thus giving a psychological basis to the study of Biblical texts, Strauss rests this claim on what must have seemed to George Eliot the inadmissible ground of Reason:

The results of the inquiry which we have now brought to a close, have apparently annihilated the greatest and most valuable part of that which the Christian has been wont to believe concerning his Saviour Jesus, have uprooted all the animating motives which he has gathered from his faith, and withered all his consolations. The boundless store of truth and life which for eighteen centuries has been the aliment of humanity, seems irretrievably dissipated; the most sublime levelled with the dust, God divested of his grace, man of his dignity, and the tie between heaven and earth broken. Piety turns away with horror from so fearful an act of desecration, and strong in the impregnable self-evidence of its faith, pronounces that, let an audacious criticism attempt what it will, all which the scriptures declare, and the church believes of Christ, will still subsist as eternal truth, nor needs one iota of it to be renounced. Thus at the conclusion of the criticism of the history of Jesus, there presents itself this problem: to re-establish dogmatically that which has been destroyed critically.[22]

This looks rather like Kant's 'saving' of God and immortality in the *Kritik der praktischen Vernunft* after he had seemed to prove them impossible in the *Kritik der reinen Vernunft*, a manoeuvre which Heine, for one, had viewed ironically:

Da erbarmt sich Immanuel Kant und zeigt, dass er nicht bloss ein grosser Philosoph, sondern auch ein guter Mensch ist, und er überlegt, und halb gutmütig und halb ironisch spricht er: "Der alte Lampe muss einen Gott haben, sonst kann der arme Mensch nicht glücklich sein – der Mensch soll aber auf der Welt glücklich sein – das sagt die praktische Vernunft – meinetwegen – so mag auch die praktische Vernunft die Existenz Gottes verbürgen." Infolge dieses Arguments unterscheidet Kant zwischen der theoretischen Vernunft und der praktischen Vernunft, und mit dieser, wie mit einem Zauberstäbchen, belebte er wieder den Leichnam des Deismus, den die theoretische Vernunft getötet.

Upon this [i.e. Kant's servant Lampe's being dismayed at Kant's sweeping away of certitudes and theological proofs] Immanuel Kant takes pity on him and shows that he is not only a great philosopher but also a good man, and he ponders it and says, half good-naturedly and half ironically, 'Old Lampe must have a God, otherwise the poor man cannot be happy – but man should be happy in this world – practical Reason says so – all right, then, practical Reason may as well guarantee the existence of God.' As a result of this argument Kant distinguishes between theoretical and practical

Reason, bringing back to life by means of the latter, as with a magic wand, the corpse of deism which the former had killed.[23]

We can guess from George Eliot's much more enthusiastic remarks while translating Feuerbach that Strauss's clinging to 'the sublimest of all religions, the Christian, which he perceives to be identical with the deepest philosophical truth'[24] did not have her full approval. Nevertheless, she was aware of Strauss's immense importance for the progress of historical research, and was wise enough to see that if German transcendental philosophy and its heirs had some short-comings, what was nonetheless needed in England was a fair welcome to such works as Strauss's, which were far in advance of British notions. It is almost as if she felt that Britain was intellectually in a more primitive stage (to use Comtian terms) than Germany, and needed to give a proper hearing to metaphysical systems before it had the right to dismiss them. Thus in an article of 1851 she praised Strauss and the tradition to which he belonged:

The introduction of a truly philosophic spirit into the study of mythology – an introduction for which we are chiefly indebted to the Germans – is a great step in advance of the superficial Lucian-like tone of ridicule adopted by many authors of the eighteenth century, or the orthodox pre-possessions of writers such as Bryant, who saw in the Greek legends simply misrepresentations of the authentic history given in the book of Genesis.[25]

It was the duty of English researchers to become acquainted with their German predecessors; George Eliot was insistent on this point in her essays and fiction alike. She castigated Dr Cumming in 1855 for his lack of attention to the progress made in Biblical criticism in Germany since the late eighteenth century, speculating on his reading during the past fifteen years and concluding that

either it has left him totally ignorant of the relation which his own religious creed bears to the criticism and philosophy of the nineteenth century, *or* he systematically blinks that criticism and that philosophy; and instead of honestly and seriously endeavouring to meet and solve what he knows to be the real difficulties, contents himself with setting up popinjays to shoot at, for the sake of confirming the ignorance and winning the cheap admiration of his evangelical hearers and readers.[26]

In *Middlemarch* Casaubon shares Cumming's fault. Will Ladislaw tells Dorothea that Casaubon's researches are rendered void by his ignorance: 'the Germans have taken the lead in historical inquiries, and they laugh at results which are got by groping about in woods with a pocket-compass while they have made good roads', and 'Do you not see that it is no use now to be crawling a little way after men of the last century – men like Bryant – and correcting their mistakes? – living in a lumber-room and furbishing up broken-legged theories about Chus and Mizraim?'[27] Casaubon further compounds his sin of omission by adducing as one of his objections to Will his having chosen 'the anomalous course of studying at Heidelberg'. The remark is intended to be damaging to the authority of the speaker, who would himself have benefited from close contacts with German Biblical critics in the late 1820s and early 1830s, the time in which the novel is set.[28]

George Eliot suggests that when once British thinkers have brought themselves up to date with German activity, they may go on to add a desirable element of common sense and freedom from systematic dogma. Mackay's *Progress of the Intellect* ranks highly with her for this reason:

It exhibits an industry in research which reminds us of Cudworth, and for which, in recent literature, we must seek a parallel in Germany rather than England, while its philosophy and its aims are at once lofty and practical. Scattered through its more abstruse disquisitions we find passages of pre-eminent beauty – gems into which are absorbed the finest rays of intelligence and feeling. We believe Mr. Mackay's work is unique in its kind. England has been slow to use or to emulate the immense labours of Germany in the departments of mythology and biblical criticism; but when once she does so, the greater solidity and directness of the English mind ensure a superiority of treatment.[29]

Like Sterling, she thought it disgraceful that English theologians paid so little attention to truth, being prepared to 'lie for God' rather than follow their German colleagues in honestly separating fact from error in the Scriptures.[30]

George Eliot's translation of Strauss had the appropriate luck – Chapman, later her co-editor of the *Westminster Review*, being its publisher – to be intelligently reviewed in the *Westminster*. Her critic, James Martineau, was not shocked by its conclusions, being well acquainted with the tradition of research of which it was the latest logical example:

The appearance of Dr. Strauss's work, in 1835, can have taken by surprise no one acquainted with the course of Biblical literature during the last half-century. The instantaneous effect produced by it was a start, less of astonishment, than of realized expectation. So completely were tendencies of the age, in themselves distinct and independent, – the historical researches of Niebuhr, the mythological speculations of Heyne, the metaphysics of Hegel, as well as the internal condition of Scripture criticism itself – converging towards such a result, that we have no doubt the 'Life of Jesus' did but disappoint, by anticipating, many a like project already floating through the German brain.

He was appreciative of the labour George Eliot had expended in translating – 'having toiled through the second German edition, we can testify that the translator has achieved a very tough work with remarkable spirit and fidelity'.[31]

J. A. Froude, who had been observed in Oxford in 1844 becoming 'regularly Germanized' and talking 'unreservedly about Strauss, miracles, &c',[32] appropriately sent a copy of his *Nemesis of Faith* (1849), care of Chapman, to 'the Translator of Strauss'.[33] The book that shocked Oxford shows direct signs of its author's reading in German historical criticism. When Markham Sutherland resigns his curacy because of doubts about the literal truth of Scripture, his friend-cum-editor presents his scattered thoughts to the reader (*Wilhelm Meister* and *Sartor* may well have provided models for the loose plot and the mingling of reflection and narrative):

People canvass up and down the value and utility of Christianity, and none of them seem to see that it was the common channel towards which all the great streams of thought in the old world were tending, and that in some form or other when they came to unite it must have been. That it crystallized round a particular person may have been an accident; but in its essence, as soon as the widening intercourse of the nations forced the Jewish mind into contact with the Indian and the Persian and the Grecian, such a religion was absolutely inevitable.[34]

To those less progressive than Sterling and Froude, George Eliot's translation made available in an accurate English text a work known to have caused a controversy even in historical research-minded Germany.[35] As Lewes wrote in 1847, reviewing a satirical pamphlet by Strauss attacking Friedrich Wilhelm IV, 'all our readers are familiar at least with the name of Strauss'.[36]

More translation: Spinoza and Feuerbach (1849–54)

The Strauss was George Eliot's first published work, and undoubtedly the discipline of translating such a scholarly work on such a subject completed her break with religious orthodoxy. But it is likely that Spinoza was at least as important in her 'conversion to disbelief'.[37] Spinoza was, of course, the grand, 'precocious' precursor of eighteenth- and nineteenth-century Biblical criticism, for in *Tractatus Theologico-Politicus* (1670) he subjected the Biblical accounts of miracles to clear-eyed scrutiny and showed an understanding of the social function of religious myth.[38] It is possible that George Eliot began translating this work about a year before she took on Strauss. By her own account, she was certainly translating it in 1849.[39] She must have felt as Arnold did, when he compared the characteristics of the *Tractatus* with those of the *Leben Jesu*:

Strauss has treated the question of Scripture miracles with an acuteness and fulness which even to the most informed minds is instructive; but because he treats it almost wholly without the power of edification, his fame as a serious thinker is equivocal. But in Spinoza there is not a trace either of Voltaire's passion for mockery or of Strauss's passion for demolition. His whole soul was filled with desire of the love and knowledge of God, and of that only.[40]

Like Goethe, Coleridge, Novalis, and Lewes before her, George Eliot was early attracted to Spinozan pantheism:

I cannot think the conviction that immortality is man's destiny indispensable to the production of elevated and heroic virtue and the sublimest resignation. I feel with Coleridge, that the notion of Revelation abandoned, there is ever a tendency towards Pantheism, and the personality of the Deity is not to be maintained quite satisfactorily apart from Christianity.[41]

Whether she finished her translation of the *Tractatus* is not known. But she did complete a translation of the *Ethics*, and it was by an unfortunate chance that the translation was not published. If it had been, it would have been the first in English.[42] Lewes had a confused arrangement with Bohn – publisher of so many translations of major German works in the nineteenth century, beginning with Black's translation of A. W. Schlegel's *Lectures on Dramatic Art and Literature* (1815) – about a translation by Lewes of the *Ethics*. He handed the work over to George Eliot in Berlin in 1854, while he got on with the *Life of Goethe*. But when he came to negotiate terms with Bohn, they could not agree. Probably Lewes was highhanded; he alienated Bohn, and George Eliot's translation remained unpublished.[43]

Spinozism is fundamental in some of its aspects not only to the

German philosophers and poets of the nineteenth century, as Froude pointed out in his *Westminster* article on Spinoza, which George Eliot admired;[44] it was also basic to Comte's positivism and those English writers, including Mill, Spencer, and Lewes, who partially accepted Comte's system.[45] If George Eliot's language describing her own development, and that used of Dorothea in *Middlemarch*, were traceable to any single source, it would be finally to Spinoza. She had felt her loss of faith in her twenties as a positive gain in clarity, a shift from excessive Evangelical piety to a wider view of human destiny. As early as October 1843 she wrote of the liberation of the soul from 'the wretched giant's bed of dogmas on which it has been racked and stretched' and her turning to 'the *truth of feeling* as the only universal bond of union'. As late as November 1874 she claimed that 'righteousness is salvation – and is not to be sought in metaphysical refinements about a 'personal God' but is to be found in our idealization of human relations and human needs'. Of her books she said in 1868 that they were 'deliberately, carefully constructed' on her conviction of 'the relative goodness and nobleness of human dispositions and motives'. Her aim was 'to help my readers in getting a clearer conception and a more active admiration of those vital elements which bind men together and give a higher worthiness to their existence; and also to help them in gradually dissociating these elements from the more transient forms on which an outworn teaching tends to make them dependent.'[46]

The language of *Middlemarch* insists that Dorothea, beginning with her disillusion with Casaubon and Rome and the planting of the seed of affection and understanding between her and Will, moves towards a 'clearness' of perception about her relation to others in society. Her growing awareness in her life with Casaubon is measured by the fact that 'she was no longer struggling against the perception of facts, but adjusting herself to their clearest perception'.[47] Towards the end of the novel, when Dorothea engages with Lydgate's problems and pays her visit to Rosamond, her voice, her eyes, her consciousness, and her effect on Lydgate are described strikingly in terms of clarity and distinctness.[48] Indeed, it is the misfortune of Lydgate that he, the scientific investigator, cannot, as he says, 'get his mind clear again' because of the 'clogging medium' of a mismatch, money troubles, and the hostility of the Middlemarchers.

These references to 'clear ideas' belong partly to the terminology of nineteenth-century optimism, of Comte's idea that successive stages of thought and investigation bring an increase in clarity and positiveness, perhaps also of Whewell, who claimed that 'the existence of clear Ideas applied to distinct Facts will be discernible in the History of Science, whenever any marked advance takes place'.[49] But 'clear ideas' probably have primary reference to Spinoza. For him the chief ethical aim of man was the pursuit of self-knowledge. By reflecting on an irrational (and involuntary) passion, by forming a clear and distinct idea of it, we gain control over it and set our energies free from the bondage of the irrational.[50] Herbert Spencer's formulation of his doctrine of sympathy as the root of justice and benevolence in a society of self-interested individuals was a contemporary restatement of the idea that was foremost in Spinoza's work (and in Feuerbach's).[51] For Spinoza, self-interest is necessarily man's motive force, but by reflecting on it and on the fact that if I am of supreme interest to myself, so also is my fellow man of supreme interest to himself, I can and must act altruistically: 'By the fact that we imagine a thing which is like ourselves, and which we have not regarded with any emotion to be affected with any emotion, we are also affected with a like emotion.'[52] George Eliot's most celebrated expression of the idea comes in *Middlemarch*:

We are all of us born in moral stupidity, taking the world as an udder to feed our supreme selves: Dorothea had early begun to emerge from that stupidity, but yet it had been easier to her to imagine how she would devote herself to Mr. Casaubon, and become wise and strong in his strength and wisdom, than to conceive with that distinctness which is no longer reflection but feeling – an idea wrought back to the directness of sense, like the solidity of objects – that he had an equivalent centre of self, whence the lights and shadows must always fall with a certain difference.[53]

Spinoza explains emotion as 'a confused idea' which can be self-contradictory: for example, when someone I hate (hatred being an irrational passion) is in distress, I am both pleased, because I hate him, and sorry, because he is of my species, is like me, and I can imagine his feelings. George Eliot works this combination on her readers when she insists that Mr Tulliver, Mrs Transome, Casaubon, Bulstrode, and Gwendolen are, as much because of as in spite of their hateful qualities, like us and demand our sympathy. By concentrating on the likeness, we can educate our feelings and widen our sympathies.

What Spinoza offered – and Feuerbach also[54] – that Strauss's work made no pretence of including was an ethic and a psychology applicable to men in their unheroic everyday (or, as George Eliot often put it, 'working day') lives.[55] Here surely is one reason why she so enjoyed translating Feuerbach's *Wesen des Christenthums* (*Essence of Christianity*) in 1854, and why she felt able to say, 'With the ideas of Feuerbach I everywhere agree.'[56] Sympathy for others of the same species[57] is of key importance not only in Spinoza but also in Feuerbach, whose aim was to show that the essence of Christianity is really 'the essence of human feeling' and that the only divinity is 'the divinity of human nature'.[58] Feuerbach follows Strauss and the higher criticism, but his study is different from Strauss's dry, thorough, 'critical' (in the Kantian sense of negating previously held theories and clearing the way for further, more positive study) analysis. He shows religion to have been an imaginative necessity for man. Spinoza, too, had been tolerant of popular religions because they kept men virtuous by means of the imagination where it was not possible by reason;[59] and George Eliot, in *Scenes of Clerical Life* and *Adam Bede*, displayed just such a knowledgeable warmth towards religious doctrines she no longer held and could not approve of intellectually. Feuerbach, with erratic brilliance, gives the fullest statement of the idea that religion is a dream in which man can fulfil his needs and assuage his feelings of imperfection and limitation: 'Man, by means of the imagination, involuntarily contemplates his inner nature; he represents it as out of himself. The nature of man, of the species – thus working on him through the irresistible power of the imagination, and contemplated as the law of his thought and action – is God.' Thus man posits God as the perfection of his own imperfect species (and his posited God then comfortingly posits man as his creature); but the real object of man's interest is man – 'homo homini Deus est', 'the consciousness of God is nothing else than the consciousness of the species'. His actions are social and require co-operation – 'only through his fellow does man become clear to himself and self-conscious', 'in isolation human power is limited, in combination it is infinite'.[60]

Furthermore, Feuerbach's welcome religion of humanity was built on an empirical base: 'I differ *toto coelo* from those philosophers who pluck out their eyes that they may see better; for *my* thought I require the senses, especially sight; I found my ideas on materials which can be appropriated only through the activity of the senses.'[61] Here is no futile *a priori* system, but one which proceeds by observation and without denying the validity of the senses, one which is in this respect 'un-German'. Feuerbach, like Gruppe whom George Eliot reviewed warmly in 1855, 'renounces the attempt to climb to heaven by the rainbow bridge of 'the high *priori* road', and is content humbly to use his muscles in treading the uphill *a posteriori* path which will lead, not indeed to heaven, but to an eminence whence we may see very bright and blessed things on earth'.[62] She positively enjoyed translating, and even proof-reading, his work. His text, she wrote to Sara in February 1854, was '*for a German* – concise, lucid and even epigrammatic now and then'.[63]

Most important of all for George Eliot was Feuerbach's allowance for goodness in human beings as a spontaneous emotion, not one extracted from them by fear of an angry God and not thwarted by the exclusiveness of a consciousness – whether Jewish or Protestant – of belonging to a 'chosen people'.[64] Her article 'Evangelical Teaching: Dr. Cumming' (1855) everywhere applies Feuerbach's points to the very dogmas with which she had grown up. As Coleridge had been distressed at Kant's exclusion of love from ethics, so George Eliot rejected Cumming:

He is most at home in the forensic view of Justification, and dwells on salvation as a scheme rather than as an experience. He insists on good works as the sign of justifying faith, as labours to be achieved to the glory of God, but he rarely represents them as the spontaneous, necessary outflow of a soul filled with Divine love.

A wife is not to devote herself to her husband out of love to him and a sense of duties implied by a close relation – she is to be a faithful wife for the glory of God.[65]

Yet this harsh opinion of the harmful, fanatical aspects of Evangelicalism is compatible in George Eliot with tolerance of the good that is done in the name of religion. All the novels testify to her unchanging belief that 'the idea of God, so far as it has been a high spiritual influence, is the ideal of a goodness entirely human (i.e. an exaltation of the human)'.[66] They do so in predominantly Feuerbachian terms, the language of I–Thou relationships, the 'divine' efficacy of human love, the redeeming influence of man on man, personality as revelation, the possibility of 'baptism and consecration' by contact with other natures.[67] For her, as for Feuerbach,

'homo homini Deus est'; in 1855 she praised *In Memoriam* specifically for its 'sanctification of human love as a religion'.[68]

In this way George Eliot widened the influence of Feuerbach's
(and more problematically Comte's[69]) religion of humanity during
twenty years of novel writing, as well as by direct transmission in
her translation. Curiously, the translation itself received less attention than the Strauss eight years before.[70] George Eliot foresaw
hostility among British critics:

Your impression of the book exactly corresponds to its effect in Germany.
It is considered *the* book of the age there, but Germany and England are
two countries. People here are as slow to be set on fire as a *stomach*. Then
there are the reviewers, who set up a mound of stupidity and unconscienti-
ousness between every really new book and the public.[71]

In fact only a few English critics noticed it. George Eliot did not
count the praise of her friend and proof-reader, Sara Hennell, in the
Coventry *Herald* in July 1854.[72] For some reason (perhaps because
she and Lewes were absent in Weimar within three weeks of its
publication, and perhaps at her own request) *The Leader*, to which
they both contributed regularly, carried no review, though Lewes
had announced the book as forthcoming on 1 July, predicting its
effect would be that of a 'bombshell thrown into the camp of
orthodoxy'.[73] James Martineau's two-page review in the *Westminster*
in October was surprisingly hostile, considering both George Eliot's
distinguished record with the *Review* and Martineau's liberal politics
and his acquaintance with German historical criticism, particularly
Strauss.[74] His tone was sarcastic:

It is a sign of "progress," we presume, that the lady-translator who maintained the anonymous in introducing Strauss, puts her name in the title-
page of Feuerbach. She has executed her task even better than before: we
are only surprised that, if she wished to exhibit the new Hegelian Atheism
to English readers, she should select a work of the year 1840, and of quite
secondary philosophical repute in its own country. Its system is nothing but
an inverse reading of the principle that "God made man in his own image,"
– a long homily on the text that "Man makes God in his own image."

He accepted that Feuerbach carried out his interpretation 'ingeni-
ously enough', but ridiculed Feuerbach's emphasis – strengthened in
the Preface to the second edition (1843) in reply to hostility from
German critics – on the efficacy and symbolic quality of baptism
and the eucharist:

The doctrine of Feuerbach receives an application at the close to the rites of baptism and the eucharist, which has been justly and universally condemned in Germany, and which the translator would have consulted his reputation by omitting. He professes to interpret the mystery of these two sacraments. Baptism means to say, that men, infants and all, cannot keep clean without washing; and the eucharist, that flour would be raw without the baker, grapes crude without the wine-grower! "If in water, we declare – Man can do nothing without nature; by bread and wine we declare – Nature needs man, as man needs nature." Alas! which is the wiser, – the dreamer, or the interpreter of dreams? Be there mocking, or be there meaning in the voice, this sort of oracle is alike deplorable.[75]

The passage from which Martineau quotes comes at the end of the *Essence of Christianity*, and is indeed an over-rapturous and perhaps intellectually weak conclusion. It is worth quoting from at length in George Eliot's translation, both to give a true sense of the controversial nature of the work and to give proof of how close to his language is George Eliot's in the more visionary passages of her novels:

The Water of Baptism is to religion only the means by which the Holy Spirit imparts itself to man. But by this conception it is placed in contradiction with reason, with the truth of things. On the one hand, there is virtue in the objective, natural quality of water; on the other, there is none, but it is a merely arbitrary medium of divine grace and omnipotence. We free ourselves from these and other irreconcilable contradictions, we give a true significance to Baptism, only by regarding it as a symbol of the value of water itself. Baptism should represent to us the wonderful but natural effect of water on man. Water has, in fact, not merely physical effects, but also, and as a result of these, moral and intellectual effects on man. Water not only cleanses man from bodily impurities, but in water the scales fall from his eyes: he sees, he thinks more clearly; he feels himself freer; water extinguishes the fire of appetite. How many saints have had recourse to the natural qualities of water in order to overcome the assaults of the devil! What was denied by Grace has been granted by Nature. Water plays a part not only in dietetics, but also in moral and mental discipline. To purify oneself, to bathe, is the first, though the lowest of the virtues. In the stream of water the fever of selfishness is allayed. Water is the readiest means of making friends with Nature. The bath is a sort of chemical process, in which our individuality is resolved into the objective life of Nature. The man rising from the water is a new, a regenerate man.

[. . .] In Baptism we bow to the power of a pure Nature-force; water is the element of natural equality and freedom, the mirror of the golden age. But we men are distinguished from the plants and animals, which together with the inorganic kingdom we comprehend under the common name of

Nature; – we are distinguished from Nature. Hence we must celebrate our distinction, our specific difference. The symbols of this our difference are bread and wine. Bread and wine are, as to their materials, products of nature; as to their form, products of man. If in water we declare: Man can do nothing without Nature; by bread and wine we declare: Nature needs man, as man needs Nature. In water, human mental activity is nullified; in bread and wine it attains self-satisfaction. Bread and wine are supernatural products, – in the only valid and true sense, the sense which is not in contradiction with reason and Nature. If in water we adore the pure force of Nature, in bread and wine we adore the supernatural power of mind, of consciousness, of man. Hence this sacrament is only for man matured into consciousness; while baptism is imparted to infants. But we at the same time celebrate here the true relation of mind to Nature: Nature gives the material, mind gives the form. The sacrament of Baptism inspires us with thankfulness towards Nature, the sacrament of bread and wine with thankfulness towards man. Bread and wine typify to us the truth that Man is the true God and Saviour of man.

Eating and drinking is the mystery of the Lord's Supper; – eating and drinking is, in fact, in itself a religious act; at least, ought to be so. Think, therefore, with every morsel of bread which relieves thee from the pain of hunger, with every draught of wine which cheers thy heart, of the God who confers these beneficent gifts upon thee, – think of man! But in thy gratitude towards man forget not gratitude towards holy Nature! Forget not that wine is the blood of plants, and flour the flesh of plants, which are sacrificed for thy well-being! Forget not that the plant typifies to thee the essence of Nature, which lovingly surrenders itself for thy enjoyment! Therefore forget not the gratitude which thou owest to the natural qualities of bread and wine! And if thou art inclined to smile that I call eating and drinking religious acts, because they are common every-day acts, and are therefore performed by multitudes without thought, without emotion; reflect, that the Lord's Supper is to multitudes a thoughtless, emotionless act, because it takes place often; and, for the sake of comprehending the religious significance of bread and wine, place thyself in a position where the daily act is unnaturally, violently interrupted. Hunger and thirst destroy not only the physical but also the mental and moral powers of man; they rob him of his humanity – of understanding, of consciousness. Oh! if thou shouldst ever experience such want, how wouldst thou bless and praise the natural qualities of bread and wine, which restore to thee thy humanity, thy intellect! It needs only that the ordinary course of things be interrupted in order to vindicate to common things an uncommon significance, *to life, as such, a religious import.* Therefore let bread be sacred for us, let wine be sacred, and also let water be sacred! Amen.[76]

Feuerbach's German contemporaries, as well as Martineau, found this absurd. And while the distinguished theologian Karl Barth, who has written an introduction for the modern reprint of the work in George Eliot's translation (1957), gives full credit to Feuerbach for taking early nineteenth-century theology logically a step further into anthropology and for showing the church the need to liberate herself from ideologies, he concludes bluntly that Feuerbach's theory is 'a platitude', 'at bottom trite beyond compare'.[77] Feuerbach had answered such criticisms by his contemporaries in the preface to the second edition by insisting that what seems trivial in his theory is meant to be understood symbolically:

I, in fact, put in the place of the barren baptismal water, the beneficent effect of real water. How "watery," how trivial! Yes, indeed, very trivial. But so Marriage, in its time, was a *very trivial truth*, which Luther, on the ground of his natural good sense, maintained in opposition to the seemingly holy illusion of celibacy. But while I thus view water as a real thing, I at the same time intend it as a vehicle, an image, an example, a symbol, of the "unholy" spirit of my work, just as the water of Baptism – the object of my analysis – is at once literal and symbolical water. It is the same with bread and wine. Malignity has hence drawn the conclusion that bathing, eating and drinking are the *summa summarum*, the positive result of my work. I make no other reply than this: If the whole of religion is contained in the Sacraments, and there are consequently no other religious acts than those which are performed in Baptism and the Lord's Supper; *then* I grant that the entire purport and positive result of my work are bathing, eating, and drinking, since this work is nothing but a faithful, rigid, historico-philosophical analysis of religion – the revelation of religion to itself, the *awakening of religion to self-consciousness*.[78]

George Eliot does not seem to have felt embarrassed at translating these passages, nor does she anywhere, as far as we know, dissent from Feuerbach's views. Indeed, in transfusing the same religious symbols into the life of her novels, and particularly in making scrupulously circumscribed use of traditional religious terms in her secular settings, she generally avoids the trap of sentimentality or weak-mindedness into which Feuerbach may be thought to have fallen in the different discipline of a work of scholarship. Interestingly, one of George Eliot's most astute critics, Richard Holt Hutton, saw that *Romola* failed to impress precisely because the setting, late fifteenth-century Florence, did not suit such a transfusion of religious terms into secular conclusions. In a letter to her in 1863 he made clear his insight into her artistic problems, and he mentioned Feuerbach as central to this. Romola herself

struck me throughout as rather modern & as separating the doubtful from the ethical germs of Savonarola's faith with too much of our modern habit of discriminating between the righteous principles which prove themselves and the divine authority on which they were proclaimed...Romola seems to me not so much to *take*, as almost to *imply* a knowledge of, such distinctions, as she might have picked up by a study of Feuerbach. I do not mean of course that any such questions come up, but that her mind seems to have that habit of hanging back – suspending belief, – before any mere accidental adjunct of what compels her faith which the study of the subtlest negative analysis of religious beliefs would give.[79]

His letters to her and the review he wrote drew from George Eliot an admission of 'excess in this effort after artistic vision' in *Romola*, but also an important defence of her method generally: 'It is the habit of my imagination to strive after as full a vision of the medium in which a character moves as of the character itself.'[80]

There were aspects of Feuerbach's work with which George Eliot did find fault. His terminology places him in the post-Kantian and post-Hegelian tradition, but his use of it is sometimes inconsistent. For instance, he describes God first as 'the pure subjectivity of man, freed from all else, from anything objective, having relation only to itself, enjoying only itself, reverencing only itself – his most subjective, his inmost self'. Yet in inverting the proposition of traditional religious speculation of God as the first being and man as the second, he writes, 'in reality the first is man, the second the nature of man made objective, namely, God'.[81] Of course, he is constantly working with two contradictory yet for his purposes complementary ideas – that of traditional theology and his own anthropological, psychological interpretation of it – so that it is not surprising to find his language stretched in this way. But he does not seem sufficiently aware of the confusion arising from his use of terms like 'subject', 'object', and 'reality'.[82] George Eliot complained in a letter to Sara of 'the laxity of Feuerbach's language', which she found 'particularly tiresome in the 2d §' of the Appendix, where Feuerbach tries to distinguish between 'feeling' (Gefühl) and 'sensation' (Empfindung).[83] Parts of the Appendix are not only lax, according to her, but 'abstract and Germanized "to a degree"', and she feared that they 'might repel the reader from the appendix, which contains a great deal of important and accessible matter'. She asked Sara's approval of her plan to omit sections two to four of the Appendix. In the end, she omitted only part of the fourth section, announcing in a footnote:

Here follows in the original a distinction between *Herz*, or feeling directed towards real objects, and therefore practically sympathetic; and *Gemüth*, or feeling directed towards imaginary objects, and therefore practically unsympathetic, self-absorbed. But the *verbal* distinction is not adhered to in the ordinary use of the language, or, indeed, by Feuerbach himself; and the *psychological* distinction is sufficiently indicated in other parts of the present work. The passage is therefore omitted, as likely to confuse the reader.[84]

Nevertheless, George Eliot owed a lot to Feuerbach for his stimulating humanism, and as a novelist she reaped benefits particularly from his emphasis on the use of the senses and the faculty of imagination as central to religious myth and the exercise of moral duty alike. Here Feuerbach joined with Spinoza and Goethe – 'der Spinoza der Poesie', according to Heine[85] – as the most telling German influences on her thought and art.

George Eliot and Goethe (1854–76)

George Eliot had read some Goethe before she met Lewes in 1851,[86] but probably her first thorough acquaintance with his works came in 1854, when she and Lewes set off for Weimar to begin life together and collect materials for the *Life of Goethe*. The journals she kept in Weimar and Berlin leave us in no doubt how closely she was connected with the final version of Lewes's work.[87] Her comments are always brief, but make it clear that she read most of Goethe's works during that time, translated extracts for the *Life*, and proofread the work, all at the same time as she translated Spinoza's *Ethics*. Here are some examples from her notebooks:

[Weimar] 14 Sept. We had a delicious walk in the open fields, came home, & finished the M.S. of Goethe's life.
1 Oct. In the evening walked & read aloud the Wahl*verw*ands. chapter.
6 Oct. We walked out into the open fields, & then read the *Wahlverwand* – 5 chapters.
20 Oct. G. got some interesting particulars from Frau Riesner about Goethe – especially about his attachment to Minna Herzlieb – which throw light on the sad experience he declares himself to have deposited "as in a burial urn" in the Wahl*verw*ands. *cha*pter. I read *Egmont* in the evening.
27 Oct. I read Götz in the morning.
[Berlin] 8 Nov. Began translating Spinoza's Ethics...Read Wilhelm Meister aloud in the evening.
11 Nov. I read Heine's poems; wrote a few recollections of Weimar & translated Genealogical Tables of the Goethe family.

1 Dec.   Finished Recollections of Weimar.[88] Began the *Italienische Reise*.
15 Dec.   Worked at Spinoza. Read G's M.S. – Weimar period.
24 Dec.   . . .copied Goethe's Discourse on Shakspeare. Read, at dinner, his wonderful observations on Spinoza. Particularly struck with the beautiful modesty of the passage in which he says he cannot presume to say that he thoroughly understands Spinoza. After coffee read aloud G's M.S. of the Leipsic & beginning of the Strasburg Period.
27 Dec.   Translated passages from the Kestner Briefe [for the *Life*].
2 January 1855.   Read Goethe's Maxims in the Wanderjahre.
9 Jan.   Finished Wanderjahre, skippingly.
10 Jan.   Read Stahr & finished translating the 2d. Book of Ethics. . .Began the West-östliche Divan.[89]

She obviously shared Lewes's admiration for Goethe's interest in science, his refusal to be led by Schiller into embracing the Kantian (or any *a priori*) philosophical system, his Spinozan insistence on the importance of observation.[90] In her article 'The Natural History of German Life' (1856), she remarked that Goethe was 'eminently the man who helps us to rise to a lofty point of observation, so that we may see things in their relative proportions'.[91]

During the stay in Berlin she found herself defending Goethe's *Wahlverwandtschaften* against German criticism of it. In December 1854 they visited Professor Stahr and 'had a long discussion about the Wahlverwandschaften [sic], with which Stahr found fault on the score of its dénouement. This dénouement, he said, was "unvernunftig." So, I said, were dénouements in real life very frequently: Goethe had given the dénouement wh. would naturally follow from the characters of the respective actors.'[92] This was not her only defence of Goethe. When she returned to England one of the first articles she wrote was the short but important one in *The Leader* (July 1855), entitled 'The Morality of Wilhelm Meister'.[93] Here she showed her understanding of why readers, particularly English readers, were invariably puzzled or shocked by the Lehrjahre, and undertook to help their appreciation of the work.[94] We may be forgiven for wondering if the article was written just when it was partly as a tactical move, as a deliberately placed precursor to Lewes's *Life*, to be published a few months later, with its easy tolerance of Goethe's 'morality' in both life and works. The article begins thus:

Perhaps Mr. Lewes's *Life of Goethe*, which we now see advertised, may throw some new light on the structure and purpose of the much debated novel – *Wilhelm Meister's Apprenticeship*. In the meantime, we are tempted by the appearance of a new translation,[95] to give the opinion

167

which our present knowledge enables us to form on one or two aspects of this many-sided work.

Its timing apart, the article is an important one, both as being un-mistakeably by the tolerant observer who later provided the guiding consciousness in the novels, and as indicating how public attitudes to Goethe had and had not changed over thirty or forty years. So many of his works had been translated and reviewed, particularly in the post-Carlyle 1830s, that George Eliot had no doubt that everyone had now read *Wilhelm Meister*, an assumption it would have been impossible to make even about some critics and reviewers of Goethe earlier in the century. But she realised that most readers, however divested of hardened prejudices against the work, had difficulties in the appreciation of it: 'Ask nineteen out of twenty moderately edu-cated persons what they think of *Wilhelm Meister*, and the answer will probably be – 'I think it an immoral book; and besides, it is awfully dull: I was not able to read it'.' She tackles the more damaging charge of immorality in a characteristically illustrative passage, in which – as in defending the *Wahlverwandtschaften* to Professor Stahr – she focuses on the difficult question of dénouements and the decision by authors to award prizes and punishments to the characters:

But is *Wilhelm Meister* an immoral book? We think not: on the contrary, we think that it appears immoral to some minds because its morality has a grander orbit than any which can be measured by the calculations of the pulpit and of ordinary literature. Goethe, it is sometimes said, seems in this book to be almost destitute of moral bias: he shows no hatred of bad actions, no warm sympathy with good ones; he writes like a passionless Mejnour, to whom all human things are interesting only as objects of in-tellectual contemplation. But we question whether the direct exhibition of a moral bias in the writer will make a book really moral in its influence. Try this on the first child that asks you to tell it a story. As long as you keep to an apparently impartial narrative of facts you will have earnest eyes fixed on you in rapt attention, but no sooner do you begin to betray symptoms of an intention to moralise, or to turn the current of facts to-wards a personal application, than the interest of your hearer will slacken, his eyes will wander, and the moral dose will be doubly distasteful from the very sweet-meat in which you have attempted to insinuate it. One grand reason of this is, that the child is aware you are talking *for it* instead of *from yourself*, so that instead of carrying it along in a stream of sympathy with your own interest in the story, you give it the impression of contriving coldly and talking artificially. Now, the moralising novelist produces the same effect on his mature readers; an effect often heightened by the perception that the moralising is rather intended to make his book eligible for family reading than prompted by any profound conviction or enthusiasm. Just as far from being really moral is the so-called moral *dénouement*, in which rewards and punishments are distributed according to those notions of justice on which the novel-writer would have recommended that the world should be governed if he had been consulted at the creation. The emotion of satisfaction which a reader feels when the villain of the book dies of some hideous disease, or is crushed by a railway train, is no more essentially moral than the satisfaction which used to be felt in whipping culprits at the cart-tail. So we dismiss the charge of immorality against *Wilhelm Meister* on these two counts – the absence of moral bias in the mode of narration, and the comfortable issues allowed to questionable actions and questionable characters.[96]

George Eliot's own tendency in her novels was to direct her readers more or less overtly towards objects of sympathy. That was her method of 'carrying [them] along in a stream of sympathy with [her] own interest in the story'. However, she recognises Goethe's restraint and artistry in writing without directing remarks, at the same time realising that this very quality often had the negative effect of misleading and repelling his readers. As Richard Holt Hutton, also a fine critic of Goethe, wrote in his review of Lewes's *Life of Goethe*:

[Goethe's works] invariably repel, at first, English readers with English views of life and duty. As the characteristic atmosphere of the man distils into your life, you find the magnetic force coming strongly over you; – you are as a man mesmerised; – you feel his calm independence of so much on which you helplessly lean, combined with his thorough insight into that desire of yours to lean, drawing you irresistibly towards the invisible intellectual centre at which such independent strength and such genial breadth of thought was possible.[97]

George Eliot's answer to the question about how proper it is for Goethe 'to depict irregular relations in all the charms they really have for human nature', in particular to make us feel the attraction of 'the lawless Philina', represents an advance even on Lewes's defence of Goethe as artist, not moralist. It is not enough, she says, to take one's stand in a naive realism, saying that 'Goethe's pictures are truthful', because 'no one can maintain that *all* fact is a fit subject for art'. Here the commentator in the novels, with her careful use of moral terms in a secular, tolerant spirit, is already apparent. Goethe joins Comte and Feuerbach as examples for George Eliot of thinkers who secularise religious feeling, channelling it into human feelings towards fellow humans, and stripping it of mean-spirited exclusiveness. Her answer in the article is made up of a mixture of the moral and artistic concerns:

The sphere of the artist has its limit somewhere, and the first question is, Has Goethe overstepped this limit, so that the mere fact of artistic representation is a mistake? The second: If his subjects are within the legitimate limits of art, is his mode of treatment such as to make his pictures pernicious? Surely the sphere of art extends wherever there is beauty either in form, or thought, or feeling. A ray of sunlight falling on the dreariest sandbank will often serve the painter for a fine picture; the tragedian may take for his subject the most hideous passions if they serve as the background for some divine deed of tenderness or heroism, and so the novelist may place before us every aspect of human life where there is some trait of love, or endurance, or helplessness to call forth our best sympathies. . .

Everywhere he brings us into the presence of living, generous humanity – mixed and erring, and self-deluding, but saved from utter corruption by the salt of some noble impulse, some disinterested effort, some beam of good nature, even though grotesque or homely. And his mode of treatment seems to us precisely that which is really moral in its influence. It is without exaggeration; he is in no haste to alarm readers into virtue by melodramatic consequences; he quietly follows the stream of fact and of life; and waits patiently for the moral processes of nature as we all do for her material processes. The large tolerance of Goethe, which is markedly exhibited in *Wilhelm Meister*, is precisely that to which we point as the element of moral superiority. We all begin life by associating our passions with our moral prepossessions, by mistaking indignation for virtue, and many go through life without awaking from this illusion. These are the 'insupportables justes, qui du haut de leurs chaises d'or narguent les misères et les souffrances de l'humanité.' But a few are taught by their own falls and their own struggles, by their experience of sympathy, and help and goodness in the 'publicans and sinners' of these modern days, that the line between the virtuous and vicious, so far from being a necessary safeguard to morality, is itself an immoral fiction. Those who have been already taught this lesson will at once recognise the true morality of Goethe's works. Like *Wilhelm Meister*, they will be able to love the good in a Philina, and to reverence the far-seeing efforts of a Lothario.[98]

This is the same George Eliot who insists that on a little reflection we have no choice but to sympathise with Casaubon, who constantly enjoins us to 'imagine' what it would be like to be Daniel Deronda, however different his aims and concerns from those that usually interest us. Her appreciation of Goethe's slow following of 'the stream of fact and life' without show of haste or manipulation, and particularly her expression of it in terms of natural processes, enlightens us both as to Goethe's love of clear, unhurried observation (so praised by Lewes in the *Life*) and her own. We have seen that Lewes incorporated a similar insight of hers into his own less tolerant criticism of the slow pace of *Die Wahlverwandtschaften*.

This essay, which has been quoted almost entire here, shows how George Eliot found in criticising *Wilhelm Meister*, which still needed explaining to English readers, expression for those basic beliefs about realism, observation, imagination, and sympathy which informed her writings from then till her death. The same questions about overt moralising and giving rewards and punishments in novels, exercised her in an article published, like 'The Morality of Wilhelm Meister', in July 1855, on Kingsley's *Westward Ho!* and Geraldine Jewsbury's *Constance Herbert*. Kingsley too readily 'drops into the homily', thus 'enfeebling the effect' of his works: 'If he would confine himself to his true sphere, he might be a teacher in the sense in which every great artist is a teacher – namely, by giving us his higher sensibility as a medium, a delicate acoustic or optical instrument, bringing home to our coarser senses what would otherwise be unperceived by us.' In *Constance Herbert* the theme of renunciation arises, and George Eliot gives strong expression to the falseness with which she sees Geraldine Jewsbury viewing it:

This moral [that 'nothing they renounce for the sake of a higher principle, will prove to have been worth the keeping'] is illustrated in the novel by the story of three ladies, who, after renouncing their lovers, or being renounced by them, have the satisfaction of feeling in the end that these lovers were extremely 'good-for-nothing', and that they (the ladies) have had an excellent riddance. In all this we can see neither the true doctrine of renunciation, nor a true representation of the realities of life; and we are sorry that a writer of Miss Jewsbury's insight and sincerity should have produced three volumes for the sake of teaching such copy-book morality. It is not the fact that what duty calls on us to renounce, will invariably prove 'not worth the keeping'; and if it *were* the fact, renunciation would cease to be moral heroism, and would be simply a calculation of prudence...The notion that duty looks stern, but all the while has her hand full of sugar-plums, with which she will reward us by-and-by, is the favourite cant of optimists, who try to make out that this tangled wilderness of life has a plan as easy to trace as that of a Dutch garden; but it really undermines all true development by perpetually substituting something extrinsic as a motive to action, instead of the immediate impulse of love or justice, which alone makes an action truly moral.[99]

It is quite possible that George Eliot is here applying to inferior writers the complex view of renunciation that she was familiar with in *Wilhelm Meister*. For example, it is by 'an immediate impulse of love' for his son Felix that Wilhelm finally comes close to Natalie, the woman who is right for him, but whom he had given up hoping to find. Wilhelm's renunciation of the wrong woman, Therese, looks rather less than heroic, as he gives her up only when he realises that the preferred Natalie can, after all, be his. But Goethe is skilful in showing how Wilhelm is bound by several threads of duty and gratitude, that his final choice affects the happiness of others than himself and the two women immediately involved. Renunciation is in this case a noble but not unmixedly heroic action, rather one that is prepared for and carried out in the context of the mutual relationships of a larger social group. That George Eliot approved of such a wide view of the morality of actions is apparent not only from the strongly-worded essays of 1855, but also from her novels. In *Daniel Deronda*, she is careful to remind us that Daniel, in marrying Mirah whom he loves and who is, in her Jewishness and blood relationship to the mentor Mordecai, 'right' for him in his future sphere of action, is nevertheless renouncing a different, perhaps more stimulating, relationship with Gwendolen. And the choice is not a black-and-white one: had he married Gwendolen, whom he also loves, he would have found an outlet for his saving gifts in helping her and fulfilling the more limited duty of a conventional bond:

Any one who knows him cannot wonder at his inward confession, that if all this had happened little more than a year ago, he would hardly have asked himself whether he loved her: the impetuous determining impulse which would have moved him would have been to save her from sorrow, to shelter her life for evermore from the dangers of loneliness, and carry out to the last the rescue he had begun in that monitary redemption of the necklace. But now, love and duty had thrown other bonds around him, and that impulse could no longer determine his life; still, it was present in him as a compassionate yearning, a painful quivering at the very imagination of having again and again to meet the appeal of her eyes and words. The very strength of the bond, the certainty of the resolve, that kept him asunder from her, made him gaze at her lot apart with the more aching pity.[100]

We do not know how often George Eliot read *Wilhelm Meister* in her life, but a journal entry suggests, not least in its punctuation, that she returned to it often. It reads for 2 December 1870, while she was composing *Middlemarch,* 'in the evening aloud, Wilhelm Meister again!'[101] George Eliot's novels are such fully-matured expressions of her wide reading and compound philosophy that it would be absurd to suggest a single direct influence from Goethe. Occasionally her German-oriented contemporaries saw parallels. Crabb Robinson read *Scenes of Clerical Life* in 1859 and saw in it something of the beautiful, wise, and moral writing without actual belief which he knew also in Goethe. In George Eliot's case, the bold use of religious terms divorced from a context of belief worried him (as did probably his knowledge of the facts of her life):

> It is so very Evangelical in its tone that it is quite unpleasant thinking of it as the writing of Miss Evans...One excuses this in so great a man as Goethe. He is the perfect artist...One is not displeased on reading (at least, I am not) Goethe's *Confessions of a Beautiful Soul,* but the *Repentance of Janet* I should have read with some pleasure from a regular Evangelical or pious High Church – Miss Sewell.[102]

Hutton also sees matter for comparison, between Goethe's 'schöne Seele' and Dinah in *Adam Bede,* finding the characterisation of Dinah superior because the story of the 'schöne Seele' is 'an episode of mere description, and the character is not delineated in action'.[103]

In spite of the occasional echo of a Goethean plot – the unfortunate mutual attraction between Maggie Tulliver and Stephen and their symbolic drifting down the Floss into undutiful action (or passivity) and disrepute reminds one of the *Wahlverwandtschaften* – George Eliot's novels are too dense and characteristic to convince us of particular debts. In this her novels need only be compared to Lewes's or to Froude's *Nemesis of Faith,* which borrows unsubtly from *Die Wahlverwandtschaften.*[104] What we can say is that Goethe was for George Eliot an artist who subscribed to many of the same philosophical and cultural beliefs as she did, whose aesthetic example was stimulating, and with whom she became thoroughly acquainted as the subject of Lewes's biography, a work which she helped him to write in the first few months of their life together. Her essay on *Wilhelm Meister,* moreover, was the most intelligent critique of it to date.

The pros and cons of the German genius

A German writer from whom George Eliot quoted in her novels almost as often as she did from Goethe, is Heine.[105] She read his

Salon in Berlin in 1854, and in June 1855 she told Charles Bray that her reading aloud in the evenings with Lewes consisted at that time of Boswell's Johnson, followed by 'the dreary dryness of Whewell's History of the Inductive Sciences', and 'winding up with Heine's wit and imagination' in the *Reisebilder* (*Travel Pictures*).[106] Heine was the subject of some of her bread-and-butter reviewing on her return from Germany.[107] She wrote one full length article of importance, 'German Wit: Heinrich Heine', in the *Westminster Review* (January 1856). Though not the first or best article on Heine yet published in a periodical,[108] it did attempt to use Heine as a striking example of a trait which was universally thought to be lacking in German literature. George Eliot agreed with Lewes that 'nothing can be more wearisome than...German *jeux d'esprit*',[109] finding little humour in the Germans and that little tiresome:

A German comedy is like a German sentence: you see no reason in its structure why it should ever come to an end, and you accept the conclusion as an arrangement of Providence rather than of the author. We have heard Germans use the word *Langeweile*, the equivalent for ennui, and we have secretly wondered *what* it can be that produces ennui in a German.

Jean Paul, 'the greatest of German humorists' (beloved of Carlyle and De Quincey) is 'unendurable to many readers, and frequently tiresome to all' in his prolixity and lack of measure and tact.[110] Heine is the one notable exception, and he deserves our attention for it – George Eliot adapts one of Lewes's favourite quotations from Goethe when she says Heine is 'no echo, but a real voice' – even though his brilliance is sometimes bedimmed by a coarseness, 'miry clay mingled with the precious metal'.[111] Most of the article consists of quotation from Heine's funny accounts of his contemporaries, as well as from some of his poems. It is chiefly interesting for its placing of Heine as the first example of mature wit in modern German literature and its praise of what that literature has achieved in the non-comic kind, praise which she offers as a counterbalance to her ironic remarks about German clumsiness and tediousness.[112] She has fun at the expense of the Germans, but, like Carlyle in *Sartor*, she turns immediately to view the positive side of such a serious national literature :

Whatever may be the stock of fun which Germany yields for home consumption, she has provided little for the palate of other lands. – All honour to her for the still greater things she has done for us! She has fought the hardest fight for freedom of thought, has produced the grandest inventions, has made magnificent contributions to science, has given us some of the divinest poetry, and quite the divinest music, in the world. No one reveres and treasures the products of the German mind more than we do. To say that that mind is not fertile in wit, is only like saying that excellent wheat land is not rich pasture; to say that we do not enjoy German facetiousness, is no more than to say, that though the horse is the finest of quadrupeds, we do not like him to lay his hoof playfully on our shoulder.[113]

If Heine's merits consisted for George Eliot partly in his un-German characteristics, so also did Lessing's. Like Coleridge, De Quincey, and Lewes, she revered Lessing as the father of German criticism, the great writer of lucid German prose, and the bold, tolerant free-thinker of the eighteenth century. Like them, she hardly wrote at all publicly on Lessing – perhaps *because* he needed no explaining to English readers, his arguments always carrying their own conviction. Her journal records her impression of *Laokoon* in 1854 as 'the most un-German of all German books that I have ever read. The style is strong clear & lively, the thought acute & pregnant'.[114] While in Berlin she saw three plays of Lessing's performed, and was particularly impressed by *Nathan der Weise*. 'Our hearts swelled & the tears came into our eyes as we listened to the noble words of the dear Lessing whose great spirit lives immortally in this crowning work of his.'[115] In a letter to Bray she indicated the reason for her admiration:

Last night we went to see "Nathan der Weise." You know, or perhaps you do not know that this play is a sort of dramatic apologue the moral of which is religious tolerance. It thrilled me to think that Lessing dared nearly a hundred years ago to write the grand sentiments and profound thoughts which this play contains for the people's theatre which he dreamed of, but which Germany has never had. In England the words which call down applause here would make the pit rise in horror.[116]

Jeffrey had found the play absurd in 1806, refusing to allow for Lessing's dramatic licence in carrying on his theological controversies (banned by the authorities) in the broad allegorical terms of the drama.[117] And the translator of Strauss and Feuerbach might have been right about its probable reception fifty years later in England, though she herself was doing more than anyone by her translations, her essays, and later her novels, to increase her readers' knowledge of German Biblical criticism and to engage their sympathies in a larger moral tolerance.

George Eliot was as amused as Lewes by the 'heaviness of *Germanity*' they found in the inhabitants of Weimar;[118] her letters and journals often record the absurdities of naively pompous Gelehrten (scholars). In *Theophrastus Such* there is a reminder of Bibundtücker in her account of two scholars, Butzkopf and Dugong, 'whose signatures were familiar to the Teutonic world in the *Seltenerscheinende Monatschrift* or Hayrick for the insertion of Split Hairs'.[119] But she recognised that intelligent English people were still using such easy preconceptions of the Germans as had been current in Jeffrey's reviewing days to dismiss unread certain difficult, important, and often troublesome works of German philosophy, history, and literature. In 1865 she wrote a short article called 'A Word for the Germans', in which she lectured 'John Bull' about his 'portable notions' of foreigners. 'We object', she said, 'to 'cloudy metaphysician' as the accepted periphrasis for a German, because it has begotten another habit of speech which the most constant familiarity could not endear to us. Views are set aside by saying that 'they are German'.' Kant, in particular, has been so labelled by those not able or too lazy to read him, though he is clear enough to anyone who has 'brains capable of following his argument'.[120] She agrees that Germans tend to write a laborious, cumbrous style, but lists their actual achievements:

If he is an experimenter, he will be thorough in his experiments; if he is a scholar, he will be thorough in his researches. Accordingly no one in this day really studies any subject without having recourse to German books, or else wishing he knew their language that he might have recourse to them; and the footnotes of every good French or English book that appears, whether in scholarship, history, or natural science, are filled with references to German authors. Without them, historical criticism would have been absolutely nowhere; take away the Germans, with their patience, their thoroughness, their need for a doctrine which refers all transient and material manifestations to subtler and more permanent causes, and all that we most value in our appreciation of early history would have been wanting to us.[121]

This is one of those generalisations which, unlike the contrary ones which collected all German works under the heading of 'obscurity' or 'mysticism', George Eliot knew from individual examples to be true enough not to represent a distorted view. Not all German writers displayed the talents she here ascribes to them, but enough of them – among them Kant, Strauss, and Feuerbach – had made such important contributions to knowledge that they could be ignored only at the cost of remaining intolerably ignorant of the areas of knowledge in which they had distinguished themselves. It was a point which needed to be made from time to time, though by the 1860s most educated people, and certainly most eminent critics and thinkers – Holt Hutton, Arnold, Jowett, Pater, and Leslie Stephen were the most notable – learned German as a matter of course, and kept an eye constantly on German researches. George Eliot spoke for herself and her generation: 'In fact, if anyone in the present day can be called cultivated who dispenses with a knowledge of German, it is because the two other greatest literatures of the world are now impregnated with the results of German labour and German genius.'[122]

The impregnation had necessarily been a slow process, of which the most important manifestations had been Coleridge's encyclopaedic knowledge and his sometimes indirect passing on of it to those inspired by his ideas and his personality; Carlyle's direct assault on his readers' imaginations with his translations of and exhortative articles on the best examples of German literary genius; those followers of Coleridge and Carlyle who translated and reviewed widely in the 1830s – Sterling, Sarah Austin, Hayward, Blackie, and others; and the generation which benefited from their enthusiasm (and often from their texts – how many Victorians read *Sartor* first, then *Wilhelm Meister*?) and grew up with an interest in German literature – Mill is a striking example. Of that last generation, George Eliot and Lewes, separately and together, were those who introduced new important German works in philosophy, aesthetics, and the higher criticism to an English public now aware of German culture but still suspicious of the tendencies of its philosophy and scholarship. Unlike their predecessors in the task of introduction, they could assume that even sceptical English readers and critics would pay some attention to what came from Germany without crying out about German bad taste, immorality, and mysticism.

NOTES

INTRODUCTION

1 Samuel Taylor Coleridge, Notebook 42 (1829), Add. MS 47,537, f. 9 (British Museum). Coleridge probably refers here to Thomas Medwin's *Conversations of Lord Byron* (London, 1824), in which Byron is reported as having said, 'If he had never gone to Germany, nor spoilt his fine genius by the transcendental philosophy and German metaphysics, nor taken to write lay sermons, he would have made the greatest poet of the day...Coleridge might have been any thing: as it is, he is a thing "that dreams are made of"', p. 266. The Coleridge notebook entry quoted here reads rather oddly, but the general drift is clear.

2 *See* Sterling to Emerson, 28 June 1842, *A Correspondence between John Sterling and Ralph Waldo Emerson*, ed. E. W. Emerson (Boston, 1897, reissued Port Washington, New York, 1971), p. 59.

3 Letter to Sterling, 28 September 1839, Mill, *Earlier Letters, The Collected Works of John Stuart Mill*, ed. F. E. L. Priestley, 17 vols (Toronto, 1963–72), xiii, 406.

4 O. B. Frothingham, *Transcendentalism in New England, A History* (New York, 1876, reprinted 1959), pp. 76, 92.

5 René Wellek, *Immanuel Kant in England, 1793–1838* (Princeton, New Jersey, 1931), gives Coleridge less credit than he deserves, largely because he is impatient with Coleridge's attempt to make Kant's doctrines fit with his religious views.

6 For A. W. Schlegel *see* A. A. Helmholtz, *The Indebtedness of Coleridge to A. W. Schlegel* (Madison, Wisconsin, 1907). For Schelling *see* in particular Thomas McFarland, *Coleridge and the Pantheist Tradition* (Oxford, 1969) and Gian N. G. Orsini, *Coleridge and German Idealism: A Study in the History of Philosophy with Unpublished Materials from Coleridge's Manuscripts* (Carbondale, Illinois, 1969).

7 Coleridge's interest in Jean Paul was greatest around 1810 and 1811. He borrowed Crabb Robinson's copies of Jean Paul's works and annotated them, but the particular reason for his interest seems to be Jean Paul's comments on marriage, a topic obviously relevant to Coleridge at that time, *see The Notebooks of Samuel Taylor Coleridge*, ed. K. Coburn, 3 double vols – (London, 1957 –), iii, 3684ff. When thinking how to embody his 'constructive Philosophy' in 1818, he considered the novel form but thought Novalis's *Heinrich von*

Ofterdingen a discouraging example, *see Collected Letters of Samuel Taylor Coleridge*, ed. E. L. Griggs, 6 vols (Oxford, 1956–71), IV, 870. Coleridge wrote to Dr Coppleston ca. 11 October 1820, that Wordsworth, Southey, Sir Walter Scott and others observed his son Hartley's lack of any conscious 'I', 'and never can I read De la Motte Fouqué's beautiful Faery Tale...of Undina, the Water-Fay, before she had a Soul, beloved by all whether they would or no, & as indifferent to all, herself included, as a blossom whirling in a May-gale, without having Hartley recalled to me, as he appeared from infancy to his boyhood...', *ibid.*, V, 110–11.

8 Walter Pater, 'Coleridge's Writings', *Westminster Review* (January 1866), *Essays on Literature and Art*, ed. Jennifer Uglow (London, 1973), p. 12.

9 *See* M. H. Abrams for the 'secularization of inherited theological ideas' and their reformulation into the 'prevailing two-term system' of subject and object, *Natural Supernaturalism: Tradition and Revolution in Romantic Literature* (London, 1971), pp. 12–13.

10 The following works are some of those which deal with aspects of Anglo-German relations in the eighteenth century: Theodor Süpfle, 'Beiträge zur Geschichte der deutschen Litteratur in England im letzten Drittel des 18. Jahrhunderts', *Zeitschrift für vergleichende Litteraturgeschichte*, VI (1893), 305–28; Ernst Margraf, 'Einfluss der deutschen Litteratur auf die englische am Ende des achtzehnten und im ersten Drittel des neunzehnten Jahrhunderts', *Studien zur vergleichenden Litteraturgeschichte* (special issue, 1901); Thomas Rea, *Schiller's Dramas and Poems in England* (London, 1906); Jean Marie Carré, *Goethe en Angleterre* (Paris, 1920); F. W. Stokoe, *German Influence in the English Romantic Period, 1788–1818* (Cambridge, 1926); Violet Stockley, *German Literature as Known in England, 1750–1830* (London, 1929); L. M. Price, *The Reception of English Literature in Germany* (Berkeley, California, 1932); Frederic Ewen, *The Prestige of Schiller in England, 1788–1859* (New York, 1932); James Boyd, *Goethe's Knowledge of English Literature* (Oxford, 1932); Carl August Weber, 'Bristols Bedeutung für die englische Romantik und die deutsch-englischen Beziehungen', *Studien zur englischen Philologie*, LXXXIX (1935), 1–304; Erich Auerbach, *Mimesis: The Representation of Reality in Western Literature*, trans. Willard Trask (Princeton, New Jersey, 1953); M. H. Abrams, *The Mirror and the Lamp: Romantic Theory and the Critical Tradition* (New York, 1953) and *Natural Supernaturalism: Tradition and Revolution in Romantic Literature* (London, 1971); Lilian Furst, *Romanticism in Perspective: A Comparative Study of Aspects of the Romantic Movements in England, France and Germany* (London, 1969).

11 18 September 1794, Coleridge, *Collected Letters*, I, 103.

12 3 November 1794, *ibid.*, I, 122.

13 William Hazlitt, 'On the Feeling of Immortality in Youth' (1827), *The Complete Works of William Hazlitt*, ed. P. P. Howe, 21 vols (London, 1930–4), XVII, 196–7.

14 Prospectus of *The Anti-Jacobin; or, Weekly Examiner*, ed. W. Gifford (London, 20 November 1797 – 9 July 1798). The chief collaborators in the venture were G. Canning, J. H. Frere, and G. Ellis.

15 It was staged at the Theatre Royal, Haymarket, in an adaptation by J. G. Holman, *The Red-Cross Knights*, in 1800. This version, as a reviewer in the *Monthly Review* approvingly pointed out, substituted 'very loyal sentiments' for the 'anarchical notions of the German original', XXXII (July 1800), 322.

16 *Anti-Jacobin*, 4 June 1798, p. 238 (Act I, Scene ii of *The Rovers*).

17 *The Castle Spectre* (1798), by 'Monk' Lewis, also has a father who has been buried alive in a subterranean dungeon for sixteen years.

18 Lessing criticised the practice of following French classical rules in the German theatre, pointing out that Shakespeare's example was greater, more natural, and more suitable for the German theatre to model itself on than Racine or Corneille, *Briefe die neueste Literatur betreffend* (*Letters relating to Recent Literature*, Berlin, 1759–65) and *Hamburgische Dramaturgie* (Hamburg, 1767–9). Herder took up the idea of Shakespeare as a genius so great that no rules could apply to him; he used natural and organic terms to describe Shakespeare's genius, and he publicly encouraged Goethe to become the German Shakespeare with *Götz von Berlichingen*, *see* Herder's Shakespeare essay in *Von deutscher Art und Kunst* (*Of German Art*, Hamburg, 1773).

19 *Anti-Jacobin*, 4 June 1798, p. 236.

20 *Ibid.*, p. 237n. Goethe himself recognised the improbability of the ending; in 1805 he produced a reworking of the play, in which Stella takes poison and Fernando shoots himself. Much later Goethe admitted to von Müller that the early ending had been illogical, unsuitable, and unprepared for: 'über Stella, deren früherer Schluss durchaus keiner gewesen, nicht konsequent, nicht haltbar, eigentlich nur ein Niederfallen des Vorhangs', Johann Wolfgang von Goethe, *Werke, Briefe und Gespräche*, Gedenkausgabe, ed. Ernst Beutler, 24 vols (Zürich, 1948–62), XXIII, 311. Only the early version was noticed in Britain.

21 The most popular were *Pizarro*, translated by Sheridan in 1799, *Menschenhass und Reue*, translated as *The Stranger* by Benjamin Thompson in 1798, and *Das Kind der Liebe*, known as *Lovers' Vows* in Mrs Inchbald's translation of 1798. *See Biographia Dramatica; or, a Companion to the Playhouse*, ed. Baker, Reed, and Jones, 3 vols (London, 1812).

22 Kotzebue's absurdities did not go unnoticed in Germany either. The brothers Schlegel lampooned him in the *Athenäum* in 1799, and Nicolai, author of a parody of *Werther*, wrote, according to Crabb Robinson, 'a clever play, in which Kotzebue's "Stranger" and the hero of Goethe's "Stella" are made to be the same, and the Stranger is represented as compromising with his wife, receiving her back on condition of her living with him in partnership with Stella', Henry Crabb Robinson, *Diary, Reminiscences and Correspondence*, ed.

Thomas Sadler, 3 vols (London, 1869), I, 160. I have not been able to find such a work by Nicolai, but he was well known as the author of attacks on and parodies of works by most of his contemporaries, including Goethe, Schiller, Kant, Fichte, and the Schlegels, *see* Jacob Minor's introduction on Nicolai, *Deutsche National-Litteratur*, ed. Joseph Kürschner, 163 vols (Berlin and Stuttgart, n.d., ?1884–6), LXXII, 277–323.

23 *See* the short notices in the 'Monthly Catalogue', *Monthly Review*, XXXII (July 1800), 322, 326.

24 *Ibid.*, XXXIII, 127ff. *See* Chapter 1.

25 *Ibid.*, XXXIX (December 1802), 383, 384.

26 Francis Jeffrey, 'Southey's *Thalaba*', *Edinburgh Review*, I (October 1802), 63, 64.

27 *Ibid.*, VIII (April 1806), 149.

28 *See* the portrait of Taylor in Chapter 23 of Borrow's *Lavengro; the scholar, the gypsy, the priest* (London, 1851).

29 In his collection of periodical articles written between 1790 and the 1820s, *A Historic Survey of German Poetry*, 3 vols (London, 1828–30), William Taylor wrote that Kotzebue was 'the greatest dramatic genius that Europe has evolved since Shakspeare', III, 102. Carlyle found this preference, along with Taylor's dislike of Goethe's later works, 'Philistine', *see* his harsh review of the *Historic Survey* in the *Edinburgh Review*, LIII (March 1831), 172.

30 *See* Scott's letter to Taylor, 25 November 1796, *Letters of Sir Walter Scott*, ed. H. J. C. Grierson, 12 vols (London, 1932–7), I, 59.

31 *See* Robinson, *Diary*, I, 42, and C. C. Southey (ed.), *The Life and Correspondence of the late Robert Southey*, 6 vols (London, 1849–50), II, 16.

32 George Henry Lewes, 'Lessing', *Edinburgh Review*, LXXXII (October 1845), 451ff.

33 *Ibid.*, XLVI (October 1827), 320.

34 Letter to Southey, 7 March 1805, *see* J. W. Robberds, *A Memoir of the Life and Writings of the late William Taylor, of Norwich*, 2 vols (London, 1843), II, 74. The collection became *A Historic Survey of German Poetry*.

35 William Taylor, 'Critical Survey of Lessing's Works', *Monthly Magazine*, XXII (August 1806), 27.

36 Coleridge, *The Friend* (1809 and 1818), ed. Barbara Rooke, *The Collected Works of Samuel Taylor Coleridge*, ed. K. Coburn, 16 vols in progress (London, 1969–), I, 34 and II, 38. *Biographia Literaria* also has several references to Lessing, including a passage in praise of him as 'a model of acute, spirited, sometimes stinging, but always argumentative and honorable, criticism', Coleridge, *Biographia Literaria*, ed. J. Shawcross, 2 vols (London, 1907), II, 87.

37 Essay on Lessing (1797), Friedrich Schlegel, *Kritische Friedrich-Schlegel-Ausgabe*, ed. Ernst Behler, 19 vols (München, 1961–71), II, 118.

38 I.e. between an ignorant article on Kant by Thomas Brown in January

1803 and a more knowledgeable one on Madame de Staël's *De L'Allemagne* by James Mackintosh in October 1813.

39 Jeffrey, 'Lessing's *Nathan the Wise*', *Edinburgh Review*, VIII (April 1806), 150. Lessing used Boccaccio's story of the three rings to signify the three religions coinciding in Jerusalem. Each is seen to have a part of the truth, and mutual tolerance is advocated, as no one denomination can lay claim to the whole truth. The weak part of the plot is the growing love between Nathan's adopted daughter and the Templar who has saved her life and the abrupt change wrought in their affections by the discovery that they are brother and sister. Uncomfortable as the solution is, it adds to the chief message of the play, that Jews, Christians, and Moslems can and should live together in brotherly harmony.

40 William Taylor, 'Critical Survey of Lessing's Works', *Monthly Magazine*, XXIV (November 1807), 338.

41 Lewes, 'Its conception is philosophical, its execution epigrammatic and polemical', 'Lessing', *Edinburgh Review*, LXXXII (October 1845), 464. George Eliot saw *Nathan*, 'a sort of dramatic apologue the moral of which is religious tolerance', performed at Berlin in 1854, *see The George Eliot Letters*, ed. Gordon S. Haight, 7 vols (London, 1954–6), II, 185.

42 William Taylor, 'Critical Survey of Lessing's Works', *Monthly Magazine*, XXIV, 338.

43 Letter of 3 June 1806, Robberds, *Memoir of the Life and Writings*, II, 135.

44 Letter to Taylor, 9 August 1808, *ibid.*, II, 259.

45 Letter of 8 October 1845, *Selection from the Correspondence of the late Macvey Napier*, ed. by his son, Macvey Napier (London, 1879), pp. 507–8.

46 *See* Harriet Martineau, *Autobiography*, ed. Maria Weston Chapman, 3 vols (London, 1877), I, 81–2, 300.

47 *See* Robinson, *Diary*, I, 135, 269, and Adolph B. Benson, 'Fourteen Unpublished Letters by Henry Crabb Robinson', *Publications of the Modern Language Association of America*, XXXI (1916), 395.

48 Hayward to Crabb Robinson, 29 July 1833, MS Henry Crabb Robinson (Dr Williams's Library).

49 Robinson, *Diary*, I, vi.

50 *See* J. M. Baker, *Henry Crabb Robinson of Bury, Jena, 'The Times', and Russell Square* (London, 1937), p. 188.

51 *See* Emma G. Jaeck, *Madame de Staël and the Spread of German Literature* (New York, 1915).

52 James Mackintosh, review of *De L'Allemagne*, *Edinburgh Review*, XXII (October 1813), 201. Similar views of Madame de Staël's work were given by Hazlitt, *Morning Chronicle* (November 1813, February, March, and April 1814), *Complete Works*, XIX and XX; William Taylor, *Monthly Review*, LXXII (December 1813), 421ff; and Reginald Heber, *Quarterly Review*, X (January 1814), 355ff.

53 *Memoirs, Journal, and Correspondence of Thomas Moore*, ed. Lord John Russell, 8 vols (London, 1853–6), II, 43.
54 Hazlitt, 'Characters of Shakespear's Plays' (1817), *Complete Works*, IV, 171–2. *See also* Leigh Hunt's review of Hazlitt's work, where he remarks that Schlegel 'had hitherto been the only writer who seemed truly to *understand* as well as feel [Shakespeare]', *Examiner*, 20 July 1817, *Leigh Hunt's Dramatic Criticism, 1808–1831*, ed. L. H. and C. W. Houtchens (New York, 1949), p. 291.
55 Statistical studies such as Stockley, *German Literature as Known in England*, B. Q. Morgan, *Critical Bibliography of German Literature in English Translation, 1481–1927*, 2nd edition revised (Stanford University Press, California, 1938), W. F. Schirmer, 'German Literature, Historiography and Theology in Nineteenth-Century England', *German Life and Letters*, new series I (1947), 165ff, and B. Q. Morgan and A. R. Hohlfeld, *German Literature in British Magazines, 1750–1860* (Madison, Wisconsin, 1949), show that interest rose ca. 1815, after the publication of *De L'Allemagne* and the end of the Napoleonic Wars.
56 *See* Hazlitt, *Complete Works*, VI, 362.
57 *See*, for example, Thomas Lovell Beddoes's references to Gillies's articles in 1827, *Letters*, ed. Edmund Gosse (London, 1894), p. 133. Later translators from German, among them J. S. Blackie, who translated *Faust* in 1834, and Sarah Austin, translator of several memoirs of Goethe by his contemporaries, acknowledged Gillies as a source.
58 *See The Collected Letters of Thomas and Jane Welsh Carlyle*, ed. C. R. Sanders and K. J. Fielding, 7 vols– (Durham, North Carolina, 1970–), III, 40.
59 Tieck criticised Schiller for thinking only of theory and not of practice, 'Die geschichtliche Entwicklung der neureren Bühne' ('The Historical Development of the Recent Stage', 1831), *Kritische Schriften*, 4 vols (Leipzig, 1848–52), II, 348. Schiller thought of theatre as an arena for moral and aesthetic play, for a liberation from everyday experience into a more ordered realm. The chorus was to distance the audience from ordinary life and encourage it to view intelligently the heightened 'game' of drama. *See* Schiller's essays on drama, particularly 'Die Schaubühne als eine moralische Anstalt betrachtet' ('The Stage viewed as a Moral Institution', 1784) and the preface to *Braut von Messina*, 'Über den Gebrauch des Chors in der Tragödie' ('On the Use of the Chorus in Tragedy', 1803). For the 1784 essay *see* Friedrich Schiller, *Sämtliche Werke*, Säkular-Ausgabe, ed. Eduard von der Hellen et al, 16 vols (Stuttgart and Berlin, 1904), XI, 89–100. For the preface to *Braut see* Friedrich Schiller, *Sämmtliche Werke*, ed. K. Goedeke, 15 vols (Stuttgart, 1867–76), XIV, 3–12. Subsequent references to Schiller's works will be to *Schillers Werke*, Nationalausgabe, 42 vols in progress (Weimar, 1943–), except where, as in the case of the two works cited here, a work has not yet appeared in it.
60 For example Solger, review of A. W. Schlegel's *Über dramatische*

Kunst und Literatur, Jahrbücher der Literatur, VII (1819), 82, and von
Schütz, 'Adolph Müllners Trauerspiele', *ibid.*, x (1820), 190.

61 Letter of 1823, MS 4721, f. 226 of Blackwood Correspondence
(National Library of Scotland). *See also* Lockhart's article on Gower's
translation of *Faust*, in which he exhorts Gillies to 'turn seriously to
the true masterpieces of German genius', and not meddle with the
mediocre examples, 'New Poetical Translations', *Blackwood's Magazine*, XIV (July 1823), 39.

62 *See*, for example, 'Noctes Ambrosianae', *Blackwood's Magazine*, XII
(December 1822), 695 and XIII (May 1823), 592. Gillies wrote most of
the articles in the series 'Horae Germanicae', he translated Hoffmann's
Die Elixiere des Teufels (The Devil's Elixir) in 1824, but he was
critically unsound and unreliable in producing his work on time.
Manuscript letters in the National Library of Scotland from Gillies to
Blackwood show Gillies's persecution complex and Blackwood's
attempts to sack him. *See* R. D. Ashton, 'The Reception of German
Literature in England from the Founding of *Blackwood's Magazine*
(1817) to the Time of Carlyle and his Disciples' (Cambridge University PhD thesis, 1974).

63 J. G. Lockhart, 'Wallenstein, translated by Coleridge', *Blackwood's
Magazine*, XIV (October, 1823), 377, 378–9.

64 *Ibid.*, XXXI (April 1832), 693.

65 Jean Paul [Richter] characterised his own writings when he described
'die komische Romantik' as 'die Regenten der Subjektivität', *Vorschule der Ästhetik (Introduction to Aesthetics*, 1804). The book is his
idiosyncratic contribution to the Romantic theory of literature, the
discussion of Greek and modern literature, classical and romantic,
objective and subjective. *See* Jean Paul [Richter], *Werke*, ed. N. Miller
and G. Lohmann, 6 vols (München, 1959–66, Darmstadt, 1967), v,
132.

66 For Beddoes *see* Carl August Weber, 'Bristols Bedeutung für die
englische Romantik und die deutsch-englischen Beziehungen'. *Studien
zur englischen Philologie*, LXXXIX (1935), number 4, 105ff. Taylor's
article, 'Anecdotes of German Authors and Authoresses residing at
Weimar in Saxony', was in the *Monthly Magazine*, XI (March 1801),
146ff.

67 Thomas De Quincey, 'John Paul Frederick Richter', *London Magazine*, IV (December 1821), 606ff, reprinted in *Collected Writings*, ed.
David Masson, 14 vols (Edinburgh, 1889–90), XI, 259ff.

68 *See* Carlyle's marginal comment on a German memoir of his life by
Althaus (1866), quoted in part by J. A. Froude, *Thomas Carlyle: A
History of the First Forty Years of his Life, 1795–1835*, 2 vols (London,
1882), I, 396.

69 De Quincey, 'Suspiria de Profundis', *Blackwood's*, LVII (March 1845),
269. For a brief discussion of De Quincey's translation of Jean Paul's
'Traum über das All' ('Dream upon the Universe', *London Magazine*,
March 1824), *see* W. A. Dunn, *Thomas De Quincey's Relation to
German Literature and Philosophy* (Strassburg, 1900), pp. 84ff. *See*

also P. Michelsen, 'Thomas De Quincey und Jean Paul', *Journal of English and Germanic Philology*, LXI (1962), 736ff.

70 Letter of 17 October [1823], De Quincey to Hessey, Add. MS 37,215, f. 30 (British Museum).

71 *See* my discussion of Coleridge and Kant in Chapter 1.

72 De Quincey, *'Wilhelm Meister's Apprenticeship'*, *London Magazine*, x (September 1824), 302, and Jeffrey, *'Wilhelm Meister's Apprenticeship*, a Novel', *Edinburgh Review*, XLII (August 1825), 414. De Quincey was later ashamed of his article, omitting it from his collected works in 1859, but only because he did not want 'to seem actually wishing and going out of my road expressly to seek a quarrel or offer petty irritations to Carlyle', letter to his publisher Hogg, 21 May 1859, W. H. Bonner, *De Quincey at Work* (Buffalo, New York, 1936), p. 100. As far as Goethe was concerned, De Quincey felt he had been 'severe, but hardly as much as he deserved', 'Autobiography', *Tait's Magazine*, VIII (February 1841), 102. Unaccountably, De Quincey was asked to write the entry on Goethe for Napier's *Encyclopaedia Britannica* in 1835. The essay is largely biographical, but in it De Quincey grudgingly adds some mainly hostile remarks on the works, *see* De Quincey, *Collected Writings*, IV, 416ff.

73 8 April 1825, Coleridge, *Collected Letters*, V, 421. The work referred to here, as in the MS Note Book of 1829 quoted at the beginning of this Introduction, is Thomas Medwin's *Conversations of Lord Byron* (London, 1824).

74 *Works of Thomas Carlyle*, Centenary Edition, ed. H. D. Traill, 30 vols (London, 1896–9), I, 3–4.

75 Conversation with Eckermann, 11 October 1828, Goethe, *Werke*, Gedenkausgabe, XXIV, 293.

76 *See* Carlyle, *Collected Letters*, IV, 360.

77 *See* S. M. Vogel, *German Literary Influences on the American Transcendentalists* (New Haven, Connecticut, 1955), p. 65.

78 Francis Espinasse, *Literary Recollections and Sketches* (London, 1893), p. 57.

79 Carlyle, XXIII, 4–5.

80 One of many examples is the frequent quotation from Goethe, Matthew Arnold, 'On Translating Homer' (1860–1), *The Complete Prose Works of Matthew Arnold*, ed. R. H. Super, 10 vols (Ann Arbor, Michigan, 1960–77), I, 97ff.

81 Letter to Carlyle, 26 October 1837, Carlyle, *Life of Sterling* (1851), *Works*, XI, 138.

82 John Sterling, 'Carlyle's Works', *London and Westminster Review*, XXXIII (October 1839), 23; letter of 12 January 1840, Sterling to Blackwood, MS 4052 (National Library of Scotland).

83 Sarah Austin, *Characteristics of Goethe: From the German of Falk, von Müller etc.*, 3 vols (London, 1833), I, 309. This work reached a second edition in 1836, renamed *Goethe and his Contemporaries*. Her letters to Carlyle are in the National Library of Scotland. Some of them are published in Janet Ross, *Three Generations of English-*

women, 2 vols (London, 1888), and some are partially quoted in Froude, *Thomas Carlyle, 1795–1835*.

84 Lord Francis Leveson Gower (trans.), Preface to *Faust. And Schiller's Song of the Bell* (London, 1823), p. iii.

85 Abraham Hayward's prose translation of 1833 reached a second edition in 1834; J. S. Blackie, a contributor on German subjects to *Blackwood's*, published his verse translation in 1834, as did David Syme; John Anster, friend of Coleridge and an early writer in *Blackwood's*, wrote his verse translation in 1835; and Robert Talbot's version was also published in 1835.

86 Carlyle, 'Varnhagen von Ense's Memoirs, *Westminster Review*, XXXII (December 1838), 60.

87 George Eliot, 'Thomas Carlyle', *Leader* (27 October 1855), *Essays of George Eliot*, ed. Thomas Pinney (New York, 1963), pp. 213–14.

88 Mark Pattison recorded that in 1837 he 'had fallen under the influence of Coleridge...The *Aids to Reflection* especially dominated me', *Memoirs* (London, 1885), p. 164.

89 Kingsley (Froude's brother-in-law) to Max Müller, 10 May 1852, MS (Bodleian). He added that Froude had had 'spiritual diarrhoea' in public, and 'must take the consequences of so offending the public nose', and that *Nemesis* had been 'a fearful mistake' because there was in it 'no positive with which to defend his negative, as Carlyle had, & was strong therein'.

90 In *Die Wahlverwandtschaften* there is a diagonal attraction of four characters and the 'guilty' Ottilie pines to death from remorse and the loss of her lover, but otherwise Froude's details are almost identical with Goethe's.

91 Mill confessed to Comte that he knew Kant and Hegel only through English and French interpretations, letter of 13 March 1843, Mill, *Collected Works*, XIII, 576.

92 In 1844 Carlyle wrote to his brother Jack about a visit paid to him by a German woman who could speak no English: 'We wished you had been here with your German. Neither Darwin nor I could make any hand of speaking...', MS 512 (National Library of Scotland).

93 E. S. Shaffer makes clear the line of connection between Coleridge and George Eliot in their interest in historical criticism of the Bible, from Coleridge's knowledge of Eichhorn in 1798 to George Eliot's translations of Strauss and Feuerbach in the mid-nineteenth century, *'Kubla Khan' and The Fall of Jerusalem* (Cambridge, 1975).

94 Matthew Arnold, 'Spinoza and the Bible' (1863), *Complete Prose Works*, III, 181.

95 *See* John Stuart Mill, *Autobiography*, ed. with introduction and notes by Jack Stillinger (London, 1971), p. 97.

96 *See* George Eliot, 'German Wit: Heinrich Heine', *Westminster Review* (January 1856), *Essays*, p. 223, and the opening paragraph of Chapter XLV of *Middlemarch*.

CHAPTER 1

1 Southey talked of his 'spawning plans…like a herring' but finally doing
nothing, Southey to Coleridge, 4 August 1802, C. C. Southey, *The
Life and Correspondence of the late Robert Southey*, II, 190. There
was the plan in 1796 to translate all the works of Schiller, and in
1798–9 to write a Life of Lessing, *see* Coleridge, *Collected Letters*, I,
209, 455, 518–19.

2 31 August and 4 September 1816, Coleridge, *Collected Letters*, IV,
663–4, 666.

3 *See*, for example, Coleridge's bitter remarks on Jeffrey in Chapter 22
of his *Biographia Literaria*. Sara Coleridge, when editing the second
edition in 1847, omitted the reference to Jeffrey.

4 De Quincey began the exposure in four articles entitled 'Samuel
Taylor Coleridge', *Tait's Magazine*, I new series (September, October,
November 1834), 509ff, 588ff, 685ff, and II (January 1835), 3ff. He was
followed by Ferrier, 'The Plagiarisms of S. T. Coleridge', *Blackwood's
Magazine*, XLVII (March 1840), 287ff. In this century there have been
notably the works of A. A. Helmholtz, *The Indebtedness of Coleridge
to A. W. Schlegel*, and Norman Fruman, *The Damaged Archangel*
(London, 1972). J. C. Hare answered De Quincey's claims, 'Samuel
Taylor Coleridge and the English Opium-Eater', *British Magazine*, VII
(January 1835), 15ff, Sara Coleridge looked at Ferrier's in her 1847
edition of *Biographia*, and recently Thomas McFarland has given a
rather shrill defence of Coleridge with respect to A. W. Schlegel,
Coleridge and the Pantheist Tradition. D. M. MacKinnon turns the
very diversity of Coleridge's remarks on Kant into a mitigation of
plagiarism, 'Coleridge and Kant', *Coleridge's Variety: Bicentenary
Studies*, ed. John Beer (London, 1974), p. 184.

5 *See* Coleridge, *Notebooks*, where the editor frequently points to possible debts of Coleridge to German authors, but prudently avoids being
dogmatic, as she is aware of the difficulty of dating some of the entries.

6 Letter to Charles Ollier, 15 October 1819, *The Letters of Percy Bysshe
Shelley*, ed. F. L. Jones, 2 vols (Oxford, 1964), II, 127.

7 *See* Coleridge, *Poetical Works*, ed. E. H. Coleridge, 2 vols (London,
1912), I, 214–15. *See also* his letter to an unknown correspondent in
1811 about the 'coincidence' between A. W. Schlegel's remarks on
Romeo and Juliet and Coleridge's own recent lecture on the same
play. Here Coleridge talks of 'springs' and 'tanks', *Collected Letters*,
III, 355.

8 Molly Lefebure states quite simply that you cannot expect a drug
addict to recognise or adhere to strict truth, Preface to *Samuel
Taylor Coleridge: A Bondage of Opium* (London, 1974).

9 *Henry Crabb Robinson on Books and their Writers*, ed. E. J. Morley,
3 vols (London, 1938), I, 335; and *Diary*, II, 390.

10 Robinson, *Diary*, I, 125–30; J. M. Baker, *Henry Crabb Robinson of
Bury, Jena, 'The Times', and Russell Square*, pp. 116–17; and letter

to his brother Thomas, 14 November 1802, MS HCR Correspondence (Dr Williams's Library). Coleridge had attended lectures at Göttingen from February to July 1799, where he heard Blumenbach and possibly Eichhorn. For Coleridge, Eichhorn, and the German higher criticism *see* E. S. Shaffer, *'Kubla Khan' and The Fall of Jerusalem.* Coleridge's study of Kant began in earnest in late 1800 or early 1801, *see* Coleridge, *Notebooks,* I, 887 and *Collected Letters,* II, 706–7.

11 Crabb Robinson contributed on German subjects, including Kant, to the *Monthly Register* in 1802–3, to the Unitarian *Monthly Repository* in 1808, *see* Robinson, *Diary,* I, 135, 269. *See* Coleridge, *Collected Letters,* III, 306, 422, 461, for Coleridge's requests for books, 1811–13.

12 Letter to Southey, 3 November 1794, Coleridge, *Collected Letters,* I, 122, and *Poetical Works,* I, 72–3.

13 5 May 1796, Coleridge, *Collected Letters,* I, 209.

14 To George Coleridge, 10 March 1798, *ibid.,* I, 397. *See* J. B. Beer, *Coleridge's Poetic Intelligence* (London, 1977) p. 102, for the suggestion that Coleridge's return to religious pietism and political orthodoxy was due to a combination of circumstances, including his horror at the turn of events in France, fears of imprisonment for criticising the Government at home, and also the sobering influences of parenthood and of Lamb's domestic tragedy of September 1795.

15 'The Rovers; or, The Double Arrangement' had a cast including the Prior of the Abbey of Quedlinburgh, a prisoner Rogero, a Polish emigrant Casimere, the Count of Saxe Weimar, Matilda Pottingen who is in love with Rogero and mother of Casimere's children, Cecilia Mückinfeldt who is Casimere's wife, etc., *The Anti-Jacobin; or, Weekly Examiner* (4 and 11 June 1798), pp. 236–9, 243–6. The poem of the knife-grinder is a 'Sapphic Imitation' (27 November 1797), p. 15.

16 Lecture 'On the German Drama' (1820), Hazlitt, *Complete Works,* VI, 362. *See also* his essay 'On the Feeling of Immortality in Youth' (1827), XVII, 196–7.

17 Bürger's 'Lenore' had circulated in literary groups in Edinburgh and Norwich. Both William Taylor and Walter Scott translated it in 1796. Other versions in 1796–7 were by H. J. Pye, W. R. Spencer, and J. T. Stanley, the last of these illustrated by Blake.

18 In 1832, Coleridge, *Collected Letters,* VI, 926.

19 For the adverse review of Coleridge's translation of the first part of *Wallenstein,* 'Die Piccolomini', *see Monthly Review,* XXXIII (October 1800), 127ff. For Coleridge's protesting letter *see Monthly Review,* XXXIII (November 1800), 336, and Coleridge, *Collected Letters,* I, 647.

20 Jeffrey, 'Southey's *Thalaba', Edinburgh Review,* I (October 1802), 63.

21 *See* Southey, 'Lyrical Ballads', *Critical Review,* XXIV (October 1798), 201.

22 *See,* for example, the play 'on the German model' by Scythrop (i.e. Shelley), Thomas Love Peacock, *Nightmare Abbey,* ed. C. E. Jones (London, 1923), pp. 188–9.

23 Hazlitt, 'On the German Drama', *Complete Works,* VI, 362.

24 Coleridge, *Notebooks,* III, 3952, f. 72 (July 1810). The entry begins on

Johnson's fault-finding criticism of Shakespeare, but Coleridge undoubtedly had Jeffrey and the *Edinburgh Review* in mind as well.

25 Coleridge, *The Friend*, II (1809), *Collected Works*, IV, 217. The Notebooks in the early years of the century show his current interest in
Goethe and particularly Schiller; for example, he experimented with
metres in 1804, and translated and adapted verses by both Goethe
and Schiller at that time.

26 Coleridge, *Notebooks*, II, 2598.

27 Letter to Poole, 26 October 1798, Coleridge, *Collected Letters*, I, 435.

28 For costs, *see* his letter to Mrs Coleridge, 26 November 1798, and for
his activities at Göttingen, letter to Josiah Wedgwood, 21 May 1799,
Coleridge, *Collected Letters*, I, 446, 518, 519.

29 Dorothy Wordsworth told Coleridge this; *see* Coleridge to his wife,
14 January 1799, Coleridge, *Collected Letters*, I, 445, 459.

30 Letter to Poole, 20 November 1798, *ibid.*, I, 445.

31 *See* letter to Poole, 20 November 1798, *ibid.*, I, 441–2, and Coleridge,
The Friend, II (1809), *Collected Works*, IV, 239ff.

32 *See* Coleridge to William Sotheby, 10 September 1802, Coleridge,
Collected Letters, II, 863.

33 Coleridge, *Monthly Review*, XXXIII (November 1800), 336, and *Collected Letters*, I, 648.

34 *See* letter to Sotheby, 10 September 1802, and to Daniel Stuart, 11–16
February 1809, Coleridge, *Collected Letters*, II, 863; III, 179.

35 27 January 1801, Henry Crabb Robinson MS correspondence (Dr
Williams's Library).

36 Coleridge, *The Friend*, I (1818), *Collected Works*, IV, 122n.

37 He refers to it again, *ibid.*, 428n.

38 Coleridge told Murray in 1814 that he had heard that Scott thought
his translation superior to the original, Coleridge, *Collected Letters*,
III, 524. Lockhart praised the translation as 'by far the best translation
of a foreign tragic drama which our English literature possesses',
'Wallenstein, translated by Coleridge', *Blackwood's*, XIV (October
1823), 377. Schlegel apparently told Coleridge in 1828 that he preferred the translation to the original, *see* Coleridge, *Collected Letters*,
VI, 747n. Coleridge reported to William Godwin in 1823 that Tieck
thought his version better than Schiller's, V, 269.

39 John Gibson Lockhart, 'Wallenstein, translated by Coleridge', *Blackwood's*, XIV, 377–9.

40 *Wallensteins Tod*, Act I, Scene iv, *Schillers Werke*, VIII, 183–4.
Coleridge translated from the 1800 MS version, in which this speech
occurs at the end of the second play, *Die Piccolomini*, not at the beginning of the third, as in the published original. *See Wallenstein,
a Drama in Two Parts* (London, 1800), pp. 155–6 for Coleridge's
translation.

41 *See*, for example, Abraham Hayward's Preface to his translation,
Faust: A Dramatic Poem (London, 1833), pp. xiiiff, and George Moir,
Preface to his translation, *Wallenstein, from the German*, 2 vols (Edin-
burgh, 1827), I, i.

42 Coleridge certainly knew 'Über naive und sentimentalische Dichtung' and possibly 'Über Anmut und Würde', *see* Coleridge, *Notebooks*, I, Appendix A, 'Coleridge's Knowledge of German as Seen in the Early Notebooks', by E. M. Wilkinson.

43 *Schillers Werke*, XXI, 170.

44 *Henry Crabb Robinson on Books*, I, 70.

45 Coleridge, *Biographia*, I, 99.

46 De Quincey, 'German Studies and Kant in Particular', *Tait's Magazine*, III (June 1836), 352.

47 4 January 1801, *Crabb Robinson in Germany, 1800–1805*, ed. E. J. Morley (London, 1929), p. 48.

48 William Drummond, *Academical Questions* (London, 1805), p. 352 (Drummond's italics).

49 *See* Thomas Love Peacock, *Nightmare Abbey* and *Melincourt*, *The Works of Thomas Love Peacock*, ed. H. F. B. Brett-Smith and C. E. Jones, 10 vols (London, 1924–34), vols III and II respectively.

50 Hazlitt, 'Coleridge's Literary Life', *Edinburgh Review*, XXVIII (August 1817), 497; *Complete Works*, XVI, 123.

51 Immanuel Kant, 'Das blosse, aber empirisch bestimmte Bewusstsein meines eigenen Daseins beweiset das Dasein der Gegenstände im Raum ausser mir', 'Transzendentale Analytik', *Kritik der reinen Vernunft* (1781, revised 1787), *Werke*, ed. Wilhelm Weischedel, 6 vols (Wiesbaden, 1956–64), II, 255.

52 Kant, 'Transzendentale Methodenlehre', *ibid.*, 646.

53 Kant, 'Wenn aber gleich alle unsere Erkenntnis mit der Erfahrung anhebt, so entspringt sie darum doch nicht eben alle aus der Erfahrung', *ibid.*, 45.

54 Kant, 'Ich nenne alle Erkenntnis transzendental, die sich nicht so wohl mit Gegenständen, sondern mit *unserer Erkenntnisart* von Gegenständen, *so fern diese* a priori *möglich sein soll*, überhaupt beschäftigt', *ibid.*, 63.

55 De Quincey confused the two terms, also occasionally Coleridge, *see* Wellek, *Kant in England*, pp. 176ff.

56 Kant, *Werke*, II, 33 (Preface to edition of 1787). This also provides the starting point for Kant's work on ethics, *Kritik der praktischen Vernunft* (1788), *Werke*, IV, 103ff.

57 Kant, *Kritik der reinen Vernunft*, *ibid.*, II, 35.

58 De Quincey, knowing of Kant's troubles with the religious censor in the reign of Friedrich Wilhelm II (1786–97) – probably one reason why Kant spelt out his orthodoxy in the preface to the second edition of the *Kritik der reinen Vernunft* in 1787 – levelled the charge of atheism against him, 'Samuel Taylor Coleridge', *Tait's Magazine*, I (September 1834), 515.

59 According to Kant, we know them as regulative, not constitutive Ideas, i.e. we must act 'as if' we knew them. The distinction is first discussed in Kant, *Kritik der reinen Vernunft*, *Werke*, II, 582ff, 693–4.

60 *See below*, pp. 45ff.

61 Coleridge, *The Philosophical Lectures*, ed. Kathleen Coburn (London,

1949), pp. 365, 388, 389, and editor's note p. 459 for Coleridge's marginalia to works by Kant and her conclusion, 'I doubt if he read any other philosopher's work as thoroughly and so often.'

62 In both cases the magnum opus (Wordsworth's 'Recluse' and Coleridge's 'Logosophia') remained uncompleted. *See* the opening paragraph of *Biographia*, where Coleridge says the book is 'introductory to the statement of my principles in Politics, Religion, and Philosophy, and an application of the rules, deduced from philosophical principles, to poetry and criticism', Coleridge, *Biographia Literaria*, I, 1. *See also* his reference to 'my *Logosophia*', *ibid.*, 179.

63 He calls himself a 'transcendental philosopher' (with Schelling), *ibid.*, 187.

64 *Ibid.*, 93–4, 193n (also 85 for the same example). The *Kritik der reinen Vernunft* appears in a footnote to the first passage, though its precise application is not made explicit. There is no acknowledgment of Kant in either of the references to eyes and seeing.

65 De Quincey, 'Letters to a Young Man whose Education has been Neglected. No. V. On the English Notices of Kant', *London Magazine*, VIII (July 1823), 94.

66 *Ibid.*, VII (January 1823), 90.

67 *Ibid.*, VIII, 92.

68 Letter from Schiller to Goethe, 28 October 1794, Goethe, *Werke*, XX, 36, and Coleridge to J. H. Green, 13 December 1817, Coleridge, *Collected Letters*, IV, 791–2.

69 Carlyle, 'Novalis', *Foreign Review*, IV (1829), 117.

70 Carlyle, *Works*, XXV, 114n.

71 Coleridge, *Biographia*, I, 99, 196.

72 Letters to Poole, 5 May 1796 and 20 November 1798, Coleridge *Collected Letters*, I, 209, 444.

73 *See* Coleridge, *Notebooks*, I, 349–54 (October 1798) for Coleridge's lists of vocabulary, and I, 887 (December 1800–January 1801) for evidence that he is taking notes from Kant.

74 *Ibid.*, 886.

75 Coleridge, *Collected Letters*, II, 676.

76 *Ibid.*, II, 677ff.

77 16 March 1801, *ibid.*, II, 706, 707.

78 Coleridge, *Biographia*, I, 81.

79 They are 'reine Formen aller sinnlichen Anschauung', Kant, *Werke*, II, 73ff.

80 *See* the Preface to the second edition, Kant, *Kritik der reinen Vernunft*, *Werke*, II, 31.

81 Kant, *Werke*, II, 675. This is the basis on which the companion work, *Kritik der praktischen Vernunft*, is founded.

82 'As to metaphysics I know little about them, and my head is at present so full of various affairs that I have not even read the letters Coleridge has written on those subjects, as I have honestly told him', MS letter in British Museum, quoted in Coleridge, *Collected Letters*, II, 677.

83 G. H. Lewes, 'Auguste Comte', *Fortnightly Review*, III (1 January 1866), 407.

84 For an analysis of Coleridge's struggles with Kant in 1803 *see* Orsini, *Coleridge and German Idealism*, pp. 153-4.
    to Green, 13 December 1817. Coleridge *Collected Letters*, IV, 791-2.

85 Coleridge, *Notebooks*, I, 1705. Here Coleridge is making notes from Kant's *Grundlegung zur Metaphysik der Sitten* (1785).

86 Kant, 'Es ist sehr schön, aus Liebe zu Menschen und teilnehmendem Wohlwollen ihnen Gutes zu tun,...aber das ist noch nicht die echte moralische Maxime unsers Verhaltens' (It is very beautiful to do good to men from love for them and from sympathetic good will,...but it is not the true moral maxim of our conduct), *Kritik der praktischen Vernunft*, *Werke*, IV, 204. Coleridge's objection to Kant's 'stoic principle' as 'false, unnatural, and even immoral' was voiced in a letter to Green, 13 December 1817, Coleridge *Collected Letters*, IV, 791-2. A. J. Harding, *Coleridge and the Idea of Love* (Cambridge, 1974), pp. 143, 163-5, deals with this aspect of Coleridge's ethics and his disagreement with Kant.

87 Coleridge, *Aids to Reflection*, 11th edition, ed. Derwent Coleridge (London, 1866), p. 65.

88 Such compound complications are difficult to do justice to, *see* A. O. Lovejoy, 'It is possible – and is not, I think, very uncommon – to harmonise the thought of a reflective writer in such a fashion that what is, historically considered, precisely the most interesting and most noteworthy fact about him – the impact upon him of traditions of differing origins and opposite tendencies, or the dim emergences in his thinking of new ideas destined to be seized upon and made much of by his successors – is wholly concealed', Preface to *Essays in the History of Ideas* (New York, 1948), pp. xiii–xiv. Wellek, *Kant in England*, shows inflexibility on just this point. He adopts a narrow attitude towards Coleridge, De Quincey, Carlyle, and the other English writers he deals with, treating each as if he should have been a second Kant but could only manage to be a poor or grudging imitator.

89 Carlyle, *Reminiscences*, ed. J. A. Froude, 2 vols (London, 1881), I, 230.

90 Orsini points out that much appears under the name of 'Plato' in *The Friend* (1818) that is really Kantian, *Coleridge and German Idealism*, p. 250.

91 13 October 1806, Coleridge, *Collected Letters*, II, 1193, 1198. *See also* a marginal comment on a copy of *The Friend*, I, (1818), 'The term, Understanding, ethically employed, is used here and elsewhere by the Friend as the Faculty of adapting means to ends, in distinction from the Reason, as that by which we pre-determine the final end', Coleridge, *Collected Works*, IV, 442n.

92 *See*, for example, Coleridge's last paragraph in *Biographia*, where he aims to unify all the faculties and see faith as 'but [reason's] continuation', and later where he describes theology as the primary science,

the 'root and trunk' of all knowledge, *On the Constitution of Church and State*, ed. John Colmer, *Collected Works*, x, 47.

93 Coleridge, *Aids*, pp. xv–xvi. For Coleridge on Understanding and Reason in the MS 'Logic' *see* James D. Boulger, *Coleridge as Religious Thinker* (New Haven, Connecticut, 1961), pp. 72ff.

94 *See* Chapter 2.

95 *See* S. M. Vogel, *German Literary Influences on the American Transcendentalists*, pp. 26, 65.

96 *Mill on Bentham and Coleridge*, ed. and with an introduction by F. R. Leavis (London, 1950), pp. 109–10.

97 His ideas of guilt and sin made a personal, loving God, whose incarnation assured forgiveness of sins, necessary to him, Coleridge, *Notebooks*, III, 3510 (April–August 1809). *See also* his 'Confessio Fidei' of 1810, III, 4005, also published in Coleridge, *Literary Remains*, ed. H. N. Coleridge, 4 vols (London, 1836–9), I, 389–95.

98 Unpublished Notebook 30, MS 47,527, f.38 (British Museum), *See also* letter to John Taylor Coleridge, 8 April 1825, Coleridge, *Collected Letters*, v, 421.

99 Letter to Green, 29 March 1832, Coleridge, *Collected Letters*, VI, 895.

100 *See*, for example, Coleridge, *Notebooks*, III, 3605 (August–September 1809). Also, Coleridge, *Aids*, particularly pp. 168, 174.

101 'Selection from Mr. Coleridge's Literary Correspondence', *Blackwood's* x (October 1821), 243–62, and Coleridge, *Collected Letters*, v, 166–71.

102 'Selection from Mr. Coleridge's Literary Correspondence', *Blackwood's*, x, 254 and Coleridge, *Collected Letters*, v, 169.

103 *See* Schiller, *Briefe über die Ästhetische Erziehung des Menschen* (*Letters on the Aesthetic Education of Man*, 1795), *Schillers Werke*, xx, 309ff. Jean Paul [Richter], *Vorschule der Ästhetik* (1804), and Hegel's lectures, collected and published posthumously as *Vorlesungen über die Aesthetik*, ed. D. H. G. Hotho (Berlin, 1835). OED says Baumgarten first used it in this sense in the 1750s. *See* M. H. Abrams, *The Mirror and the Lamp*, on 'Coleridge and the Aesthetics of Organism'.

104 Kant, *Kritik der Urteilskraft* (1790), divided into two parts, 'Kritik der ästhetischen Urteilskraft' and 'Kritik der teleologischen Urteilskraft', *Werke*, v, 279ff.

105 Kant, 'Urteilskraft überhaupt ist das Vermögen, das Besondere als enthalten unter dem Allgemeinen zu denken', *ibid.*, 251.

106 Edward Caird, who also pointed out that the third Critique was an afterthought, not part of Kant's original plan, *The Critical Philosophy of Immanuel Kant*, 2 vols (Glasgow, 1889), I, 232; II, 406.

107 Kant, 'Von der Kunst überhaupt', *Werke*, v, 402.

108 Goethe, 'Als ich die Kantische Lehre, wo nicht zu durchdringen, doch möglichst zu nutzen suchte, wollte mir manchmal dünken, der köstliche Mann verfahre schalkhaft ironisch, indem er bald das Erkenntnisvermögen aufs engste einzuschränken bemüht schien, bald über die Grenzen, die er selbst gezogen hatte, mit einem Seitenwink hinaus-

deutete' (When I tried, if not to penetrate, then at least to make use of the Kantian doctrine, I often began to think that the dear man was dealing ironically, for he first seemed intent on limiting the faculty of knowledge, but then began to suggest, as it were with a sideways gesture, ways of crossing the boundaries he himself had set), essay on 'Anschauende Urteilskraft', *Werke*, xvi, 877–8.

109 10 September 1802, Coleridge, *Collected Letters*, ii, 864–6.

110 There are also two notebook entries of 1809 on Taste and its mediation between Sense and Idea, Coleridge, *Notebooks*, iii, 3584, 3587. *See also Statesman's Manual* (1816), 'Imagination. . .that reconciling and mediating power, which incorporating the Reason in Images of the Sense,. . .gives birth to a system of symbols. . .', Coleridge, *Lay Sermons*, ed. R. J. White, *Collected Works*, vi, 29.

111 Coleridge, *Biographia*, i, 202. For Schiller, following Kant, the 'Einbildungskraft' brings about the cooperation of intuition and understanding, but depends on the laws of the understanding for its operation; it is itself an unconscious function which produces images involuntarily in accordance with the law of association, unless controlled by the understanding. Coleridge separates the 'shaping power' from the involuntary function with his Imagination and Fancy. *See* E. M. Wilkinson and L. A. Willoughby, glossary to their edition with parallel translation of Schiller's *Briefe über die Ästhetische Erziehung des Menschen* (1795), *On the Aesthetic Education of Man* (Oxford, 1967), pp. 306–7.

112 As MacKinnon points out, *Dejection* celebrates the misery of our slavery to a mood of depression, 'Coleridge and Kant', *Coleridge's Variety*, ed. John Beer, pp. 188–9. I. A. Richards takes the psychological implications of Coleridge's theory, based on Hartley, to be the most important part of his work, *Coleridge on Imagination* (London, 1934).

113 Kant, *Werke*, ii, 149.

114 Coleridge, *Biographia*, i, 73.

115 *See*, for example, Coleridge, *Notebooks*, iii, 4498, f. 139 (March 1819) and note.

116 Friedrich Schlegel defined 'Romantic' and 'Classic' in his essays of the 1790s in terms close to Schiller's both before and after reading 'Über naive und sentimentalische Dichtung', *see* A. O. Lovejoy, 'The Meaning of "Romantic" in Early German Romanticism', *Essays in the History of Ideas*, pp. 183–227. A. W. Schlegel classified the characteristics of classical versus modern drama in his lectures *Über dramatische Kunst und Literatur* (1809–10). Jean Paul talked of 'modern' literature as subjective, self-conscious, even parodic, *Vorschule der Ästhetik* (1804).

117 Letter to unknown correspondent, ca. 15–21 December 1811, Coleridge, *Collected Letters*, iii, 360. *See also* Coleridge, *Biographia*, i, 102–3.

118 *See* Thomas McFarland, *Coleridge and the Pantheist Tradition*, Excursus Note 1 on Coleridge and A. W. Schlegel and the aesthetic climate they shared.

119 *Schillers Werke*, xx, 437–8n.

120 *Ibid.*, xx, 473n. In the letters *Über die Ästhetische Erziehung des Menschen* also Schiller discusses man's aesthetic faculty, or Spieltrieb (play-drive), as the necessary middle term reconciling his Formtrieb (form-drive) and his 'Sinnlicher Trieb' (sense-drive), but reminds us that there never was a time when man was at a purely physical stage of development, nor one when he had entirely freed himself from it. The distinction is thus a *theoretical* one. *See* letters xiv and xxv, Wilkinson and Willoughby, *On the Aesthetic Education of Man*, pp. 97, 183n.

121 *See* Chapter 3.

122 Coleridge, *Biographia*, ii, 12. Note from Chapter 1 that Coleridge's aim is twofold, to argue with Wordsworth's prefaces about poetic diction and the *Lyrical Ballads*, and to trace his own poetic, philosophical, and religious studies, deducing from them the theory of the Imagination.

123 *Schillers Werke*, xx, 433.

124 Notes for a lecture in 1813, Coleridge, *Shakespearean Criticism*, ed. T. M. Raysor, 2 vols (London, 1960), i, 69.

125 Coleridge, *Biographia*, ii, 15–16.

126 Letter to John Thelwall, 31 December 1796, Coleridge, *Collected Letters*, i, 294.

127 Letter to Goethe, 31 August 1794, Goethe, *Werke*, xx, 20. Schiller also described modern man with his aching sense of the gulf between his desires and their fulfilment in *Philosophische Briefe* (1784–6), *Schillers Werke*, xx, 112. *See* Erich Heller, *The Disinherited Mind: Essays in Modern German Literature and Thought* (London, 1971), and M. H. Abrams, *Natural Supernaturalism*, two excellent studies of the plight of the Romantic and post-Romantic sensibility.

128 *See* Orsini on Coleridge's essay 'On Poesy or Art' as 'Kantian', *Coleridge and German Idealism*, pp. 167–8. Sara Coleridge answered the first notices of the plagiarisms from Schelling by appealing to Coleridge's method of studying and taking notes without referring to their sources, Coleridge, *Biographia* (1847), p. viii. *See also* Orsini, *Coleridge and German Idealism*, pp. 198ff and McFarland, *Coleridge and the Pantheist Tradition*, pp. 146ff; both give very detailed accounts of Coleridge's debts to Schelling in *Biographia*.

129 *Henry Crabb Robinson on Books*, i, 52, 107.

130 *See* his algebraic caricature of Fichte, letter to Dorothy Wordsworth, 9 February 1801, Coleridge, *Collected Letters*, ii, 673–4; and his absurd poem, Coleridge, *Biographia*, i, 101–2n. Schiller was similarly scornful of Fichte, *see* letter to Goethe, 28 October 1794, Goethe, *Werke*, xx, 37.

131 Ferrier had suggested that Coleridge stopped abruptly in *Biographia* because Schelling himself had no more to say; Sara Coleridge argued Coleridge's illness and lack of ability to concentrate and complete a long argument, Coleridge, *Biographia* (1847), p. xxi. Neither of these explanations is adequate.

132 *See* Coleridge's objection to Schelling on this ground, Coleridge, *Notebooks*, III, 4449 (October 1818) and 4497 (March 1819).

133 Coleridge, *Biographia*, I, 187.

134 *See* the final paragraph of Coleridge, *Biographia*, also *The Friend*, I (1818), Coleridge, *Collected Works*, IV, 515n.

135 Barbara Rooke notices two trends in Coleridge's distinctions: one 'takes the whole into consideration,...the other the limited; one embraces the total personality or situation, the other a part; one makes life an affair of thought infused with feeling, the other subordinates or eliminates one or the other', Introduction to *The Friend*, I, *Collected Works*, IV, cii.

136 The poem 'Human Life', first published in 1817.

137 Letter to Green, 30 September 1818, Coleridge, *Collected Letters*, IV, 874, and letter to Tulk, 24 November 1818, *ibid.*, IV, 883. Coleridge had heard that Schelling was now a Roman Catholic, which helps to account for the vehemence of his antagonism.

138 He retained a 'reverence' for Boehme and Spinoza, defending Boehme as an enthusiast rather than a fanatic, Coleridge, *Biographia*, I, 95–8, and maintaining a double attitude towards Spinoza, admiring but clear-sighted about Spinoza's pantheism, *see* annotations to his copy of F. H. Jacobi, *Ueber die Lehre des Spinoza* (1789), p. xliv (in British Museum), and Coleridge, *Collected Letters*, II, 1196 (1806).

139 Hazlitt, 'Coleridge's Literary Life', *Complete Works*, XVI, 121–3 (*Edinburgh Review*, XXVIII, August 1817).

140 Schelling, *Ueber das Verhältniss der bildenden Künste zu der Natur* (München, 1807), translated as *The Philosophy of Art* by A. Johnson (London, 1845). The *System des transcendentalen Idealismus* (Tübingen, 1800) was first translated by T. Davidson in 1871. B. Q. Morgan and A. R. Hohlfeld, *German Literature in British Magazines, 1750–1860*, record only two brief references to Schelling in periodicals, one in the *Athenaeum* in 1833, the other in the *Dublin University Magazine* in 1845.

141 Hazlitt, 'Lectures on the Age of Elizabeth', *Complete Works*, VI, 302.

142 De Quincey, 'The Poetry of Pope' (1848), *Collected Writings*, XI, 54. De Quincey uses 'reason' and 'understanding' in Coleridge's sense in this essay.

143 Letter to Coleridge, 20 February 1818, E. L. Griggs 'Ludwig Tieck and Samuel Taylor Coleridge', *Journal of English and Germanic Philology*, LIV (April 1955), 266.

144 Only one of Murray's letters about the translation, that of 29 August 1814, is published, Samuel Smiles, *A Publisher and his Friends: Memoir and Correspondence of John Murray*, 2 vols (London, 1891), I, 299–300.

145 Letter of 26 August 1814, *The Letters of Charles Lamb*, ed. E. V. Lucas, 3 vols (London, 1935), II, 135.

146 Coleridge, *Notebooks*, III, 4301.

147 Letter from Lamb to Coleridge, 26 August 1814, Lamb, *Letters*, II, 134.

148 In 1812 he asked Robinson to lend him any works which might keep him in touch with the 'neuere, neueste, und allerneueste Filosophie', in 1821 he commented to Green on one of Kleist's plays, and in 1830 he was still showing an interest in new German works, asking Green about the novels of Hoffmann and Steffens, Coleridge, *Collected Letters*, III, 422; V, 190; VI, 828.

149 *See* Coleridge, *Notebooks*, III, 3685–706. It is chiefly Jean Paul's remarks on marriage which Coleridge notes.

150 Coleridge, *Collected Works*, VI, 42; letter of 8 April 1828, Coleridge, *Collected Letters*, V, 422.

151 *Specimens of the Table Talk of Samuel Taylor Coleridge*, 2nd edition corrected, ed. H. N. Coleridge (London, 1836), p. 199.

152 Coleridge, *Collected Letters*, III, 521–2.

153 *Ibid.*, 522, 523.

154 Samuel Smiles, *A Publisher and his Friends*, I, 299.

155 Coleridge, *Collected Letters*, III, 523–4, 528.

156 *Ibid.*, IV, 562.

157 Letter of 13 August 1812, *Henry Crabb Robinson on Books*, I, 107.

158 Letter of 10 May 1820, Coleridge, *Collected Letters*, V, 43–4. Coleridge's attempted withdrawal from the opium habit in 1814 may help to explain the complex contradictoriness of the letters to Murray at that time.

159 *Ibid.*, V, 43n.

160 Carlyle, 'State of German Literature', *Edinburgh Review*, XLVI (October 1827), 305.

161 Letters of 12 January and 10 April 1822, Shelley, *Letters*, II, 376, 407.

162 No further reference need be made to the vexed problem of Coleridge's plagiarisms from A. W. Schlegel – they clearly exist, though the exact dating and extent of the influence are still undecided, *see* Coleridge, *Notebooks*, III, xviii.

163 *See* Wordsworth's 1800 preface to the *Lyrical Ballads* for the remark about German tragedies and his 1815 *Essay supplementary to the Preface* for his praise of 'the Germans' and their appreciation of Shakespeare. *See also* Hazlitt, 'Characters of Shakespear's Plays' (1817) and 'On the German Drama' (1820), *Complete Works*, IV, 171–4; VI, 360–3. Coleridge was offended that Wordsworth had 'affirmed *in print*, that a German critic *first* taught us to think correctly concerning Shakespeare', lecture of 1818, Coleridge, *Shakespearean Criticism*, II, 245.

164 Lockhart, 'Translations of Goethe's Faust', *Quarterly Review*, XXXIV (June 1826), 140. Statistical studies such as Morgan and Hohlfeld, *German Literature in British Magazines, 1750–1860*, show that interest in German literature generally rose ca. 1815. *See also* F. W. Stokoe, *German Influence in the English Romantic Period, 1788–1818*, and Violet Stockley, *German Literature as Known in England, 1750–1830*.

165 Coleridge wrote to Anster 'as a Son', advising him about his career, 18 February 1824, Coleridge, *Collected Letters*, V, 334.

166 William Taylor, 'Goethe's *Faustus, a Tragedy*', *Monthly Review*, LXII

(August 1810), 492, 495. Taylor wrote to Henry Crabb Robinson, 9 September 1810 '[Goethe] has attained that *divine* morality which looks down on all the forms of human conduct with equal eye, & sees in the lewdness of Faustus...that exact adaptation of effect to cause... which characterises the constitution of things', MS HCR Correspondence (Dr Williams's Library).

167 Thomas Medwin, *Conversations of Lord Byron*, I, 181-2.

168 Hazlitt, *Complete Works*, XII, 313. *See also* Scott's objection to the dramatisation of the Book of Job in the Prologue, J. G. Lockhart, *Memoirs of the Life of Sir Walter Scott, Bart*, 7 vols (Edinburgh, 1837-8), IV, 192-3.

169 Carlyle, 'Goethe's Faust', *New Edinburgh Review*, II, (April 1822), 319.

170 *See* W. E. Houghton, *The Victorian Frame of Mind, 1830-1870* (New Haven, Connecticut, 1957), part 3, chapter 13.

171 Lockhart, 'Translations of Goethe's Faust', *Quarterly Review*, XXXIV (June 1826), 137-8.

172 *See* Sterling, 'Carlyle's Works', *London and Westminster Review*, XXXIII (October 1839), 2-68, and Mill, *Autobiography*, p. 97, and *Collected Works*, XII, 85, 111.

173 Probably 1833, Carlyle MSS (Yale University Library).

174 James White, 'A Discourse on Goethe and the Germans', *Blackwood's Magazine*, XLV (February 1839), 250.

CHAPTER 2

1 Jeffrey, '*Wilhelm Meister's Apprenticeship*, a Novel', *Edinburgh Review*, XLII (August 1825), 414.

2 Lewes, 'Character and Works of Göthe', *British and Foreign Review*, XIV (1843), 78.

3 Carlyle to his brother Jack, 4 June 1827, Carlyle, *Collected Letters*, IV, 228.

4 Crabb Robinson to Goethe, 31 January 1829, Henry Crabb Robinson, *Diary*, II, 390, and Goethe, *Werke*, XIV, 956.

5 Carlyle, 'State of German Literature', *Edinburgh Review* (October 1827), *Works*, XXVI, 28, 35, 37.

6 *Ibid.*, XXVI, 38, 35.

7 Gillies wrote most of the 'Horae Germanicae' articles for *Blackwood's* in the early 1820s. The articles were known to most of his contemporaries, including Byron, Thomas Moore, and Thomas Lovell Beddoes, who mentioned them in their letters and journals. Carlyle's letter was written 2 March 1824, Carlyle, *Collected Letters*, III, 40.

8 *See* Carlyle's letter to Goethe, 18 April 1828, *ibid.*, IV, 364, and to Scott, 13 April 1828, *ibid.*, IV, 354-5.

9 De Quincey's first article on Jean Paul appeared in the *London Magazine*, IV (December 1821), 606ff.

10 This is a marginal comment of Carlyle's on Althaus's biographical essay on him (1866), quoted in part in J. A. Froude, *Thomas Carlyle: A History of the First Forty Years of his Life, 1795–1835*, I, 396.

11 *See* Carlyle, *Collected Letters*, III, 220, and *Henry Crabb Robinson on Books*, I, 319, 347; *see also* Crabb Robinson to Carlyle, 8 May 1825, MS 1765, f. 32 (National Library of Scotland).

12 Letter of 21 January 1831, Carlyle, *Collected Letters*, V, 213.

13 Letter of 22 January 1831, *ibid.*, 220.

14 Lockhart, 'Memoirs of William Taylor, of Norwich', *Quarterly Review*, LXXIII (December 1843), 33–4.

15 Letter of 25 October 1843, Jane Welsh Carlyle, *Letters to her Family, 1839–63*, ed. Leonard Huxley (London, 1924), p. 160.

16 *Fraser's Magazine*, III (March 1831), 127ff.

17 Letters of 22 January 1831 and 10 June 1831, Carlyle, *Collected Letters*, V, 219–20, 288–9.

18 Letters of 21 March and 1 May 1833, *ibid.*, VI, 350, 377.

19 *See* Carlyle, *Collected Letters*, IV, 300n.

20 *Ibid.*, IV, 245n, Froude, *Thomas Carlyle: 1795–1835*, II, 39 and letters of Jeffrey to Carlyle, MS 787 (National Library of Scotland).

21 Carlyle, 'State of German Literature', *Works*, XXVI, 70.

22 *Ibid.*, 76, 72, 81.

23 *Ibid.*, 76ff. *See* my discussion of Carlyle and German philosophy below.

24 Letter to Thomas Murray, 4 August 1820, Carlyle, *Collected Letters*, I, 268.

25 *See* Carlyle, *Sartor Resartus*, Book III, Chapter viii, entitled 'Natural Supernaturalism', in which Carlyle gives an idealist view of the mystery and miracles in Nature. Abrams took the phrase as the title of his book, as representative of the secularisation of religious belief in the works of the German and English Romantics.

26 Leslie Stephen, 'Carlyle's Ethics', *Hours in a Library*, new enlarged edition, 3 vols (London, 1872), III, 277.

27 Heinrich Heine, *Die Romantische Schule* (1833), Book II, *Werke und Briefe*, ed. Hans Kaufmann, 10 vols (Berlin, 1961–4), V, 89.

28 Carlyle, *Life of Sterling* (1851), *Works*, XI, 56.

29 For a list of parallelisms between 'Wotton Reinfred' and *Sartor*, *see* C. F. Harrold's edition of *Sartor Resartus* (Michigan, 1937), p. 318.

30 'Wotton Reinfred', *Last Words of Thomas Carlyle* (London, 1892), pp. 80–1, and Carlyle to his brother Jack, 22 January 1825, Carlyle, *Collected Letters*, III, 260.

31 Carlyle, *Last Words*, pp. 102–4.

32 Carlyle, *Works*, XXVII, 59, 65, 58, 68. *See also* 'Characteristics', where he attacks 'your frightful theory of Materialism' and 'the fever of Scepticism', *ibid.*, XXVIII, 4, 40.

33 Carlyle, *Foreign Review* (1829), *Works*, XXVII, 3.

34 *See* Coleridge to H. F. Cary, 6 February 1818, on Blake: 'You perhaps smile at *my* calling another Poet, a *Mystic*; but verily I am in the

very mire of common-place common-sense compared with Mr Blake, apo- or rather ana-calyptic Poet and Painter!' Coleridge, *Collected Letters*, IV, 834; on Boehme *see* Coleridge, *Biographia Literaria*, I, 95–8.

35 Letter of 18 July 1833, Carlyle, *Collected Letters*, VI, 413.
36 Jeffrey to Carlyle in 1827, quoted in Carlyle, *Collected Letters*, IV, 245n.
37 Jeffrey to Carlyle, 27 June 1828, MS 787 (National Library of Scotland), and Carlyle to James Johnston, quoting Jeffrey, 19 November 1827, Carlyle, *Collected Letters*, IV, 278.
38 Letter to Mrs Montagu, 17 August 1828, Carlyle, *Collected Letters*, IV, 390.
39 Carlyle, *Works*, XXVI, 51, 55.
40 Letter of 18 April 1828, Carlyle, *Collected Letters*, IV, 364–5.
41 *See* D. F. S. Scott, 'English Visitors to Weimar', *German Life and Letters*, II new series (1948–9), 330–41.
42 Letter of 20 December 1824, Carlyle, *Collected Letters*, III, 236.
43 William Allingham, *A Diary*, ed. H. Allingham and D. Radford (London, 1907), p. 79.
44 Letter of 20 July 1827, Goethe, *Werke*, XXI, 745.
45 Carlyle, *Collected Letters*, IV, 165, 245.
46 Carlyle described the house so in a letter to Goethe, 23 May 1830, *ibid.*, V, 104.
47 Goethe to Carlyle, 1 January 1828, *Correspondence between Goethe and Carlyle*, ed. C. E. Norton (London, 1887), p. 38. (This letter is not published in the Gedenkausgabe of Goethe's works.)
48 *New Letters of Thomas Carlyle*, ed. Alex. Carlyle, 2 vols (London, 1904), II, 319.
49 Letter to John Fergusson, 4 October 1821, Carlyle, *Collected Letters*, I, 389.
50 *Ibid.*, IV, 360.
51 *The George Eliot Letters*, II, 185.
52 Varnhagen to Carlyle, 22 June 1837, Rodger L. Tarr, 'Some Unpublished Letters of Varnhagen von Ense to Thomas Carlyle', *Modern Language Review*, LXVIII (January 1973), 23.
53 Varnhagen von Ense's diary, 1 October 1852, *Aus dem Nachlass Varnhagen's von Ense, Tagebücher*, ed. Ludmilla Assing, 15 vols (Leipzig, Hamburg, Zürich, 1861–70, Berlin, 1905), IX, 374.
54 Letter of 13 March 1853, MS Egerton 3032 (British Museum).
55 Sterling, 'Carlyle's Works', *London and Westminster Review*, XXXIII (October 1839), 27.
56 G. H. Lewes, 'Character and Works of Göthe', *British and Foreign Review*, XIV (1843), 128.
57 Letters of 25 August 1819, 29 March and 19 April 1820, Carlyle, *Collected Letters*, I, 193, 236, 240.
58 Letter of 3 June 1820, *ibid.*, 254–5.
59 To Alex. Carlyle, 12 January 1822, *ibid.*, II, 9.
60 Carlyle, 'Goethe's *Faust*', *New Edinburgh Review*, II (April 1822), 330.

This article was not included by Traill in his edition of Carlyle's works.

61 Bulwer Lytton compared Disraeli's *Contarini Fleming* with *Wilhelm Meister*, in both of which 'the Author is often allegorical and actual at the same time', 'Asmodeus at Large', *New Monthly Magazine*, xxxv (July 1832), 27. *See* Susanne Howe, *Wilhelm Meister and his English Kinsmen; apprentices to life* (New York, 1930), chapter vi, for the effect of *Wilhelm Meister* on Bulwer Lytton's novel theory and practice.

62 Letter of 25 March 1825, Thomas Lovell Beddoes, *Letters*, p. 61.

63 *See* Carlyle, *Collected Letters*, ii, 434, 437, and *Two Note Books*, ed. C. E. Norton (New York, 1898), p. 32; and Novalis (Freiherr Friedrich von Hardenberg): 'Göthe ist ganz practischer Dichter. . .So ist Wilhelm Meister ganz ein Kunstproduct – ein Werck des Verstandes' ('Goethe is a. . .quite practical writer. . .Thus *Wilhelm Meister* is an artificial product – a work of the understanding'), 'Über Goethe', *Schriften*, ed. P. Kluckhohn and R. Samuel, 4 vols– (Stuttgart, 1960–), ii, 640, 641.

64 To Jane, 18 September 1823, and to James Johnston, 21 September 1823, Carlyle, *Collected Letters*, ii, 434, 437.

65 Coleridge, *Confessions of an Inquiring Spirit*, ed. H. N. Coleridge (1849), Letter i; *Henry Crabb Robinson on Books*, i, 309.

66 Carlyle, *Works*, xxiii, 6.

67 Schiller thought the *Hamlet* criticism too long and suggested Goethe intersperse it with some action, and he criticised the theatrical part of Book v as disproportionate to the larger idea of the work, 22 February and 15 June 1795, Goethe, *Werke*, xx, 62, 85.

68 Conversation with von Müller, 22 January 1821, *ibid.*, xxiii, 119.

69 Carlyle, *Works*, xxiii, 10. For Carlyle's tendency to heaviness in his translation *see* Howe, *Wilhelm Meister and his English Kinsmen*, p. 102, and for his toning down of suggestive references, particularly in connection with the flirt Philina *see* C. T. Carr, 'Carlyle's Translations from German', *Modern Language Review*, xlii (1947), 223ff.

70 De Quincey, '*Wilhelm Meister's Appenticeship*', *London Magazine*, x (August 1824), 190.

71 See Friedrich Schlegel, *Athenäum* (1798), *Kritische Friedrich-Schlegel-Ausgabe*, ii, 126–46, and *Heidelbergische Jahrbücher*, ii (1808), 166–7, for defences of Goethe against such criticisms. Carlyle quotes Friedrich Schlegel in the preface: '"To judge", says he, "of this book, – new and peculiar as it is, and only to be understood and learned from itself, by our common notion of the novel, a notion pieced together and produced out of custom and belief, out of accidental and arbitrary requisitions, – is as if a child should grasp at the moon and stars, and insist on packing them into its toy-box"', Carlyle, *Works*, xxiii, 7.

72 Conversation with Eckermann, 25 December 1825, Goethe, *Werke*, xxiv, 166.

73 Henry James, 'Carlyle's Translation of Goethe's *Wilhelm Meister*',

North American Review (July 1865); *Literary Reviews and Essays by Henry James*, ed. Albert Mordell (New York, 1957), pp. 267–8.

74 Carlyle, *Works*, XXIII, 6.
75 Carlyle, 'Goethe's Works', *Foreign Quarterly Review* (August 1832), *Works*, XXVII, 422.
76 Goethe, *Wilhelm Meisters Lehrjahre*, Book I, Chapter v, *Werke*, VII, 22–3, and Carlyle, *Works*, XXIII, 48–9.
77 Goethe, *Wilhelm Meisters Lehrjahre*, Book I, Chapter xiv, *Werke*, VII, 56, and Carlyle, *Works*, XXIII, 81–2.
78 The first verse of the Goethe poem is as follows:

> Kennst du das Land, wo die Citronen blühn,
> Im dunklen Laub die Gold-Orangen glühn,
> Ein sanfter Wind vom blauen Himmel weht,
> Die Myrte still und hoch der Lorbeer steht –
> Kennst du es wohl?
> Dahin! Dahin!
> Möcht ich mit dir, o mein Geliebter, ziehn!

Carlyle translates this:

> Know'st thou the land where citron-apples bloom,
> And oranges like gold in leafy gloom,
> A gentle wind from deep blue heaven blows,
> The myrtle thick, and high the laurel grows?
> Knowst thou it then?
> 'Tis there! 'tis there!
> O my true lov'd one, thou with me must go!

Coleridge's version is closer in sense to the original and moves more smoothly (he translated only the first verse):

> Know'st thou the land where the pale citrons grow?
> The golden fruits in darker foliage glow?
> Soft blows the wind that breathes from that blue sky!
> Still stands the myrtle and the laurel high!
> Know'st thou it well, that land, beloved Friend?
> Thither with thee, O, thither would I wend!

79 Letter of 15 November 1830, Carlyle, *Collected Letters*, V, 194.
80 Carlyle, 'Faust's Curse [from Goethe]', *Athenaeum*, 7 January 1832, p. 5.
81 Carlyle, *Collected Letters*, II, 118ff. Carlyle was critical of other translators; he referred to Tytler's 1792 version of *Die Räuber* as 'a yeasty vehicle', to Charles Des Voeux's *Tasso* as 'trivial', and Coleridge's *Wallenstein* was merely 'the only sufferable translation from the German with which our literature has yet been enriched'. *See* Carlyle, 'Schiller', *Fraser's Magazine*, III (March 1831), 146, *Collected Letters*, IV, 366, and *Life of Schiller*, *Works*, XXV, 151n.
82 Richard Holt Hutton, essay on Emerson (1882), *Criticisms on Contemporary Thought and Thinkers*, 2 vols (London, 1894), I, 46.

83 Letter of 25 November 1839, MS 531 (National Library of Scotland).
84 Carlyle, Preface to *Wilhelm Meister* and *Collected Letters*, II, 59.
85 James, *Literary Reviews and Essays*, p. 267.
86 Letters to Sterling, 29 September 1839, and to Geraldine Jewsbury, 26 April 1840, MSS 531 and 3823 (National Library of Scotland).
87 Carlyle, 'Goethe's Works', *Works*, XXVII, 438.
88 Carlyle, *Two Note Books*, pp. 31, 56–7, in which he quotes Goethe's advice in *Wilhelm Meisters Lehrjahre*, Book VII, Chapter i, *Werke*, VII. Carlyle adopted the phrase as a motto which he often used to encourage himself and others.
89 Letter of 20 August 1827, Carlyle, *Collected Letters*, IV, 248.
90 Letter of 3 March 1858, *New Letters of Thomas Carlyle*, II, 189.
91 Carlyle, 'Gallery of Literary Characters. No. XXII. The Baron von Goethe', *Fraser's Magazine* (March 1832), *Works*, XXVII, 372.
92 Carlyle, 'Goethe', *Foreign Review* (1828), *Works*, XXVI, 208. *See also* Carlyle, 'Death of Goethe', *New Monthly Magazine* (June 1832), *Works*, XXVII, 374–84.
93 Carlyle, *Works*, I, 128–57.
94 Letter to Zelter, 3 December 1812, Goethe, *Werke*, XIX, 681.
95 *See* C. F. Harrold, *Carlyle and German Thought: 1819–34* (New Haven, Connecticut, 1934, reprinted London, 1963), pp. 214ff, and C. E. Vaughan, 'Carlyle and His German Masters', *Essays and Studies*, I (1910), 168–96.
96 Goethe, *Wilhelm Meisters Lehrjahre*, Book VIII, *Werke*, VII.
97 Carlyle, 'Goethe's *Works*', *Foreign Quarterly Review* (August 1832), *Works*, XXVII, 435.
98 Carlyle, *Works*, I, 181–2.
99 *Letters of Matthew Arnold*, ed. G. W. E. Russell, 2 vols (London, 1895), II, 144.
100 Letter to Carlyle, 17 September 1832, Mill, *Earlier Letters, Collected Works*, XII, 118–19.
101 Carlyle, 'Death of Goethe', *New Monthly Magazine* (June 1832), *Works*, XXVII, 375.
102 *Henry Crabb Robinson on Books*, I, 402, and Holt Hutton, reviewing Lewes's *Life of Goethe*, *Essays Theological and Literary*, 2nd edition, 2 vols (London, 1877), II, 8.
103 *See*, for example, John Morley, 'Carlyle', *Fortnightly Review*, VIII new series (1 July 1870), 3, where he quotes Lewes's dedication in the *Life of Goethe*: 'It was he, as has been said, "who first taught England to appreciate Goethe;" and not only to appreciate Goethe, but to recognise and seek yet further knowledge of the genius and industry of Goethe's countrymen'.
104 G. H. Lewes, *Life and Works of Goethe*, 2 vols (London, 1855), II, 375, and *British and Foreign Review*, XIV, 111–12.
105 *See* Preface to the 2nd edition of the *Life of Goethe* (1864), and George Eliot, *The George Eliot Letters*, III, 274 and V, 218.
106 Lewes, 'Character and Works of Göthe', *British and Foreign Review*, XIV, 80.

107 *See* Carlyle, 'Jean Paul Friedrich Richter', *Foreign Review* (1830), 'Biography', *Fraser's Magazine* (April 1832), and 'Goethe's *Works*', *Foreign Quarterly Review* (August 1832), *Works*, XXVII, 96ff; XXVIII, 44ff, and XXVII, 385ff.

108 Carlyle, *Life of Schiller, Works*, XXV, 43.

109 Schiller, 'Die Schaubühne als eine moralische Anstalt betrachtet' ('The stage regarded as a moral institution', 1784), *Sämtliche Werke*, Säkular-Ausgabe, XI, 97.

110 *See*, for example, Schiller, 'Über die tragische Kunst' ('On tragic art', 1792), 'Über das Pathetische' ('On the pathetic', 1793), 'Über das Erhabene' ('On the sublime', 1801), *Werke*, Nationalausgabe, XX, 148ff, 196ff, XXI, 38ff. *See also* Schiller, 'Über die Ästhetische Erziehung des Menschen' ('On the aesthetic education of man', 1795), Letters XIV and XV, *ibid.*, XX, 352ff.

111 He defended *Die Jungfrau*, a romantic distortion of history in which the plot is overloaded with supernatural devices and improbable events, praising the beauty of the sentiment and 'the mere human grandeur of Joanna's spirit.' In Wilhelm Tell he found the 'simple yeoman', the man without education but with a natural nobility, a type which Carlyle particularly admired – we meet it again in *Sartor* with Teufelsdröckh's 'noble peasant' who tills the earth for the good of mankind, and in his reminiscence of his father, the Scottish peasant noted for his devotion to duty, honesty, and industriousness, Carlyle, *Works*, I, 181, and *Reminiscences*, I, 1ff.

112 To Jane, 27 September 1826, Carlyle, *Collected Letters*, IV, 137, and *Two Note Books*, pp. 112-13.

113 Annotation to his copy of the *Kritik, see* Orsini, *Coleridge and German Idealism*, p. 99.

114 Carlyle, *Two Note Books*, p. 46.

115 Carlyle, *Life of Schiller, Works*, XXV, 108.

116 Carlyle, *Two Note Books*, p. 51.

117 Carlyle, *Works*, XXV, 114.

118 Carlyle, 'Schiller', *Fraser's Magazine* (March 1831), *Works*, XXVII, 211.

119 S. H. Nobbe, 'Four Unpublished Letters of Thomas Carlyle', *Publications of the Modern Language Association of America*, LXX (September 1955), 880, and Francis Espinasse, *Literary Recollections*, p. 59.

120 George Eliot, 'Thomas Carlyle', *Leader* (1855), *Essays*, p. 215.

121 Espinasse, *Literary Recollections*, p. 66; Alex. Carlyle, 'Thomas Carlyle and Thomas Spedding', *Cornhill Magazine*, L new series (May 1921), 513ff; C. R. Sanders, 'The Correspondence and Friendship of Thomas Carlyle and Leigh Hunt', *Bulletin of the John Rylands Library*, XLV (March 1963), 465; and *The Journals and Miscellaneous Notebooks of Ralph Waldo Emerson*, ed. W. H. Gilman and A. R. Ferguson, 9 vols– (Cambridge, Mass., 1960–), IV, 302. Emerson soon grew more critical, *see* Emerson, *Journals*, V, 111.

122 René Wellek, among others, has pointed out the inconsistencies – the journal comments, the figure of Dalbrook, the ambiguities in the *Life of Schiller*, and the praise of Kant's 'iron strictness' of reasoning in

the 'State of German Literature' article. Wellek notices Carlyle's admission in the article that he has only a poor knowledge of Kant, but he draws the wrong conclusion when he supposes that Carlyle 'knew more about Kant than he cared to say in a popular essay', and that the admissions of lack of knowledge 'cannot exonerate him from the charge of confusing all the German idealists and misinterpreting an essential part of Kant's doctrine in a way which cannot be justified as mere popularization', *Kant in England*, pp. 183ff, 193. Far from knowing more than he wanted to say in an *Edinburgh* article, Carlyle really knew too little to be able to say more. The misinterpretations were genuine, not deliberately expressed in order not to frighten the empirical British reader of the *Edinburgh* by too much transcendental or 'mystical' philosophy. Of course Carlyle was acting as the champion of German literature and might wish to seem publicly more enthusiastic about Kant than he showed himself to be in his journal. But it is not a simple matter of the private view on the one hand and the public image on the other.

123 Carlyle, *Works*, XXVI, 78, 83, 81–2.
124 Novalis, 'Der ächte philosophische Act ist Selbsttödtung; dies ist der reale Anfang aller Philosophie, dahin geht alles Bedürfniss des philosophischen Jüngers, und nur dieser Act entspricht allen Bedingungen und Merckmalen der transscendenten Handlung' ('The real philosophical act is self-annihilation; this is the true beginning of all philosophy, this is what the disciple of philosophy needs, and this is the only act which corresponds to the character and conditions of transcendent action'), 'Fragmentblatt', *Novalis Schriften*, II, 395.
125 *See Glauben und Liebe (Faith and Love*, 1798), written to celebrate the accession of Friedrich Wilhelm III and Luise, *ibid.*, II, 475ff.
126 He confided in his journal that he found Novalis 'unfathomable', Carlyle, *Two Note Books*, pp. 135ff.
127 Carlyle, *Works*, XXVII, 5.
128 *Ibid.*, 21–2.
129 *Ibid.*, 23. For Carlyle and Fichte *see* C. F. Harrold, *Carlyle and German Thought*, pp. 101ff, 165ff.
130 *See Novalis Schriften*, II, 104ff.
131 Kant's discussion of Time and Space as 'reine Formen aller sinnlichen Anschauung' ('pure forms of sensible intuition') comes at the beginning of the *Kritik*. The argument is difficult, and clearly Carlyle did not grasp the fact that Kant does not deny 'empirische Realität' to the two forms of perception but only 'absolute and transzendentale', Kant, *Werke*, II, 83–6.
132 Carlyle, *Works*, XXVII, 26. Carlyle admitted in his journal in 1830 that he 'only half' understood Kant on Time and Space, *Two Note Books*, p. 161.
133 Teufelsdröckh's student days are so described, Carlyle, *Works*, I, 90.
134 Carlyle, *Two Note Books*, p. 150.
135 *Henry Crabb Robinson on Books*, II, 593.
136 The main difference is the worship of Reason as an intuitive visionary

power. *See* Emerson's lecture of 1842, 'The Transcendentalist', in which he says, 'what is popularly Transcendentalism among us, is Idealism', and the transcendentalist 'believes in miracle, in the perpetual openness of the human mind to new influx of light and power; he believes in inspiration, and in ecstasy', *Works*, Riverside Edition, 12 vols (Boston, Mass., 1894), I, 311, 317.

137 Frothingham, *Transcendentalism in New England*, p. 94.
138 Spencer wrote this in a notebook 'About Carlyle' (1882 or 1883), MS 791/355/4 (University of London Library). *See also* a similar comment, Herbert Spencer, *Autobiography*, 2 vols (London, 1904), I, 380, 381.
139 Mill, *Autobiography*, p. 105.
140 Letter to Carlyle, 7 April 1838, MS 1796, f. 52 (National Library of Scotland).
141 Frothingham, *Transcendentalism*, p. 52.
142 *See* Harrold, *Carlyle and German Thought*, p. 8.
143 Letter to Zelter, 20 August 1831, *Briefwechsel zwischen Goethe und Zelter in den Jahren 1796 bis 1832*, ed. F. W. Riemer, 6 vols (Berlin, 1833–4), VI, 259. (This letter is not published in the Gedenkausgabe of Goethe's works.)
144 Edward Lytton Bulwer, *England and the English*, 2 vols (London, 1833), II, 171.
145 Carlyle, 'Goethe's *Works*', *Foreign Quarterly Review* (August 1832) and 'Schiller', *Fraser's Magazine* (March 1831).
146 Carlyle, journal of October 1831, *Two Note Books*, p. 203, and letter to Sarah Austin, 18 July 1833, Janet Ross, *Three Generations of Englishwomen*, I, 78.
147 Letter to his mother, 5 August 1834, Carlyle, *Collected Letters*, VII, 258, and *Two Note Books*, pp. 81, 152, 276.
148 To Jack, 26 November 1828, and to Eckermann just before the move to London, 6 May 1834, Carlyle, *Collected Letters*, IV, 423; VII, 144.
149 Carlyle, *Works*, I, 153, 25, 28, 91. For a detailed study of his German sources for *Sartor see* Harrold, *Carlyle and German Thought*, pp. 79ff. *See also* Harrold's introduction and notes to *Sartor*, and the thorough, rather over-systematic study by G. B. Tennyson, *'Sartor' Called 'Resartus', the Genesis, Structure, and Style of Thomas Carlyle's First Major Work* (Princeton, New Jersey, 1965).
150 Carlyle, *Works*, I, 43.
151 *Ibid.*, I, 49, 211, 95.
152 *Ibid.*, I, 154. For the importance of Carlyle's idea of symbolism, *see* M. H. Abrams, *Natural Supernaturalism*, pp. 36ff.
153 Leigh Hunt confessed that he was 'mystified', Sanders, 'The Correspondence and Friendship of Thomas Carlyle and Leigh Hunt', *Bulletin of the John Rylands Library*, XLV (March 1963), 464; Mill said in his *Autobiography* that when he read *Sartor* in manuscript he 'made little of it', p. 105.
154 Carlyle, *Works*, XXVIII, 40–1.
155 *Ibid.*, I, 3.

156 *Ibid.*, I, 62–3.

157 Mill to Carlyle, 5 September 1833, Mill, *Earlier Letters, Collected Works*, XII, 176, and Carlyle to Mill, 24 September 1833, Carlyle, *Collected Letters*, VI, 449. Mill likewise advised Carlyle to omit his other German professor, Sauerteig, from the 'Chartism' pamphlet in 1839, Mill, *Collected Works*, XIII, 414.

158 Sterling to Carlyle, 29 May 1835, Carlyle, *Life of Sterling, Works*, XI, 113.

159 *Henry Crabb Robinson on Books*, I, 440, 556.

160 Espinasse, *Literary Recollections*, p. 57, and Amelia H. Stirling, *James Hutchison Stirling: his life and work* (London and Leipzig, 1912), p. 48.

161 Draft of a letter to Carlyle, 30 November 1839, Carlyle MSS (Yale University Library).

162 Carlyle to Geraldine Jewsbury, 12 April 1840, MS 3823, f. 71 (National Library of Scotland), and 26 April 1840, Nobbe, 'Four Unpublished Letters of Thomas Carlyle', *Publications of the Modern Language Association of America*, LXX, 879.

163 Letter of 6 May 1834, Carlyle, *Collected Letters*, VII, 142–3.

CHAPTER 3

1 G. H. Lewes, *The Life of Goethe*, I, 42n.

2 Lewes, 'Our Continental Pantheon. No. III. K. A. Varnhagen von Ense', *British Miscellany*, I, 235.

3 Lewes's copy of Hegel's *Vorlesungen über die Aesthetik*, ed. D. H. G. Hotho, 3 vols (Berlin, 1835), inscribed 'The pencil marks throughout are by Varnhagen von Ense, who gave me the work' (I, v), and heavily annotated in preparation for the articles, is in Dr Williams's Library.

4 *See* Gordon S. Haight, 'The Carlyles and the Leweses', *Carlyle and his Contemporaries*, ed. John Clubbe (Durham, North Carolina, 1976), pp. 181–204.

5 J. S. Blackie, 'Germany – by Charles Julius Weber', *Blackwood's Magazine*, XLVIII (July 1840), 120.

6 For example, George Moir, translator of *Wallenstein* in 1827, contributor on German literature to *Blackwood's Magazine*, and avowed pupil of Carlyle, as is evident from his letters to Carlyle (National Library of Scotland); Abraham Hayward, who translated *Faust* in 1833; and Sarah Austin, translator and populariser of German literature, particularly Goethe, and friend of Sterling and Mill, to whom she taught German, *see* Mill, *Collected Works*, XII, 10n.

7 Mill, *Autobiography*, p. 97. *See also* Mill's famous article in the *Westminster Review* (1840) on Coleridge, reprinted with its companion essay on Bentham and with an introduction by Leavis, as *Mill on Bentham and Coleridge*, pp. 108–9.

8 Matthew Arnold, *Complete Prose Works*, X, 166.

9 Sterling, 'Carlyle's Works', *London and Westminster Review*, XXXIII (October 1839), 23.

10 Carlyle published some of the letters in his *Life of Sterling* (1851), *Works*, XI; others are published by Anna K. Tuell, *John Sterling, a Representative Victorian* (New York, 1941). *See also A Correspondence between John Sterling and Ralph Waldo Emerson.* Many more letters are in the National Library of Scotland.

11 *See* Mill's diary for 6 February 1954, published by Hugh Elliot, *Letters of John Stuart Mill*, 2 vols (London, 1910), II, 368, and Matthew Arnold's letter to his sister in December 1877, *Letters of Matthew Arnold*, II, 144.

12 Lewes, 'Character and Works of Göthe', *British and Foreign Review*, XIV (1843), 80.

13 Leslie Stephen, *Studies of a Biographer*, 4 vols (London, 1898-1902), II, 71.

14 Leslie Stephen, 'Coleridge' (1888), *Hours in a Library*, III, 367.

15 To Julius Charles Hare in 1836, *see* Hare's introduction to his edition of Sterling's *Essays and Tales*, 2 vols (London, 1848), I, xv; also Tuell, *John Sterling*, p. 242.

16 Tuell, *John Sterling*, pp. 262, 261.

17 Sterling, 'On Coleridge's Christabel', reprinted in *Essays and Tales*, I, 101.

18 Lewes chides Coleridge for his abuse of Hobbes in his marginalia to his copy of *The Friend*, ed. H. N. Coleridge, 3 vols (London, 1837), I, 36, and again for his attack on Voltaire, I, 172-3 (Dr Williams's Library).

19 Lewes, marginalia to *The Friend*, III, 107.

20 Lewes paid tribute to Coleridge and Schelling, from whom Coleridge 'borrowed' the idea, for introducing him to the theory of life, and particularly of individuation, Lewes, *Comte's Philosophy of the Sciences* (London, 1853), pp. 167-8.

21 Lewes, 'The Student', *National Magazine*, I (August, September, and November 1837), 4, 97, 323-4, 328.

22 *See* Lewes, 'Hints towards an Essay on the Sufferings of Truth', *Monthly Repository*, I (1837), 311-19, where Lewes again uses Tissot for Kant.

23 A reviewer of his *Study of Psychology* made this appropriate comment, *Athenaeum*, 27 September 1879, p. 398.

24 Lewes to Hunt, 3 October 1838, MS letter (Keats Memorial House, Hampstead).

25 This is an allusion to a life of Shelley which he never finished; nor did he ever publish the *Tasso* translation.

26 To Leigh Hunt, 15 November 1838, MS Add. 38,523, f. 182 (British Museum).

27 Lewes, 'Hegel's Aesthetics', *British and Foreign Review*, XIII (1842), 1-2. He had already made a similar plea for the absorption of German ideas into English reviewing in an article on Leigh Hunt in the *Monthly Chronicle* in March 1840.

28 Lewes, *Ranthorpe* (London, 1847), Chapters 5–10; Goethe, *Wilhelm Meisters Lehrjahre*, Books i–v, *Werke*, vii. *See also* the amusing wrangle between poet, theatre manager, and merry andrew in the Prologue in the Theatre to *Faust*, part one, *Werke*, v. As for Lewes's own experience, there is a sharp exchange in letters between him and his actor-manager Charles Kean in 1852 about a melodrama, *Mont St. Michel*, on which Lewes had collaborated with a Mr Bernard and which Kean was producing at the Princess Theatre, and the misunderstandings which had arisen between them, MS letter in Osborn Files (Yale University Library).

29 Goethe, *Wilhelm Meisters Lehrjahre*, Book ii, Chapter 14, and Lewes, *Ranthorpe*, heading to Book ii.

30 Lewes, *Ranthorpe*, p. 350.

31 *Ibid.*, heading to Chapter 10.

32 *Ibid.*, p. 171.

33 Goethe gives impartial portraits of artists, businessmen, and wise men in both parts of *Wilhelm Meister*. Lewes may also have had Comte's classification of a positive society in mind, as well as his programme of initiation into positivist belief from the metaphysical stage of education. For assessments of Lewes's novels *see* Susanne Howe, *Wilhelm Meister and his English Kinsmen*, pp. 220ff, and Anna T. Kitchel, *George Lewes and George Eliot; a review of records* (New York, 1933), pp. 51ff.

34 Lewes, 'Prospectus of an intended course of lectures on the philosophy of humbug. By Professor Wolfgang von Bibundtücker', *Bentley's Miscellany*, vi (1839), 599; 'Aesthetical Considerations on the World-Drama, revealed in the Popular Poem of "The Milkmaid's Courtship". By Herr Wolfgang von Bibundtücker', with a 'Note by the Translator', *British Miscellany*, i (April 1841), 185–8. Lewes repeated the second sketch in the *Monthly Magazine*, vii new series (February 1842), 148–51.

35 Lewes, 'Hegel's Aesthetics', *British and Foreign Review*, xiii (1842), 1–2, 2–3.

36 Mill to Lewes, 24 April 1841, Mill, *Collected Works*, xiii, 470.

37 Lewes to Napier, 11 November 1841, MS Add. 34,622, f. 269–70 (British Museum).

38 Mill to Kemble, 7 May 1841, Mill, *Collected Works*, xiii, 475–6. Mill also furnished Lewes with introductions to Cousin, Comte, and De Tocqueville (in 1842) and to J. W. Parker (in 1844), who published Lewes's *Biographical History of Philosophy*, 4 vols (London, 1845–6), *see* Mill, *Collected Works*, xiii, 517, 527, 537, 627.

39 *See* Alice R. Kaminsky, *George Henry Lewes as Literary Critic* (New York, 1968), p. 47, where she points out that the article is 'a potpourri of quotations from many sources, and it suffers as well from the confusion resulting from his use of Hegelian terminology in a positivistic sense'.

40 Lewes, 'Hegel's Aesthetics', *British and Foreign Review*, xiii, 5, and Coleridge, *Biographia Literaria*, Chapter 14.

41 Wordsworth's chief confusion in his Preface (1800) to *Lyrical Ballads* stems from this distinction and the corollary aim to discuss the language of poetry as no different from that of prose. Coleridge takes issue with Wordsworth in *Biographia*, but gets into hot water in Chapter 14 when he tries to differentiate 'poetry' from 'poem' – 'a poem of any length neither can be, nor ought to be, all poetry'. Coleridge changes tack here and begins to write brilliantly about the poet's activity, but he here hints at a double definition of poetry which is not unlike Hegel's own – i.e. poetry as abstract (the sensuous utterance of Spirit) and poetry as concrete (the metrical utterance of emotion).

42 Lewes, 'Hegel's Aesthetics', *British and Foreign Review*, XIII, 9, 15, 11, 14, 18, 23, 24–5.

43 *Ibid.*, 8–9.

44 Hegel, *Vorlesungen über die Aesthetik*, I, 74ff, 'Historische Deduktion des wahren Begriffs der Kunst' (Historical Deduction of the true Concept of Art).

45 T. M. Knox, Preface to his translation of the *Aesthetics*, 2 vols (Oxford, 1975), I, viii. This is only the second complete translation of the work, the first being by F. P. B. Osmaston, *Hegel's Philosophy of Fine Art*, 4 vols (London, 1916–20).

46 For example on Schlegel, Lewes, 'Augustus William Schlegel', *Foreign Quarterly Review*, XXXII (October 1843).

47 *See* his chapter on Hegel in the *Biographical History of Philosophy*, discussed below.

48 Letter to Bain, 4 November 1867, Mill, *Collected Works*, XVI, 1324.

49 Hegel, *Aesthetik*, I, 74. The translation is mine, but *see also* Knox, *Aesthetics*, I, 56. For a lucid account of Hegel's inheritance from Kant, *see* John Casey's review of Knox's translation, 'Beauty, Truth and Necessity', *Times Literary Supplement*, 2 January 1976.

50 Hegel, 'Das höhere Erfassen der wahren Einheit von Nothwendigkeit und Freiheit, Besonderem und Allgemeinem, Sinnlichem und Vernünftigem', *Aesthetik* (Introduction), I, 80.

51 Lewes, 'Hegel's Aesthetics', *British and Foreign Review*, XIII, 45.

52 Hegel, *Aesthetik*, I, 11–12. The translation is mine but *see also* Knox, *Aesthetics*, I, 7–8.

53 *Ibid.*, I, 16. *See also* Knox, *Aesthetics*, I, 11.

54 He wrote in the margin opposite the latter passage, 'Here I presume to differ – we are here as wide as the poles asunder but I think Hegel is not strictly logical from his *standpunkt aus* – see p. 11', Lewes's copy, Hegel, *Aesthetik*, I, 16.

55 Hegel divides art into Symbolical, Classical, and Romantic art, and applies these categories both historically (Eastern, Greek, and Christian) – *see* Hegel, *Aesthetik*, Part two – and to the arts themselves (thus architecture is fundamentally the symbolic art, sculpture the classical, and painting, music, and poetry are the romantic or Christian arts) – *see* Hegel, *Aesthetik*, Part three.

56 Lewes, *Biographical History*, IV, 208, 209.

57 Lewes, 'Hegel's Aesthetics', *British and Foreign Review*, XIII, 4, 5, 14–15.
58 This may be compared to Coleridge's definition in *Biographia*, Chapter 14, of a poem as that which carries the reader forward 'by the pleasurable activity of mind excited by the attractions of the journey itself.' I. A. Richards took off from here in *Coleridge on Imagination* (London, 1934); and in *Principles of Literary Criticism* he everywhere takes his lead from Coleridge, especially from 'the Fourteenth chapter of *Biographia Literaria*, that lumber-room of neglected wisdom which contains more hints towards a theory of poetry than all the rest ever written on the subject', second edition (London, 1926), p. 140.
59 Lewes, 'Hegel's Aesthetics', *British and Foreign Review*, XIII, 8–9.
60 'Your notion of the essentially religious nature of poetry seems to me to need a world of explanation. . .I think it will give entirely false ideas to English readers, & is only true in *any* degree if we, *more Germanico*, call every idea a religious idea which either grows out of or leads to, feelings of infinity & mysteriousness', 1 March 1840, Mill, *Collected Works*, XIII, 466.
61 Lewes, 'Hegel's Aesthetics', *British and Foreign Review*, XIII, 19–20.
62 *Ibid.*, p. 33.
63 The upsurge of Hegelianism in England in the last few decades of the nineteenth century happened predominantly in Oxford, and more particularly at Balliol, where Jowett was tutor to T. H. Green, Edward Caird, and William Wallace, all of whom wrote philosophical works on Hegel. J. H. Stirling lectured in Edinburgh and was famous for his introduction to Hegel, *The Secret of Hegel*, 2 vols (London, 1865). This movement in philosophy left Lewes cold, though he corresponded regularly with Caird (one of the many Scots of the school) and with the German Hegelian Arnold Ruge (*see* MS letters in the Eliot Collection in Yale University Library).
64 Lewes, 'Hegel's Aesthetics', *British and Foreign Review*, XIII, 44, 44–5, 45–6.
65 *Ibid.*, p. 49.
66 B. Q. Morgan and A. R. Hohlfeld, *German Literature in British Magazines, 1750–1860*, contains only three references to Hegel in periodicals before 1860, one a brief piece of translation in the *Athenaeum* in 1833, the second Lewes's article of 1842, and the third an article on Hegel and other German philosophers and critics in the *English Review* in 1848.
67 Lewes, 'Augustus William Schlegel', *Foreign Quarterly Review*, XXXII (October 1843), 160.
68 *Ibid.*, pp. 161–3. His copy of the *Literary Remains* of Coleridge (1836) is annotated to this effect, showing he has noted Ferrier's charge of plagiarism in *Blackwood's* (1840). The copy is in the Folger Shakespeare Library.
69 'This doctrine [of sympathetic criticism, looking for what is good in a subject] we are anxious to see enforced, and to see the polemical fault-finding and superficial criticism of this analytic age give place to

a deeper and truer spirit of synthetical exposition', Lewes, 'The French Drama', *Westminster Review*, XXXIV (September 1840), 287. The article was written in 1838–9 in Berlin and Vienna, according to Lewes's note on his list of periodical contributions, which is in the Folger Shakespeare Library.

70 Lewes, 'Augustus William Schlegel', *Foreign Quarterly Review*, XXXII, 163–4.

71 *Ibid.*, pp. 168–9.

72 *Ibid.*, pp. 170–1. Nietzsche insists on the Dionysian side of the Greek character and art, as well as the Apollonian, Friedrich Nietzsche, *Werke*, ed. Giorgio Colli and Mazzino Montinari, 19 vols– (Berlin, 1967–), III, i, 5ff. *See also* George Steiner's contention that a society dominated by a redemptive theology no longer produces tragedy – he adduces Goethe's *Faust* as a major example – *The Death of Tragedy* (London, 1961), Chapter 4.

73 Lewes, 'Augustus William Schlegel', *Foreign Quarterly Review*, XXXII, 180.

74 Coleridge's copy of A. W. and F. Schlegel, *Athenäum*, 3 vols in one (Berlin, 1798–1800), I, 110–11 (British Museum).

75 Letter of 12 March 1832, MS in Speck Collection in Yale University Library.

76 *See* A. W. Schlegel, *Kritische Schriften und Briefe*, ed. Edgar Lohner, 7 vols (Stuttgart, 1962–74), V, 22; VI, 126, 165; John Black (trans.), *Schlegel's Lectures on Dramatic Art and Literature*, 2 vols (London, 1815), revised edition (London, 1861), I, 23, 358, 362, 400. And *see* Coleridge's similar comments, e.g. 'The moderns, blending materials, produced one striking whole. This may be illustrated by comparing the Pantheon with York Minster or Westminster Abbey [Schlegel had compared the Pantheon with Westminster Abbey or St Stephen's Cathedral in Vienna]. Upon the same scale we may compare Sophocles with Shakespeare', Coleridge, *Shakespearean Criticism*, II, 262. On Shakespeare's judgment Coleridge comments in *Biographia Literaria*, noticing his coincidence with Schlegel's point (Chapter 2), and on the Protean aspect of Shakespeare, to which Coleridge adds Milton by way of contrast (Chapter 15).

77 For a brief but useful study of Lewes's critical views, *see* R. L. Brett, 'George Henry Lewes: Dramatist, Novelist and Critic', *Essays and Studies*, XI new series (1958), 101–20.

78 Lewes, 'New German Book on Shakspeare', *Leader*, 30 March 1850, p. 15. *See also* Lewes's criticism of Schlegel as 'overrated', review of Oxenford's translation of Eckermann's *Conversations with Goethe*, *Leader*, 14 December 1850, p. 904, and his remarks about Schlegel's criticism as stimulating but perverse, 'Causeries', *Fortnightly Review*, III (1 February 1866), 772.

79 Lewes, *Life of Goethe*, II, 201–2.

80 Letter to Napier, 31 May 1844, MS Add. 34,624, f. 470–1 (British Museum), published in Macvey Napier, *Selection from the Correspondence of the late Macvey Napier*, pp. 463–4.

81 *'Lessing* is over-praised, and yet it is soberly and cleverly written', Jeffrey to Napier, 8 October 1845, *ibid.*, pp. 507–8.

82 *See* Mill's complaint about the Shelley article of 1841 and the Goethe article of 1843. Mill admits the same faults of style in his own early of Schelling and Hegel, 31 December 1844, Mill, *Collected Works*, XII, 449, 557–8.

83 Lewes, 'Lessing', *Edinburgh Review*, LXXXII (October 1845), 453.

84 October 1845, MS Add. 34,625, f. 476 (British Museum), and Lewes's note on his own copy in his collection of his articles in the Folger Shakespeare Library.

85 Letter of 29 May 1845, MS Lytton Collection (Hertford County Records Office).

86 James Sully, 'George Henry Lewes', *New Quarterly Magazine*, II new series (October 1879), 361–2, 359. A proof copy of the article with George Eliot's detailed marginal notes is in the Sully Collection at University College London.

87 Lewes, 'Lessing', *Edinburgh Review*, LXXXII, 468.

88 There is a short translation of a piece of Schiller's criticism, 'Thoughts on the Use of the Vulgar and the Mean in Art', with very little comment by Lewes, *Monthly Chronicle*, VII (January 1841), 170–4.

89 Lewes, 'Character and Works of Göthe', *British and Foreign Review*, XIV (1843), 119, 121.

90 Letter to Lewes, 28 January 1843, MS Speck Collection (Yale University Library).

91 Letter of 11 February 1843, MS Speck Collection.

92 Letter of 15 February 1843, MS Lytton Collection. The poem recognises that man as creature, phenomenon, is limited and imperfect and cannot bridge the gap to the noumenal world: 'Kein Erschaffner hat dies Ziel erflogen/Über diesen grauenvollen Schlund' (No created being has ever reached this goal across the horrifying chasm). But, as with Kant, the will is free and can bridge the gap ethically: 'Nehmt die Gottheit auf in euren Willen' (Take God up into your will).

93 Letter of 29 May 1843, MS Lytton Collection.

94 Lewes, *Biographical History*, IV, 245.

95 In an article on Shakespeare criticism, Lewes, 'Shakspeare's Critics: English and Foreign', *Edinburgh Review*, XC (July 1849), 71. *See also* Mill to Comte, complaining that the English were now going to Germany, not France, for new ideas, 22 March 1842, Mill, *Collected Works*, XIII, 509.

96 Rudolf Metz noted its success and described it as 'philosophically worthless' but 'stylistically clever', *Die Philosophischen Strömungen der Gegenwart in Grossbritannien*, 2 vols (Leipzig, 1935), I, 108. Lewes greatly changed and added to the work in its subsequent editions, *see* Jack Kaminsky, 'The Empirical Metaphysics of George Henry Lewes', *Journal of the History of Ideas*, XIII (June 1952), 314–32. There is a letter to Lewes's publisher, Parker, from one John Sharpe of Leicester, advocating a cheap edition of 'this, the best work of its class' which 'would be an invaluable boon to many to whom

expensive books are inaccessible', 12 November 1857, MS Eliot Collection in Yale University Library.

97 Herbert Spencer, *Autobiography*, I, 379.

98 Frederic Harrison, 'George Henry Lewes', *Academy*, XIV (7 December 1878), 543.

99 Lewes wrote in 1866 that his *Westminster Review* article had attracted attention as 'the first attempt to vindicate the great philosopher before the English public', Lewes, 'Spinoza', *Fortnightly Review*, IV (1 April 1866), 388.

100 Lewes prefers Spinoza's unifying to Descartes's dividing impulse, 'Spinoza's Life and Works', *Westminster Review*, XXXIX (May 1843), 388.

101 *Ibid.*, p. 398. *See* Kaminsky, 'A strong interest in metaphysics pervaded his article on Spinoza and he frankly admitted that Spinoza's pantheism did assume "an aspect of science"', 'The Empirical Metaphysics of George Henry Lewes', *Journal of the History of Ideas*, XIII, 317.

102 Lewes, *Biographical History*, III, 154.

103 'Spinozas are almost all sold...not above a dozen left. It is about to be translated into German: an honor which was paid me before in the case of the article on Göthe', [4] September 1843, MS Eliot Collection.

104 There is a letter from Lewes probably to Mitchell, publisher of the Spinoza pamphlet in the series 'Library of Reason', [?June 1843], MS Johns Hopkins University Library.

105 The Eliot Collection at Yale has drafts of two letters which Lewes planned to send to Bohn in June 1856, expressing his annoyance that Bohn had backed out of what Lewes took to be a long-standing agreement to publish the Spinoza.

106 Lewes, *Life of Goethe*, I, 283n.

107 *Ibid.*, I, 283.

108 Lewes, 'Spinoza', *Fortnightly Review*, IV (1 April 1866), 387.

109 Lewes, 'Spinoza's Life and Works', *Westminster Review*, XXXIX, 406, and 'Spinoza', *Fortnightly Review*, IV, 387. *See also* J. A. Froude's article on Spinoza, in which he wrote, '[Spinozism] has appeared in the abstract Pantheism of Schelling and Hegel, in the Pantheistic Christianity of Herder and Schleiermacher. Passing into practical life it has formed the strong shrewd judgment of Goethe, while again it has been able to unite with the theories of the most extreme materialism', *Westminster Review*, LXIV (July 1855), 33.

110 Lewes, *Biographical History*, IV, 93, 96ff. *See* Frothingham, *Transcendentalism in New England*, p. 14, for a commendation of Lewes's account.

111 Lewes, *Biographical History*, IV, 97, 119.

112 *Ibid.*, 121–2, 134.

113 *Ibid.*, 195, 202, 208, 219, 212–13.

114 Lewes's Notebook (Miscellaneous), MS Eliot Collection.

115 *See* his remark to Michelet about the importance of venturing 'seriously [to] study *Comte*, leaving the ontologists, from Hegel to Maine

de Biran, to settle their logomachies amongst themselves', letter of December 1843, MS Michelet Papers (Bibliothèque Historique de la Ville de Paris).

116 Lewes, 'Literature', *The Leader* (24 August 1850), p. 521.

117 F. A. Hayek points out some of the similarities between Comte and Hegel, *The Counter-Revolution of Science: Studies in the Abuse of Reason* (Glencoe, Illinois, 1952), pp. 192ff.

118 Mill, like George Eliot and Lewes, was an early disciple of Comte, see his letters to Comte in 1843–4. In one he expresses the hope that positivism will soon supersede 'le vague' and 'les tendances quiétistes' of Schelling and Hegel, 31 December 1844, Mill, *Collected Works*, XIII, 652. All of them moved away from Comte on the publication of his *Système de politique positive* (Paris, 1851–4), because of its dogmatic, neo-religious doctrine. For a survey of Comtism in England, see W. M. Simon, *European Positivism in the 19th Century, an Essay in Intellectual History* (Ithaca, New York, 1963).

119 Lewes, *Biographical History*, IV, 226–7.

120 E. Abbott and L. Campbell, *Life and Letters of Benjamin Jowett*, 2 vols (London, 1897), I, 261.

121 His diaries and notebooks record his regular reading of Kant and works on Kant in 1862, 1870–3, 1877, and of Hegel in 1870–4, see MS journals in Eliot Collection. The Eliot Collection also contains letters on philosophical subjects between Lewes and Edward Caird, author of *A Critical Account of the Philosophy of Kant* (Glasgow, 1877), and a monograph on Hegel (1883), and between Lewes and his fellow empiricist Alexander Bain.

122 Lewes, *Problems of Life and Mind*, first series, *The Foundations of a Creed*, 2 vols (London 1874), I, 17. See Kaminsky's article in the *Journal of the History of Ideas*, mentioned earlier in this chapter.

123 *See* Rudolf Metz, *Die Philosophischen Strömungen der Gegenwart in Grossbritannien*, I, 109. Lewes's reviewers were on the whole unenthusiastic about his ability as a philosopher-scientist. Frederic Harrison, Sully, and W. K. Clifford all praised his energy and ingenuity, but took his late works less seriously than Lewes would have wished.

124 Sully, 'George Henry Lewes', *New Quarterly Magazine*, II new series (October 1879), 366.

125 *See*, for example, the obituary notice of Lewes in *The Times*, 3 December 1878, as the well-known author of the *Life of Goethe*, the 'best of existing biographies'.

126 Letter to Napier, 31 May 1844, MS Add. 34,624, f. 470 (British Museum).

127 To Lewes, ?25 November 1842, Mill, *Collected Works*, XIII, 558.

128 Letter to Kemble, 23 March 1843, MS Eliot Collection.

129 Lewes, 'Character and Works of Göthe', *British and Foreign Review*, XIV (1843), 89.

130 *Ibid.*, pp. 111–12.

131 George Eliot, 'Life of Goethe', *Leader* (3 November 1855), pp. 1,058, 1,060.
132 *See* MS letter to William Bell Scott, June 1846 – 'I am now writing a Life of Göthe' (Princeton University Library).
133 Undated MS letter in Eliot Collection.
134 It was suggested in the obituary notice in *The Times* that Lewes also felt himself unfairly treated by professional scientists. Certainly some of his letters and journals show sensitivity about his reputation. He was, for example, anxious about his standing in physiology, noting in his journal on Christmas Day, 1868, 'I went to Oxford whither Acland invited me to attend the Meeting of the Medical Association ...Gratified to find how the medical profession accepted my physiological labors', MS Eliot Collection. On the whole, the opinion of his colleagues in physiology and psychology was low; for example, Bain wrote to G. C. Robertson, Professor of Logic at University College London, '[Lewes's] affectation being always beyond his powers, and always after the appearance of novelty, it is hard to give him the credit that he expects', 4 November ?1877, MS Robertson Collection (University College London).
135 Lewes, 'Goethe as a Man of Science', *Westminster Review*, II new series (October 1852), 479, and Lewes, *Life of Goethe*, II, 114.
136 Lewes, 'Goethe as a Man of Science', *Westminster Review*, II, 481, 490–2, and *Life of Goethe*, II, 135–8, 116ff.
137 *See* Gordon S. Haight, *George Eliot, a Biography* (Oxford, 1968), pp. 157, 169–71.
138 Varnhagen von Ense, *Aus dem Nachlass Varnhagen's von Ense, Tagebücher*, XI, 301, 312, 440, and George Eliot's journal 'Recollections of Berlin 1854–5', MS Eliot Collection.
139 Undated MS letter (Dr Williams's Library). From the address, East Sheen, we can date it between May 1855 and the publication of the work in November 1855, as Lewes moved to East Sheen on 2 May, *see* Haight, *George Eliot*, pp. 181, 192.
140 *See* Chapter 4.
141 George Eliot, 'Life of Goethe', *Leader*, 3 November 1855, p. 1,058.
142 Lewes, *Life of Goethe*, II, 12, 17.
143 *Ibid.*, II, 26.
144 Letter of 26 June 1864, Anthony Trollope, *Trollope Letters*, ed. B. A. Booth (London, 1951), pp. 154–5.
145 Lewes, *Life of Goethe*, I, 66, 193–4.
146 'The most interesting moment of the novel is improper for translation here', William Taylor, 'Goethe's *Elective Attractions, a Novel*', *Monthly Review*, LXVIII (August 1812), 541.
147 Lewes, *Life of Goethe*, II, 379.
148 *Ibid.*, II, 204.
149 Goethe, *Wilhelm Meisters Lehrjahre*, Book VIII, Chapter x.
150 Jarno points this out to Wilhelm, *ibid.*, Chapter v.
151 Lewes, *Life of Goethe*, II, 202–3.
152 *Ibid.*, I, 74–5.

153 *Ibid.*, II, 207-8.
154 Goethe, *Wilhelm Meisters Lehrjahre*, Book IV, Chapter V. Wilhelm has just been elected director of the group of travelling actors, and they are rehearsing *Hamlet* in the open, when they are attacked and robbed. Wilhelm is wounded, and the actors desert him (and later blame his bad management for the loss of their belongings). Only Philina stays behind to tend him. In doing so, nevertheless, she manages to hide her own trunk, so that only her belongings are saved from the robbers.
155 Lewes may have been following Shelley's example here. Shelley had found 'a striking similarity' between *Faust* and *El mágico prodigioso*, and had published translations of scenes from both plays in 1822, *see* Shelley, *Letters*, II, 407 and note.
156 Lewes, 'The three Fausts', *British and Foreign Review*, XVIII (1844), 51-92, and *Life of Goethe*, II, 278-340.
157 Lewes, *Life of Goethe*, II, 283.
158 *Ibid.*, 290.
159 *Ibid.*, 313, 307.
160 *Ibid.*, 423, 426.
161 *Ibid.*, 90-1.
162 *Ibid.*, I, 143-7.
163 Letter of 19 December 1855, MS Eliot Collection.
164 Lewes, *Life of Goethe*, I, 357-62; II, 93.
165 In three volumes, this was a translation of German memoirs of Goethe by Falk, von Müller, and others.
166 Sarah Austin, 'Goethe's Character and Moral Influence', *Edinburgh Review*, CVI (July 1857), 203, 223.
167 *Athenaeum* (10 November 1855), p. 1,304.
168 *Henry Crabb Robinson on Books*, II, 756.
169 His comment is quoted at the end of this chapter.
170 Matthew Arnold, Preface to *Merope*, and 'A French Critic on Goethe', *Complete Prose Works*, I, 39, VIII, 261.
171 Letter to Lewes, 3 November 1855, MS Speck Collection. Carlyle was rather less complimentary about it in a letter to his brother, 'The Book is decidedly good as such Books go, but by no means very interesting if you have a strict taste in Books', 27 November 1855, Carlyle, *New Letters*, II, 177.
172 Letter of 19 December 1855, MS Eliot Collection.
173 MS Journal, Eliot Collection.
174 Adolf Schöll, 'Ueber Goethes Leben und Schriften von G. H. Lewes', *Weimarer Sonntags-Blatt*, L (13 December 1857), 479.
175 *See* Varnhagen von Ense, *Tagebücher*, XI, 373ff.
176 Lewes, *Life of Goethe*, I, 323, and George Eliot, *Essays*, pp. 83, 84. Karl Biltz's outraged reply came in *Die dramatische Frage der Gegenwart, mit Bezugnahme auf die Lewes'sche Kritik der Dramen Göthe's* (Potsdam, 1859), p. 2.
177 Letter of 10 September 1879, *George Eliot Letters*, VII, 198.

178 Adolf Schöll, 'Ueber Goethes Leben und Schriften von G. H. Lewes', *Weimarer Sonntags-Blatt*, L (13 December 1857), 473.
179 MS letter of 4 February 1858 (Kestner-Museum, Hanover).
180 Lewes to his son Charles from Munich, 20 April 1858, MS Eliot Collection.
181 27 April 1858, MS Journal, Eliot Collection.
182 Lewes describes the meeting in a letter to Barbara Bodichon, 6 June 1876, MS Eliot Collection.
183 For example, L. A. Willoughby, 'Schiller in England and Germany', *Publications of the English Goethe Association*, XI new series (1935), 11, who says that the *Life of Goethe* is 'the first competent biography of Goethe published in any language.' *See also* W. F. Schirmer, 'German Literature, Historiography and Theology in 19th-Century England', *German Life and Letters*, I new series (1947), 167.
184 Richard Holt Hutton, 'Characteristics of Goethe', *National Review* (April 1856), reprinted as 'Goethe and his Influence', *Essays Theological and Literary*, second edition (London, 1877), II, 8.
185 Lytton to Lewes [?1868], MS Eliot Collection.
186 Margaret Fuller Ossoli met Lewes in 1846 and thought him 'a witty, French, flippant sort of man', 'unfit' to write a *Life* of Goethe, *Memoirs of Margaret Fuller Ossoli*, ed. R. W. Emerson and W. H. Channing, 3 vols (London, 1852), III, 98. Eliza Lynn Linton wrote, 'He was the first of the audacious men of my acquaintance, and about the most extreme. He had neither shame nor reticence in his choice of subjects', *My Literary Life*, ed. with preface by Beatrice Harraden (London, 1899), pp. 18-19. Frederic Harrison thought that others underrated Lewes's 'brilliant intelligence' because of his 'vagrant breeding and a somewhat effervescent manner', *Autobiographic Memoirs*, 2 vols (London, 1911), II, 109.
187 Spencer admitted, for example, that *Sartor Resartus* did not affect him as it did others who were 'more impressible than I was', *Autobiography*, I, 242.

CHAPTER 4

1 *See The George Eliot Letters*, I, 38, 43. She read *Maria Stuart* in October 1840, and studied *Wallenstein* with Mrs Bray in December 1842, *ibid.*, I, 69, 153.
2 Letter to Martha Jackson, 16 December 1841, *ibid.*, I, 122-3.
3 Elinor Shaffer rightly insists on the importance of the early German Biblical critics, from Lessing to Eichhorn, for Coleridge and his circle of Unitarians in Bristol in the 1790s, and sees the resurgence of interest in Strauss and others among the Unitarians of Coventry in the 1830s and 1840s as continuous with the early movement, '*Kubla Khan*' *and The Fall of Jerusalem*, pp. 230, 231.
4 Baden Powell, 'The Study of the Christian Evidences', *Edinburgh Review*, LXXXVI (October 1847), 416.

5 J. C. Hare, Introduction to his edition of Sterling's *Essays and Tales*, cxxxiii, cxxxvi.

6 Letters to Emerson, 30 April 1841 and 28 June, 1842, Sterling, *A Correspondence between John Sterling and Ralph Waldo Emerson*, pp. 41, 59–60.

7 Another anonymous translation, noticed by Sterling, existed, *see George Eliot Letters*, I, 171n.

8 The history of the translation is minutely documented in her letters, *ibid.*, I, 171, 174, 176, 197, 206.

9 To Sara Hennell [1845], *ibid.*, 203.

10 To the same, 27 November 1847 and 4 March 1846, *ibid.*, 241, 207.

11 David Friedrich Strauss, *Life of Jesus*, trans. George Eliot, 3 vols (London, 1846), I, ix–x.

12 'The celebrated *Das Leben Jesu* which created a scandal all over Europe on its publication in 1835 was only an uncompromising extension of Eichhorn's methods to the whole fabric of the New Testament', Shaffer, '*Kubla Khan*', p. 128.

13 Strauss, *Life of Jesus*, I, 99, 108–21.

14 G. S. Haight concludes that she was never happy about Strauss's 'narrow intellectual approach', *George Eliot, a Biography*, p. 151.

15 Letter of [August? 1845], *George Eliot Letters*, I, 197.

16 Matthew Arnold, 'God and the Bible' (1875), *Complete Prose Works*, VII, 171.

17 *Essays of George Eliot*, pp. 148–9.

18 *Ibid.*, p. 151.

19 Letter of May? 1846, *George Eliot Letters*, I, 216.

20 Letter of August? 1845, *ibid.*, 197.

21 Strauss, *Life of Jesus*, Preface, I, xi.

22 *Ibid.*, III, 396. On Strauss's reinstatement of Christian beliefs as truths of reason, not history, *see* G. A. Wells, *Herder and After: A Study in the Development of Sociology, Anglica Germanica* (1959), pp. 186–7.

23 Heinrich Heine, *Zur Geschichte der Religion und Philosophie in Deutschland* (1834), *Werke und Briefe*, V, 270.

24 Strauss, *Life of Jesus*, Concluding Dissertation, III, 397.

25 George Eliot, review of Mackay's *Progress of the Intellect*, *Westminster Review, Essays*, p. 36.

26 George Eliot, 'Evangelical Teaching: Dr. Cumming', *Westminster Review* (October 1855), *Essays*, p. 174.

27 George Eliot, *Middlemarch*, Chapter xxi, xxii, *The Works of George Eliot*, Cabinet edition, 20 vols (Edinburgh and London, 1878–80), XII. *See* W. J. Harvey on Bryant and Casaubon belonging to the lunatic fringe of Biblical studies, *Middlemarch: Critical Approaches to the Novel*, ed. Barbara Hardy (London, 1967), pp. 30–5.

28 Not only Strauss but the Tübingen School, and Paulus, whose *Leben Jesu* – giving a natural explanation of Bible texts – was published at Heidelberg in 1828, would be relevant here.

29 George Eliot, *Essays*, pp. 29–30.

30 Sterling, following Coleridge's honesty in searching through the Bible and facing up to the problems presented, wrote to William Coningham, 6 May 1840: 'More than half of all German theology, for the last fifty years, has turned upon the controversy about the literal accuracy and plenary inspiration of the book we call the Bible...No English book gives a plausible share of this kind of information. After long and very painful resistance of mind, I was forced to admit, that if I am to follow honestly the best light afforded me, I must own there is error in the Scriptures, and that the denial of this is, in an adequately instructed man, a mere *lying for God*, – one of the most absurd and suicidal of all human superstitions', *Twelve Letters by John Sterling* (London, 1851), p. 3.

31 James Martineau, 'Strauss and Parker', XLVII (April 1847), 139, 161-2. Professor Walter Houghton of the Wellesley Index kindly identified the reviewer for me.

32 Benjamin Jowett to B. C. Brodie, 24 November 1844, E. Abbott and L. Campbell, *Life and Letters of Benjamin Jowett*, I, 111.

33 *See George Eliot Letters*, I, 279n. George Eliot reviewed the novel favourably in the Coventry *Herald*, 16 March 1849; Haight quotes part of the short review in *George Eliot, a Biography*, p. 68.

34 J. A. Froude, *The Nemesis of Faith* (London, 1849), pp. 88-9.

35 She translated from the fourth edition, in which Strauss angrily defended himself against criticism, *see* Haight, *George Eliot, a Biography*, p. 151, and Strauss, Preface to the *Life of Jesus*.

36 Lewes, 'Julian the Apostate and Frederick William IV', *Edinburgh Review*, LXXXVIII (July 1948), 103.

37 Shaffer, '*Kubla Khan*', p. 232.

38 *See* Stuart Hampshire, *Spinoza* (London, 1951, reprinted 1956), p. 152.

39 Letter to Francis Watts, February 1843, and to Sara Hennell, 18 April 1849, *George Eliot Letters*, I, 158 and n., 280 and n. (according to Haight the translation of the *Tractatus* has not been found).

40 Arnold, 'Spinoza and the Bible', a reworking of two articles of 1863, *Complete Prose Works*, III, 179.

41 Letter to Francis Watts, 11 April 1842, *George Eliot Letters*, I, 136. For a summary of George Eliot's reading and development in the early 1840s, including her taking refuge in pantheism, *see* U. Knoepflmacher, *Religious Humanism and the Victorian Novel* (Princeton, New Jersey, 1965), pp. 44ff.

42 Matthew Arnold regretted that there was no English translation of the *Ethics* in 1863, Arnold, 'Spinoza and the Bible', *Complete Prose Works*, III, 175.

43 The drafts of two very angry letters from Lewes to Bohn are in the Eliot Collection in Yale. For a succinct account of the arrangement with Bohn, *see* Haight, *George Eliot, a Biography*, pp. 199-200.

44 Froude, 'Spinoza', *Westminster Review*, LXIV (July 1855), 32-3, and *George Eliot Letters*, II, 211.

45 'Spinoza has made his distinction of adequate and inadequate ideas

a current notion for educated Europe', Arnold, 'Spinoza and the Bible', *Complete Prose Works*, III, 181.

46 *George Eliot Letters*, I, 162; VI, 87; IV, 472.

47 George Eliot, *Middlemarch*, Chapter xxxvii. In Chapter lxxx Dorothea is described as crying 'after her lost belief which she had planted and kept alive from a very little seed since the days in Rome'.

48 Daniel Deronda is also described throughout in terms of clarity of voice, of appearance, of thought.

49 The theological stages of civilisation (divided into polytheistic and monotheistic) are discussed in volume V, Auguste Comte, *Cours de Philosophie Positive*, 6 vols (Paris, 1830-42), as is the metaphysical. The positive stage, with Comte's hopes for an appropriate education of the Western nations towards embracing a positive society, is discussed in volume VI. For Whewell's 'clear Ideas' *see* the Introduction to his *History of the Inductive Sciences* (London, 1827), *Historical and Philosophical Works*, ed. G. Buchdahl and L. L. Laudan, 6 vols— (London, 1967–), II, 7.

50 'An emotion which is a passion ceases to be a passion as soon as we form a clear and distinct idea of it', Benedict de Spinoza, *Ethics* (part 5, 'Concerning the power of the intellect or human freedom'), trans. A. Boyle (London, 1948), p. 203. *See* Dorothea's struggle with confused emotions in Rome, also Esther's 'getting more clearly into her imagination what it would be to abandon her own past' when she discovers her title to the Transome estate in *Felix Holt*. George Levine writes persuasively of George Eliot's determinist ethic, 'a deterministic universe is the *only* kind of universe in which moral acts are possible. In a wholly or even partially undetermined universe, every act would be capricious because it need not be the result of one's own past thinking and experience or of one's consciousness of its possible effects', 'Determinism and Responsibility in the Works of George Eliot', *Publications of the Modern Language Association of America*, LXVII (March 1962), 277-8.

51 Herbert Spencer, *Social Statics* (London, 1851), pp. 96-8.

52 Spinoza, *Ethics* (part 3, 'Concerning the Origin and Nature of the Emotions'), p. 102.

53 George Eliot, *Middlemarch*, Chapter xxi.

54 Feuerbach praised Spinoza's system for its honesty, its spirituality, and its bold intelligence, though he found the identification of God and Nature 'ein mystisches, amphibolisches Zwitterding' ('a mystical, amphibolic hybrid'), *Geschichte der neuern Philosophie von Bacon bis Spinoza*, *Sämmtliche Werke*, 7 vols (Leipzig, 1846-9), IV, 392.

55 As Pinney points out, George Eliot uses 'working day' in several of her essays and in novels, p. 302n. It is a key phrase in her conception of realism. *See* B. J. Paris, *Experiments in Life: George Eliot's Quest for Values* (Detroit, Michigan, 1965), p. 92, where he says Feuerbach offered what Strauss and Hennell had stopped short of – a psychological dimension, which appealed to George Eliot the novelist. Paris

gives a good summary of Feuerbach's work, pp. 94ff. *See also* Shaffer, '*Kubla Khan*', pp. 238ff.

56 Letter to Sara, 29 April 1854, *George Eliot Letters*, II, 153.
57 Note that Lydgate thinks of Rosamond 'as if she were an animal of another and feebler species' (Chapter lxv), which seems to be partly an indictment of Rosamond's minimal humanity and partly a criticism of Lydgate's lack of imaginative sympathy.
58 Ludwig Feuerbach, *The Essence of Christianity*, trans. George Eliot (London, 1854, reprinted New York, 1957), p. 140, xxxvi.
59 *See* Stuart Hampshire, *Spinoza*, p. 152.
60 Feuerbach, *Essence of Christianity*, pp. 208, 270–1, 82–3.
61 *Ibid.*, p. xxxiv.
62 George Eliot, 'The Future of German Philosophy', *Leader* (28 July 1855); *Essays*, p. 153.
63 *George Eliot Letters*, II, 141, 155.
64 'Love identifies man with God and God with man, consequently it identifies man with man; faith separates God from man, consequently it separates man from man, for God is nothing else than the idea of the species invested with a mystical form, – the separation of God from man is therefore the separation of man from man, the unloosening of the social bond', 'faith has fellowship with believers only; unbelievers it rejects', 'it is essential to faith to condemn, to anathemise', Feuerbach, *Essence of Christianity*, pp. 247, 252, 253.
65 George Eliot, *Essays*, pp. 162, 186. Compare Feuerbach, 'Faith... infuses into [man] no really moral dispositions...No! he does good not for the sake of goodness itself, not for the sake of man, but for the sake of God', *Essence of Christianity*, p. 262.
66 Letter to Mrs Ponsonby, 10 December 1874, *George Eliot Letters*, VI, 98.
67 *See*, for example, the last two chapters of *Amos Barton*, in which others adjust their attitudes towards Amos in the light of his sorrow, and he benefits from their sympathy; in *Middlemarch* the effect Dorothea's understanding, born of her own sorrow, of Lydgate's plight has on him; Romola's 'new baptism' in the need to help those stricken by the plague; and especially the developing effectiveness of Daniel Deronda's personality on Gwendolen and others. Several of the essays in Barbara Hardy (ed.), *Middlemarch: Critical Approaches to the Novel* and in *Critical Essays on George Eliot* (London, 1970), look at Feuerbachian language in the novels.
68 George Eliot, *Essays*, p. 191.
69 How committed George Eliot was to Comtism is not quite clear. She certainly accepted his stages of civilisation, and something of his belief that women were special vessels of sympathy. She more or less admitted to Frederic Harrison in 1866 that *Romola* had been an attempt at making incarnate Comtian 'normal' ideas of society, and she made no demur at Congreve's describing *The Spanish Gypsy* (1868) as 'the mass of Positivism', *George Eliot Letters*, IV, 300–1, 496. B. J. Paris, *Experiments in Life: George Eliot's Quest for Values*, assumes her to

NOTES TO PAGES 161-5

have been a thoroughgoing Positivist. But she did object to Comte's distortion of history to glorify medieval Catholicism and recommend a new priesthood, see her note on 'Historic Guidance', Pinney, 'More Leaves from George Eliot's Notebook', *Huntington Library Quarterly*, XXIX (1966), 353–76.

70 Sibilla Pfeiffer, in a rather dully systematic work, *George Eliots Beziehungen zu Deutschland, Anglistische Forschungen*, LX (Heidelberg, 1925), pp. 255–6, makes the plausible suggestion that Feuerbach was little noticed in England because attention was already occupied with Comte's version of the religion of humanity.

71 Letter to Sara, 18 January 1854, *George Eliot Letters*, II, 137.

72 To Sara, 10 July 1854, *ibid.*, 164.

73 Lewes, 'Literature', *Leader* (1 July 1854), p. 617; *George Eliot Letters*, II, 165n.

74 Martineau studied Hegel and the Tübingen School at Göttingen in 1848.

75 Martineau, 'Contemporary Literature, Theology and Philosophy', *Westminster Review*, VI new series (October 1854), 559, 560. George Eliot omitted the first four pages of Feuerbach's Preface to the second edition, because of its 'reference to transient German polemics', *Essence of Christianity*, p. xxxiiin. Feuerbach does not mince words, beginning his preface with a scornful reference to 'die albernen und perfiden Urtheile' ('the stupid and perfidious judgments') of his work, *Sämmtliche Werke*, VII, 5. In volume I of this collected edition, Feuerbach replies vigorously to hostile reviews, including one by J. Müller, *Theologische Studien und Kritiken* (1842), pp. 200–48, 249–58.
collected edition, Feuerbach replies vigorously to hostile reviews, including one by J. Müller, *Theologische Studien und Kritiken* (1842), pp. 200–48, 249–58.

76 Feuerbach, *Essence of Christianity*, pp. 275–8. In *Theophrastus Such* (1879), the most tendentious of her published works, she talked of 'a beneficent river of sympathy', 'the grand stream of human affairs', the 'smoke and flame' of egoism and the 'dews of fellowship and pity' ('Looking Inward', 'Moral Swindlers', 'The Watchdog of Knowledge').

77 Feuerbach, *Essence of Christianity*, Introductory Essay, pp. xxi, xxvii.

78 *Ibid.*, pp. xl–xli.

79 Letter of 10 August 1863, MS Eliot Collection. In his article on *Romola* in *The Spectator* (1863), Richard Holt Hutton wrote: 'The *soupçon* of hardness of which one is conscious as somewhat detracting from her power, the skill with which the author has prepared us for a mental struggle exactly similar, even in its minutest features, to what might occur to-day between the claims of a sublime faith appealing to the conscience, and a distaste for a miracle or vision in its prophet ...render it a little difficult to say whether we know her intimately, or whether we have only a very artistic idea of what she is *not*, and what she *is* only by inference and contrast...she is a shade more modern-

ized than the others', 'George Eliot', *Essays Theological and Literary*, 2 vols (London, 1871), II, 344.

80 Letter of 8 August 1863, *George Eliot Letters*, IV, 97. As if in continuation of Hutton's point, Elinor Shaffer thinks George Eliot found at last with *Daniel Deronda* 'the right Feuerbachian milieu: one saturated with religion, yet essentially secular and modern, where she could unite the primitive ground of religion with the most advanced consciousness of it', '*Kubla Khan*', p. 244.

81 Feuerbach, *Essence of Christianity*, pp. 98, 118.

82 Feuerbach explained, in the face of critical misunderstanding of his debts to and relationship with Hegel's philosophy, that 'was nämlich bei Hegel die Bedeutung des Secundären, Subjectiven, Formellen hat, das hat bei mir die Bedeutung des Primitiven, des Objectiven, Wesentlichen' ('what is in Hegel the secondary, the subjective, and the formal, is for me, the primitive [primary?], the objective, and the essential'), *Sämmtliche Werke*, I, 249.

83 The chief difficulty for George Eliot is in translating Feuerbach's two terms 'Gefühl' and 'Empfindung' into exact English equivalents; she correctly gives 'feeling' for the first, but has to use both 'sensation' and 'emotion' for the second, as neither English word alone conveys the sense. One can understand her difficulty in rendering Feuerbach's sentence, 'Empfindungen empfinden, heisst fühlen', which she expands to 'To feel is to have a sense of sensations, to have emotion in the perception of emotion', *Essence of Christianity*, p. 283. Feuerbach omitted this section from the *Sämmtliche Werke* (1846–9), but it appears in the second edition of 1843, pp. 417–19.

84 To Sara, 7 May 1854, *George Eliot Letters*, II, 154, and *Essence of Christianity*, p. 287n. Feuerbach's section IV is eight pages long, George Eliot's only two and a half.

85 Heine, *Zur Geschichte der Religion und Philosophie in Deutschland*, *Werke und Briefe*, V, 284.

86 She was reading an unspecified work of Goethe's in August 1853, *George Eliot Letters*, II, 115.

87 Haight points out that she was a 'silent collaborator' and quotes or paraphrases a few of her journal entries, *George Eliot, a Biography*, pp. 172–4.

88 George Eliot worked up these recollections into an article, 'Three Months in Weimar', *Fraser's Magazine* (June 1855), *Essays*, pp. 82–95.

89 George Eliot Journal 1854–61, MS Eliot Collection.

90 She was fond of quoting 'Goethe's wise words about reading Spinoza – "I always preferred knowing what an author himself said, to knowing what others thought he ought to have said"', letter to Alex. Main, 4 September 1871, *George Eliot Letters*, V, 182; *see also ibid.*, IV, 207.

91 George Eliot, 'The Natural History of German Life', *Westminster Review* (July 1856), *Essays*, p. 297.

92 George Eliot, 'Recollections of Berlin 1854–5', Journal 1854–61, MS Eliot Collection. By the dénouement Stahr probably means in particular Ottilie's reaction to the accident with the child and her

guilt at being in love with a married man. She fades away and dies of guilt and listlessness.

93 One scholar assumes Lewes to be the author of this article, but he gives no grounds for his supposition, *see* Richard Stang, *The Theory of the Novel in England, 1850–1870* (London, 1959), p. 222. Pinney includes the article in his volume of George Eliot's essays, assigning it on the basis of an entry in her journal for 8 July 1855: 'Wilhelm Meister & Art. on Gruppe for the Leader', George Eliot, *Essays*, p. 144. I would suggest from the tone of the article that its author was George Eliot, though she probably collaborated closely with Lewes, their interest both in Goethe and in helping the forthcoming *Life of Goethe* towards success being a shared one.

94 When George Eliot refers to 'Wilhelm Meister' in her essays, letters, and journals, she generally means the controversial *Lehrjahre*, not the tamer, religio-symbolic *Wanderjahre*.

95 By B. Dillon Boylan, in the series of Goethe's works published by Bohn's Standard Library. As Pinney points out, George Eliot, *Essays*, p. 144, this is only the ostensible occasion of George Eliot's article.

96 George Eliot, 'The Morality of Wilhelm Meister', *The Leader* (21 July 1855), *Essays*, pp. 144–5. Some of George Eliot's novels show signs of strain where she is trying not to deal out trite, obvious judgments and rewards. She could be accused of turning the screw against Amos Barton in allowing him to lose his curacy (arbitrarily) as well as his wife; and does Maggie have to die at the end of *Mill on the Floss*? Also, she wrote three versions of the last paragraph of *Middlemarch*, each different in the degree of its belief in the chances of character rising above environment, *see* Jerome Beaty, *Middlemarch from Notebook to Novel: A Study of George Eliot's Creative Method* (Urbana, Illinois, 1960).

97 Richard Holt Hutton, 'Goethe and his Influence', *National Review*, II (April 1856), 245, reprinted, *Essays Theological and Literary*, second edition enlarged (London, 1877), II, 7.

98 George Eliot, *Essays*, pp. 146–7.

99 George Eliot, '*Westward Ho!* and *Constance Herbert*', *Westminster Review* (July 1855); *Essays*, pp. 126, 134–5.

100 Chapter lxv. *See* Shaffer for *Daniel Deronda* embodying fully the Feuerbachian terms of religion as having a psychological, pathological, and sexual basis, '*Kubla Khan*', pp. 234, 256–7.

101 George Eliot, journal, July 1861–December 1877, MS Eliot Collection.

102 *Henry Crabb Robinson on Books* (his journal, 21 August 1859), II, 789–90.

103 Richard Holt Hutton, 'George Eliot', *Essays Theological and Literary* (1871), II, 307.

104 *See* the summary of *Nemesis* given in the Introduction above. It was Froude who translated *Die Wahlverwandtschaften* in 1854 for Bohn's edition of Goethe's works.

105 Her 'Commonplace Notebook' in the Eliot Collection is full of

quotations from several sources, including Goethe and Heine. *Daniel Deronda* has several references to Heine.

106 George Eliot, journal, 27 December 1854, MS Eliot Collection, and letter of 17 June 1855, *George Eliot Letters*, II, 203.

107 She wrote four articles on him in 1855–6; only one of them is of any length, *see* George Eliot, *Essays*, p. 216.

108 Pinney claims too much when he accepts S. L. Wormley's estimate of this article as one which did more than any other to introduce English readers to Heine, George Eliot, *Essays*, p. 216. There had been several interesting articles on Heine, including two in the *Quarterly Review* in 1835, one by Hayward in February, and the other by Lockhart in December.

109 Lewes, 'Julian the Apostate and Frederick William IV', *Edinburgh Review*, LXXXVIII (July 1848), 94.

110 George Eliot, 'German Wit: Heinrich Heine', *Westminster Review* (January 1856), *Essays*, p. 221.

111 George Eliot, *Essays*, pp. 223–4.

112 Sibilla Pfeiffer tries to find close similarities between Heine's drama *Almansor* and *The Spanish Gypsy*, but these exist only in the externals of plot and setting, *George Eliots Beziehungen zu Deutschland*, pp. 210–11.

113 George Eliot, *Essays*, pp. 222–3.

114 Letter of 19 November 1854, MS Eliot Collection.

115 George Eliot, 'Recollections of Berlin', MS Eliot Collection.

116 Letter of 12 November 1854, *George Eliot Letters*, II, 185.

117 Jeffrey, 'Lessing's *Nathan the Wise*', *Edinburgh Review*, VIII (April 1806), 148ff. Jeffrey calls it 'a genuine German drama' with a story 'in point of absurdity...fairly entitled to bear away the palm from the celebrated German play in the poetry of the Antijacobin [i.e. *The Rovers*]; the moral is no less comfortable, and the diction, though not altogether so lofty, is, upon the whole, entitled to equal admiration', p. 149.

118 George Eliot, 'Three Months in Weimar', *Fraser's Magazine*, *Essays*, p. 83.

119 George Eliot, 'How We Encourage Research', *Impressions of Theophrastus Such* (Edinburgh, 1879), p. 53.

120 George Eliot, 'A Word for the Germans', *Pall Mall Gazette* (7 March 1865), *Essays*, pp. 386–7, 388. George Eliot wrote nothing on Kant (though she briefly reviewed Meiklejohn's translation of the *Kritik der reinen Vernunft*, 'Translations and Translators', *The Leader*, 20 October 1855, *Essays*, pp. 207–11), but she undoubtedly knew his works. When she met Renan in Paris in 1866, she was not impressed: 'I could not help probing him when he was talking about Kant, and finding that, as I expected, he only knew Kant at second hand, and that inaccurately', George Eliot, journal, 31 December 1866, *George Eliot Letters*, IV, 328.

121 George Eliot, *Essays*, p. 389.

122 *Ibid.*, p. 390.

SELECT BIBLIOGRAPHY

Abbott, E. and Campbell, L. *The Life and Letters of Benjamin Jowett*, 2 vols, London, 1897.

Abrams, M. H. *The Mirror and the Lamp: Romantic Theory and the Critical Tradition*, New York, 1953.

Natural Supernaturalism: Tradition and Revolution in Romantic Literature, London, 1971.

Allingham, William. *A Diary*, ed. H. Allingham and D. Radford, London, 1907.

Anster, John (trans.). *Faustus: A Dramatic Mystery*, London, 1835.

Arnold, Matthew. *The Complete Prose Works of Matthew Arnold*, ed. R. H. Super, 10 vols, Ann Arbor, Michigan, 1960–77.

Letters of Matthew Arnold, ed. G. W. E. Russell, 2 vols, London, 1895.

The Note-Books of Matthew Arnold, ed. H. F. Lowry and W. H. Dunn, London, 1952.

Ashton, R. D. 'Carlyle's Apprenticeship: His Early German Criticism and His Relationship with Goethe (1822–32)', *Modern Language Review*, LXXI, January 1976, 1–18.

'Coleridge and *Faust*', *Review of English Studies*, XXVIII, May 1977, 156–67.

Auerbach, Erich. *Mimesis: The Representation of Reality in Western Literature*, trans. Willard Trask, Princeton, New Jersey, 1953.

Austin, Sarah. *Characteristics of Goethe: From the German of Falk, von Müller etc.*, 3 vols, London, 1833.

Fragments from German Prose-Writers, London, 1841.

Baker, J. M. *Henry Crabb Robinson of Bury, Jena, 'The Times', and Russell Square*, London, 1937.

Bauer, Josephine. 'The London Magazine, 1820–29', *Anglistica*, I, Copenhagen, 1953, 1–362.

Beaty, Jerome. *Middlemarch from Notebook to Novel: A Study of George Eliot's Creative Method*, Urbana, Illinois, 1960.

Beddoes, Thomas Lovell. *Letters*, ed. Edmund Gosse, London, 1894.

Beer, John. *Coleridge's Poetic Intelligence*, London, 1977.

(ed.). *Coleridge's Variety: Bicentenary Studies*, London, 1974.

Biltz, Karl. *Die dramatische Frage der Gegenwart, mit Bezugnahme auf die Lewes'sche Kritik der Dramen Göthe's*, Potsdam, 1859.

Biographia Dramatica; or, a Companion to the Playhouse, ed. Baker, Reed, and Jones, 3 vols, London, 1812.

Black, John (trans.). *Schlegel's Lectures on Dramatic Art and Literature*, 2 vols, London, 1815, revised edition, London, 1861.

Blackie, John Stuart (trans.). *Faust: A Tragedy*, Edinburgh and London, 1834.

On Self-Culture, Edinburgh, 1874.

The Wisdom of Goethe, Edinburgh, 1883.

Bollacher, Martin. *Der junge Goethe und Spinoza*, Tübingen, 1969.

Bonner, W. H. *De Quincey at Work*, Buffalo, New York, 1936.

Boulger, James D. *Coleridge as Religious Thinker*, New Haven, Connecticut, 1961.

Boyd, James. *Goethe's Knowledge of English Literature*, Oxford, 1932.

Brandl, Alois. 'Die Aufnahme von Goethes Jugendwerken in England', *Goethe–Jahrbuch*, III, 1882, 27–76.

Brett, R. L. 'George Henry Lewes: Dramatist, Novelist and Critic', *Essays and Studies*, XI new series, 1958, 101–20.

Brookfield, Frances M. *The Cambridge 'Apostles'*, London, 1906.

Bruford, W. H. 'Goethe and some Victorian Humanists', *Publications of the English Goethe Society*, XVIII new series, 1949, 34–67.

Bulwer, Edward Lytton. *Caxtoniana: A Series of Essays on Life, Literature, and Manners*, 2 vols, Edinburgh, 1863.

The Disowned, 4 vols, London, 1828.

England and the English, 2 vols, London, 1833.

Pelham; or the Adventures of a Gentleman, 3 vols, London, 1828.

(trans.). *The Poems and Ballads of Schiller*, 2 vols, Edinburgh, 1844.

Byron, Lord George Gordon. *Letters and Journals*, ed. R. E. Prothero, 6 vols, London, 1898–1901.

Letters and Journals, ed. Leslie A. Marchand, 7 vols– , London, 1973– .

Caird, Edward. *The Critical Philosophy of Immanuel Kant*, 2 vols, Glasgow, 1889.

Carlyle, Jane Welsh. *Letters to her Family, 1839–63*, ed. Leonard Huxley, London, 1924.

Carlyle, Thomas. *The Collected Letters of Thomas and Jane Welsh Carlyle*, ed. C. R. Sanders and K. J. Fielding, 7 vols– , Durham, North Carolina, 1970– .

Correspondence between Goethe and Carlyle, ed. C. E. Norton, London, 1887.

'Four Unpublished Letters of Thomas Carlyle', ed. S. H. Nobbe, *Publications of the Modern Language Association of America*, LXX, September 1955, 876–84.

Last Words of Thomas Carlyle, London, 1892.

New Letters of Thomas Carlyle, ed. Alex. Carlyle, 2 vols, London, 1904.

Reminiscences, ed. J. A. Froude, 2 vols, London, 1881.

Sartor Resartus, ed. C. F. Harrold, Michigan, 1937.

Two Note Books, ed. C. E. Norton, New York, 1898.

Works of Thomas Carlyle, Centenary Edition, ed. H. D. Traill, 30 vols, London, 1896–9.

Carr, C. T. 'Carlyle's Translations from German', *Modern Language Review*, XLII, 1947, 223–32.

Clubbe, John (ed.). *Carlyle and his Contemporaries*, Durham, North Carolina, 1976.

Cockburn, Henry Lord. *Life of Lord Jeffrey: With a Selection from his Correspondence*, 2 vols, Edinburgh, 1852.

Coleridge, Samuel Taylor. *Aids to Reflection*, 11th edition, ed. Derwent Coleridge, London, 1866.

Biographia Literaria, ed. J. Shawcross, 2 vols, London, 1907.

Collected Letters of Samuel Taylor Coleridge, ed. E. L. Griggs, 6 vols, Oxford, 1956–71.

The Collected Works of Samuel Taylor Coleridge, ed. K. Coburn, 16 vols, in progress, London, 1969– .

Confessions of an Inquiring Spirit, ed. H. N. Coleridge, London, 1849.

Literary Remains, ed. H. N. Coleridge, 4 vols, London, 1836–9.

The Notebooks of Samuel Taylor Coleridge, ed. K. Coburn, 3 double vols– , London, 1957– .

The Philosophical Lectures, ed. K. Coburn, London, 1949.

Poetical Works, ed. E. H. Coleridge, 2 vols, London, 1912.

Shakespearean Criticism, ed. T. M. Raysor, 2 vols, London, 1960.

Specimens of the Table Talk of Samuel Taylor Coleridge, 2nd edition corrected, ed. H. N. Coleridge, London, 1836.

(trans.). *Wallenstein, a Drama in Two Parts*, London, 1800.

Comte, Auguste. *Cours de Philosophie Positive*, 6 vols, Paris, 1830–42.

De Quincey, Thomas. *Collected Writings*, ed. David Masson, 14 vols, Edinburgh, 1889–90.

A Diary of Thomas De Quincey, 1803, ed. H. A. Eaton, London, 1927.

New Essays, ed. S. M. Tave, Princeton, New Jersey, 1966.

Drummond, William. *Academical Questions*, London, 1805.

Dunn, William A. *Thomas De Quincey's Relation to German Literature and Philosophy*, Univ. Diss. Strassburg, 1900.

Durand, Walter Y. 'De Quincey and Carlyle in their Relation to the Germans', *PMLA*, XXII, 1907, 521–30.

Eckermann, Johann Peter. *Gespräche mit Goethe in den letzten Jahren seines Lebens*, Leipzig and Magdeburg, 1836–48.

Eliot, George. *Essays of George Eliot*, ed. Thomas Pinney, New York, 1963.

The George Eliot Letters, ed. Gordon S. Haight, 7 vols, London, 1954–6.

Impressions of Theophrastus Such, Edinburgh, 1879.

The Works of George Eliot, Cabinet edition, 20 vols, Edinburgh and London, 1878–80.

Emerson, Ralph Waldo. *English Traits*, ed. Howard Mumford Jones, Cambridge, Mass., 1966.

The Journals and Miscellaneous Notebooks of Ralph Waldo Emerson, ed. W. H. Gilman and A. R. Ferguson, 9 vols– , Cambridge, Mass., 1960– .

Works, Riverside Edition, 12 vols, Boston, Mass., 1894.

Espinasse, Francis, *Literary Recollections and Sketches*, London, 1893.

Ewen, Frederic. 'John Gibson Lockhart, Propagandist of German Literature', *Modern Language Notes*, XLIX, April 1934, 260–5.

The Prestige of Schiller in England, 1788–1859, New York, 1932.

Feuerbach, Ludwig. *The Essence of Christianity*, trans. George Eliot, London, 1854, reprinted New York, 1957.

Sämmtliche Werke, 7 vols, Leipzig, 1846–9.

Frothingham, O. B. *Transcendentalism in New England, A History*, New York, 1876, reprinted 1959.

Froude, J. A. (trans.). *Elective Affinities, Novels and Tales by Goethe*, London, 1854.

The Nemesis of Faith, London, 1849.

Thomas Carlyle: A History of the First Forty Years of his Life, 1795–1835, 2 vols, London, 1882.

Thomas Carlyle: A History of his Life in London, 1834–1881, 2 vols, London, 1884.

Fuller, Margaret, afterwards Ossoli. *Memoirs*, ed. R. W. Emerson and W. H. Channing, 3 vols, London, 1852.

Furst, Lilian. *Romanticism in Perspective: A Comparative Study of Aspects of the Romantic Movements in England, France and Germany*, London, 1969.

Gillies, Robert Pearse (trans.). *The Devil's Elixir, by E. T. A. Hoffmann*, 2 vols, Edinburgh, 1824.

German Stories, 3 vols, Edinburgh, 1826.

(trans.). *Guilt, by Müllner*, Edinburgh, 1819.

Memoirs of a Literary Veteran, 3 vols, London, 1851.

Goethe, Johann Wolfgang von. *Briefwechsel zwischen Goethe und Zelter in den Jahren 1796 bis 1832*, ed. F. W. Riemer, 6 vols, Berlin, 1833–4.

Ueber Kunst und Alterthum, 6 vols, 1818–28, reprinted Bern, 1970.

Werke, Briefe und Gespräche, Gedenkausgabe, ed. E. Beutler, 24 vols, Zürich, 1948–62.

Gower, Lord Francis Leveson (trans.). *Faust. And Schiller's Song of the Bell*, London, 1823.

Griggs, E. L. 'Ludwig Tieck and Samuel Taylor Coleridge', *Journal of English and Germanic Philology*, LIV, April 1955, 262–8.

Haight, Gordon S. *George Eliot, a Biography*, Oxford, 1968.

Hampshire, Stuart. *Spinoza*, London, 1951.

Harding, A. J. *Coleridge and the Idea of Love*, Cambridge, 1974.

Hardy, Barbara (ed.). *Critical Essays on George Eliot*, London, 1970.

Middlemarch: Critical Approaches to the Novel, London, 1967.

Hare, Julius Charles and Augustus William. *Guesses at Truth, by Two Brothers*, 2 vols, London, 1827.

Harrison, Frederic. *Autobiographic Memoirs*, 2 vols, London, 1911.

Harrold, C. F. *Carlyle and German Thought: 1819–34*, New Haven, Connecticut, 1934, reprinted London, 1963.

Hayek, F. A. *The Counter-Revolution of Science: Studies in the Abuse of Reason*, Glencoe, Illinois, 1952.

Hayward, Abraham (trans.). *Faust: A Dramatic Poem*, London, 1833.

Hazlitt, William. *The Complete Works of William Hazlitt*, ed. P. P. Howe, 21 vols, London, 1930–4.

Hegel, Georg Wilhelm Friedrich. *Aesthetics*, trans. T. M. Knox, 2 vols, Oxford, 1975.

Vorlesungen über die Aesthetik, ed. D. H. G. Hotho, 3 vols, Berlin, 1835.
Heine, Heinrich. *Werke und Briefe*, ed. Hans Kaufmann, 10 vols, Berlin, 1961–4.
Heller, Erich. *The Disinherited Mind: Essays in Modern German Literature and Thought*, London, 1971.
Helmholtz, A. A. *The Indebtedness of Coleridge to A. W. Schlegel*, Madison, Wisconsin, 1907.
Herder, Johann Gottfried. *Sämmtliche Werke*, ed. Bernhard Suphan, Berlin, 1877–1913.
Herzfeld, Georg. *William Taylor von Norwich: Eine Studie über den Einfluss der neueren deutschen Litteratur in England*, Halle, 1897.
Houghton, Walter E. *The Victorian Frame of Mind, 1830–1870*, New Haven, Connecticut, 1957.
Howe, Susanne, *Wilhelm Meister and his English Kinsmen; apprentices to life*, New York, 1930.
Hunt, Leigh. *Leigh Hunt's Dramatic Criticism, 1808–1831*, ed. L. H. and C. W. Houtchens, New York, 1949.
Hutton, Richard Holt. *Criticisms on Contemporary Thought and Thinkers*, 2 vols, London, 1894.
Essays Theological and Literary, 2 vols, London, 1871, and 2nd edition revised and enlarged, 2 vols, London, 1877.
Jaeck, Emma G. *Madame de Staël and the Spread of German Literature*, New York, 1915.
James, Henry. *Literary Reviews and Essays*, ed. Albert Mordell, New York, 1957.
Kaminsky, Alice R. *George Henry Lewes as Literary Critic*, New York, 1968.
Kaminsky, Jack. 'The Empirical Metaphysics of George Henry Lewes', *Journal of the History of Ideas*, XIII, June 1952, 314–32.
Kant, Immanuel. *Werke*, ed. Wilhelm Weischedel, 6 vols, Wiesbaden, 1956–64.
Kitchel, Anna T. *George Lewes and George Eliot; a review of records*, New York, 1933.
Knoepflmacher, U. *Religious Humanism and the Victorian Novel*, Princeton, New Jersey, 1965.
Lamb, Charles. *The Letters of Charles Lamb*, ed. E. V. Lucas, 3 vols, London, 1935.
Lang, Andrew. *The Life and Letters of John Gibson Lockhart*, 2 vols, London, 1897.
Lefebure, Molly. *Coleridge: A Bondage of Opium*, London, 1974.
Lessing, Gotthold Ephraim. *Briefe die neueste Literatur betreffend*, Berlin, 1759–65.
Hamburgische Dramaturgie, Hamburg, 1767–9.
Lewes, George Henry. *Biographical History of Philosophy*, 4 vols, London, 1845–6.
Comte's Philosophy of the Sciences, London, 1853.
The Life and Works of Goethe, 2 vols, London, 1855, and 2nd edition revised, 1864.

Problems of Life and Mind, first series, *The Foundations of a Creed*, 2 vols, London, 1874.

Ranthorpe, London, 1847.

Lockhart, John Gibson (trans.). *Lectures on the History of Literature, Ancient and Modern, by Friedrich Schlegel*, 2 vols, Edinburgh, 1818.

Memoirs of the Life of Sir Walter Scott, Bart, 7 vols, Edinburgh, 1837–8.

Lovejoy, A. O. *Essays in the History of Ideas*, New York, 1948.

McFarland, Thomas. *Coleridge and the Pantheist Tradition*, Oxford, 1969.

Mandelkow, Karl Robert (ed.). *Goethe im Urteil seiner Kritiker, Teil I, 1773–1832*, München, 1975.

Margraf, Ernst. 'Einfluss der deutschen Litteratur auf die englische am Ende des achtzehnten und im ersten Drittel des neunzehnten Jahrhunderts', *Studien zur vergleichenden Litteraturgeschichte*, special issue, 1901.

Martineau, Harriet, *Autobiography*, ed. Maria Weston Chapman, 3 vols, London, 1877.

Medwin, Thomas. *Conversations of Lord Byron*, London, 1824.

Metz, Rudolf. *Die Philosophischen Strömungen der Gegenwart in Grossbritannien*, 2 vols, Leipzig, 1935.

Mill, John Stuart. *Autobiography*, ed. Jack Stillinger, London, 1971.

The Collected Works of John Stuart Mill, ed. F. E. L. Priestley, 17 vols, Toronto, 1963–72.

Letters, ed. Hugh S. R. Elliot, 2 vols, London, 1910.

Mill on Bentham and Coleridge, ed. and with an introduction by F. R. Leavis, London, 1950.

Miller, J. Hillis. *The Disappearance of God*, Cambridge, Mass., 1963.

Minor, Jacob (ed.). *Das Schicksalsdrama*, Berlin, ca. 1880.

Moir, George (trans.). *Wallenstein, from the German*, 2 vols, Edinburgh, 1827.

Moore, Thomas. *Memoirs, Journal, and Correspondence*, ed. Lord John Russell, 8 vols, London, 1853–6.

Morgan B. Q. *A Critical Bibliography of German Literature in English Translation, 1481–1927*, 2nd edition revised, Stanford, California, 1938.

Morgan, B. Q. and Hohlfeld, A. R. *German Literature in British Magazines, 1750–1860*, Madison, Wisconsin, 1949.

Morley, E. J. *Crabb Robinson in Germany 1800–1805*, London, 1929.

The Life and Times of Henry Crabb Robinson, London, 1935.

Muirhead, John H. *Coleridge as Philosopher*, London, 1930.

Mutschmann, Heinrich. 'Sarah Austin und die deutsche Literatur', *Die Neueren Sprachen*, xxvII, June–July 1919, 97–128.

Nangle, B. C. *The Monthly Review: Second Series, 1790–1815*, Oxford, 1955.

Napier, Macvey. *A Selection from the Correspondence of the late Macvey Napier*, ed. his son Macvey Napier, London, 1879.

Needler, G. H. *Goethe and Scott*, Toronto, 1950.

Neff, Emery. *Carlyle and Mill: An Introduction to Victorian Thought*, 2nd edition revised, New York, 1964.

Nicolai, Friedrich. *Werke*, ed. J. Minor, *Deutsche National-Litteratur*, ed. Joseph Kürschner, 163 vols, Berlin and Stuttgart, [?]1884–6.

Nietzsche, Friedrich. *Werke*, ed. Giorgio Colli and Mazzino Montinari, 19 vols– , Berlin, 1967– .

Nordmeyer, H. W. 'Zu Goethe's "Faust" in England – J. G. Lockhart', *Journal of English and Germanic Philology*, xvii, 1918, 198–213.

Novalis (Freiherr Friedrich von Hardenberg). *Schriften*, ed. P. Kluckhohn and R. Samuel, 4 vols– , Stuttgart, 1960– .

Oliphant, Mrs. *Annals of a Publishing House; William Blackwood and his Sons*, 3 vols, Edinburgh, 1897.

Orsini, Gian N. G. *Coleridge and German Idealism: A Study in the History of Philosophy with Unpublished Materials from Coleridge's Manuscripts*, Carbondale, Illinois, 1969.

Paris, B. J. *Experiments in Life: George Eliot's Quest for Values*, Detroit, Michigan, 1965.

Pater, Walter. *Essays on Literature and Art*, ed. Jennifer Uglow, London, 1973.

Pattison, Mark. *Memoirs*, London, 1885.

Peacock, Thomas Love. *The Works of Thomas Love Peacock*, ed. H. F. B. Brett-Smith and C. E. Jones, 10 vols, London, 1924–34.

Pfeiffer, Sibilla. *George Eliots Beziehungen zu Deutschland, Anglistische Forschungen*, lx, Heidelberg, 1925.

Pinney, Thomas. 'More Leaves from George Eliot's Notebook', *Huntington Library Quarterly*, xxix, 1966, 353–76.

Pollitt, Charles. *De Quincey's Editorship of the Westmorland Gazette*, Kendal, 1890.

Rea, Thomas. *Schiller's Dramas and Poems in England*, London, 1906.

Redinger, Ruby V. *George Eliot: The Emergent Self*, London, 1975.

Renan, Ernest. *Vie de Jésus*, Paris, 1863.

Richards, I. A. *Coleridge on Imagination*, London, 1934.
Principles of Literary Criticism, 2nd edition, London, 1926.

[Richter] Jean Paul. *Werke*, ed. N. Miller and G. Lohmann, 6 vols, München, 1959–66, Darmstadt, 1967.

Robberds, J. W. *A Memoir of the Life and Writings of the late William Taylor, of Norwich*, 2 vols, London, 1843.

Robinson, Henry Crabb. *Blake, Coleridge, Wordsworth, Lamb etc.: Being Selections from the Remains of Henry Crabb Robinson*, ed. E. J. Morley, Manchester, 1922, reissued 1932.
The Correspondence of Henry Crabb Robinson with the Wordsworth Circle, 1808–66, ed. E. J. Morley, 2 vols, Oxford, 1927.
Diary, Reminiscences and Correspondence, ed. Thomas Sadler, 3 vols, London, 1869.
'Fourteen Unpublished Letters by Henry Crabb Robinson', ed. A. B. Benson, *PMLA*, xxxi, 1916, 395–420.
Henry Crabb Robinson on Books and their Writers, ed. E. J. Morley, 3 vols, London, 1938.

Rose, William. *From Goethe to Byron: The Development of 'Weltschmerz'
in German Literature*, London, 1924.

'German Literary Exiles in England', *German Life and Letters*, 1 new
series, 1947, 175–85.

Ross, Janet. *Three Generations of Englishwomen*, 2 vols, London, 1888.

Schiller, Friedrich. *Briefwechsel zwischen Schiller und Goethe in den
Jahren 1794 bis 1805*, 6 vols, Stuttgart and Tübingen, 1828–9.

Sämmtliche Werke, ed. K. Goedeke, 15 vols, Stuttgart, 1867–76.

Sämtliche Werke, Säkular-Ausgabe, ed. Eduard von der Hellen et al,
16 vols, Stuttgart and Berlin, 1904.

Werke, Nationalausgabe, 42 vols in progress, Weimar, 1943– .

*Über die Ästhetische Erziehung des Menschen, On the Aesthetic Educa-
tion of Man*, ed. with parallel translation by E. M. Wilkinson and
L. A. Willoughby, Oxford, 1967.

Schlegel, A. W. *Kritische Schriften und Briefe*, ed. Edgar Lohner, 7 vols,
Stuttgart, 1962–74.

Schlegel, Friedrich. *Kritische Friedrich-Schlegel-Ausgabe*, ed. Ernst
Behler, 19 vols, München, 1961–71.

Scott, D. F. S. *Some English Correspondents of Goethe*, London, 1949.

Scott, Sir Walter. *Journal*, ed. W. E. K. Anderson, Oxford, 1972.

Letters of Sir Walter Scott, ed. H. J. C. Grierson, 12 vols, London,
1932–7.

Shaffer, E. S. *'Kubla Khan' and The Fall of Jerusalem*, Cambridge,
1975.

Shelley, Percy Bysshe. *Essays, Letters from Abroad, Translations and Fragments*, ed. Mary Shelley, 2 vols, London, 1840.

The Letters of Percy Bysshe Shelley, ed. F. L. Jones, 2 vols, Oxford,
1964.

Simon, W. M. *European Positivism in the 19th Century, an Essay in
Intellectual History*, Ithaca, New York, 1963.

Smiles, Samuel. *A Publisher and his Friends: Memoir and Correspondence of John Murray*, 2 vols, London, 1891.

Southey, C. C. (ed.). *The Life and Correspondence of the late Robert
Southey*, 6 vols, London, 1849–50.

Southey, Robert. *Poetical Works*, 10 vols, London, 1837–8.

Spencer, Herbert. *Autobiography*, 2 vols, London, 1904.

Social Statics, London, 1851.

Spinoza, Benedict de. *Ethics*, trans. A. Boyle, London, 1948.

Stephen, Leslie. *Hours in a Library*, new enlarged edition, 3 vols, London,
1892.

Studies of a Biographer, 4 vols, London, 1898–1902.

Sterling, John. *A Correspondence between John Sterling and Ralph Waldo
Emerson*, ed. E. W. Emerson, Boston, Mass., 1897, reissued Port
Washington, New York, 1971.

Essays and Tales, ed. J. C. Hare, 2 vols, London, 1848.

Twelve Letters by John Sterling, ed. W. Coningham, London, 1851.

Stirling, Amelia H. *James Hutchison Stirling: his life and work*, London
and Leipzig, 1912.

Stirling, James Hutchison. 'De Quincey and Coleridge upon Kant', *Fortnightly Review*, II new series, October 1867, 377–95.
   The Secret of Hegel, 2 vols, London, 1865.
Stockley, Violet. *German Literature as Known in England, 1750–1830*, London, 1929.
Stoddart, Anna M. *John Stuart Blackie: A Biography*, 2 vols, Edinburgh, 1895.
Stokoe, F. W. *German Influence in the English Romantic Period, 1788-1818*, Cambridge, 1926.
Strauss, David Friedrich. *Das Leben Jesu, kritisch bearbeitet*, 4th edition, 1840); *The Life of Jesus*, trans. George Eliot, 3 vols, London, 1846.
Strout, A. L. *A Bibliography of Articles in Blackwood's Magazine, 1817-1825*, Lubbock, Texas, 1959.
Syme, David (trans.). *Faust: A Tragedy*, Edinburgh, 1834.
Talbot, Hon. Robert (trans.). *Faust, attempted in English Rhyme*, London, 1835.
Taube, Edward. 'German Influence on the English Vocabulary in the Nineteenth Century', *Journal of English and Germanic Philology*, XXXIX, 1940, 488–93.
Taylor, William. *A Historic Survey of German Poetry*, 3 vols, London, 1828–30.
Tennyson, G. B. *'Sartor' Called 'Resartus', the Genesis, Structure, and Style of Thomas Carlyle's First Major Work*, Princeton, New Jersey, 1965.
Tieck, Ludwig. *Kritische Schriften*, 4 vols, Leipzig, 1848–52.
Trollope, Anthony. *Trollope Letters*, ed. B. A. Booth, London, 1951.
Tuell, Anna K. *John Sterling, a Representative Victorian*, New York, 1941.
Varnhagen von Ense. *Aus dem Nachlass Varnhagen's von Ense, Tagebücher*, ed. Ludmilla Assing, 15 vols, Leipzig, Hamburg, Zürich, 1861–70, Berlin, 1905.
   'Some Unpublished Letters of Varnhagen von Ense to Thomas Carlyle', ed. Rodger L. Tarr, *Modern Language Review*, LXVIII, January 1973, 22–7.
Vogel, S. M. *German Literary Influences on the American Transcendentalists*, New Haven, Connecticut, 1955.
Weber, Carl August. 'Bristols Bedeutung für die englische Romantik und die deutsch-englischen Beziehungen', *Studien zur englischen Philologie*, LXXXIX, 1935, number 4, 1–304.
Wellek, René. *A History of Modern Criticism, 1750–1950*, 4 vols, London, 1955–66.
   Immanuel Kant in England, 1793–1838, Princeton, New Jersey, 1931.
The Wellesley Index to Victorian Periodicals, 1824–1900, ed. W. E. Houghton, 2 vols– , Toronto, 1966– .
Wells, G. A. *Herder and After: A Study in the Development of Sociology, Anglica Germanica*, The Hague, 1959.
Whewell, William. *Historical and Philosophical Works*, ed. G. Buchdahl and L. L. Laudan, 6 vols– , London, 1967– .

Willoughby, L. A. 'English Translations and Adaptations of Schiller's "Robbers"', *Modern Language Review*, XVI, 1921, 297–315.

Wordsworth, William. *The Letters of William and Dorothy Wordsworth*, ed. E. De Selincourt, 6 vols, Oxford, 1935–9, and 2nd edition revised and enlarged, ed. C. L. Shaver et al, Oxford, 1967– .

Young, G. M. (ed.). *Early Victorian England, 1830–1865*, 2 vols, London, 1934.

INDEX

Abrams, M. H., 179n9
Allingham, William, 77
Anster, John, 22, 63, 186n85
Anti-Jacobin; or, Weekly Examiner,
18, 25, 64, 68; parody of German
drama, 6–8, 9, 30, 188n15,
226n117
Arnold, Matthew, 2, 106, 177; on
Carlyle, 90, 106; on Goethe, 20;
on Lewes's *Life of Goethe,* 143; on
Spinoza, 24, 220n42; on Strauss,
150, 156
Athenaeum, 86, 107, 142
Austin, Sarah, 22, 177, 183n57;
Carlyle and, 21, 207n6; translator
of Goethe, 21; on Lewes's *Life of
Goethe,* 23, 142

Barth, Karl, 163–4
Beddoes, Thomas, 16, 25
Beddoes, Thomas Lovell, 82, 183n57,
198n7
Bentham, Jeremy, 93, 100, 106,
207n7
Biltz, Karl, 144
Black, John, 13, 63, 156
Blackie, John Stuart, 142, 143, 177,
183n57; Carlyle and, 105; translation of *Faust,* 22, 186n85
Blackwood's Magazine, 113, 207n6;
important for its German interest,
14–16, 63, 65, 68; Coleridge sends
metaphysical letter to, 48; De
Quincey translates Lessing for, 12,
16; Gillies's articles on German
drama in, 14–15, 184n62, 198n7;
Lockhart's articles on German
literature in, 15–16, 184n61
Blake, William, 4–5, 188n17, 199n34
Boehme, Jacob, 96; Coleridge's
interest in, 55, 74, 196n138

Bohn, Henry George, 127, 156,
214n105
Boosey, Thomas, 27, 61, 80
Borrow, George, 10
Bray, Charles, 150, 174, 175
British and Foreign Review, Lewes's
articles in, 112, 113, 116, 124, 139
Brougham, Henry Peter, 1st Baron,
74
Bryant, Jacob, 153, 154
Bürger, Gottfried August, 3, 4–5,
10, 30, 56, 188n17
Bulwer, Edward Lytton, 25, 99, 124,
131, 201n61; influence of
Wilhelm Meister on, 22; on
Schiller, 125; on A. W. Schlegel,
121
Byron, Lord George Gordon, 28, 57,
61, 64, 70, 78, 198n7; on
Coleridge, 1, 17, 58, 178n1; on
Faust, 63

Caird, Edward, 193n106, 211n63,
215n121
Canning, George, 6, 30, *see also
Anti-Jacobin; or, Weekly
Examiner*
Carlyle, Jane Welsh, 69, 78, 86, 87
Carlyle, Thomas, 1–6, *passim,* 10,
11,14–15, 18–25 *passim,* 62, 65,
66, 67–104 *passim,* 108, 131,
168, 181n29, 186n92
and the *Edinburgh Review,* 18–19,
64, 67–76 *passim,* 91, 96, 100,
106, 113; 'The State of German
Literature', 10, 18, 67–8, 70–1,
74, 75–6, 94–5, 100, 110,
204n122; relationship with
Jeffrey, 18–19, 24, 67, 70, 74–5,
76, 101, 102, 113
and Goethe, 4, 20–1, 23, 25, 70,

237

INDEX

Carlyle, Thomas, *cont.*
76–91 *passim*, 99, 100, 104,
106–7; translation of *Wilhelm
Meister*, 14–15, 17–21 *passim*,
67, 69, 70, 76, 111, 201n69;
Carlyle begins the translation,
82; sends translation to Goethe,
76; Carlyle's criticisms of
Wilhelm Meister, 82–5 *passim*,
87; examples from his translation, 85–6, 202n78; influence of
his translation on other translators, 21–2; De Quincey's
criticism of his translation, 17,
84, 185n72; Jeffrey's criticism
of his translation, 17, 67, 76;
Carlyle on *Faust*, 63–4, 80–1;
translation from *Faust*, 86;
Carlyle idealises Goethe, 21,
88–91 *passim*; Goethe praises
his *Life of Schiller*, 77
and German philosophy, 19, 71,
91–9 *passim*, 100; and Kant, 3,
21, 25, 46, 72, 75, 99, 100, 101,
204n122; takes Kant for an
idealist, 42, 47, 71, 94–5, 96–7,
100–1; finds Kant obscure,
92–4; and German 'mysticism',
68, 70–1, 74–5, 93, 95–6, 101,
204n122; and transcendentalism,
72, 93–4, 97, 98, 204n122
Sartor Resartus, 19–20, 21, 71–5
passim, 88, 95, 97–8, 99–104
passim, 105, 111, 176, 177,
204n111; importance of German
thought for, 100–3 *passim*,
206n149; influence of Goethe
on, 89; George Eliot on, 22,
147; response of British readers
to, 21, 94, 103–4, 107, 218n187;
response of American readers
to, 98, 103; influence on other
English novelists, 22, 155,
186n89; 'Wotton Reinfred',
72–3
and Schiller, 18, 79, 86, 99, 100,
204n111; *Life of Schiller*, 42,
70, 76–9 *passim*, 91–4 *passim*,
99; Goethe praises the *Life*, 77;
Carlyle's problems with the
Life, 92–4 *passim*
and Jean Paul [Richter], 17, 69,
99, 100, 174

and Novalis (Friedrich von
Hardenberg), 4, 73–4, 89, 95–7
passim, 99, 100, 101
and German aesthetics, 73, 94
and Coleridge, 68, 71, 79, 82, 93,
99, 101, 202n81; importance of
Coleridge's writings for, 19, 47,
71–4 *passim*, 95–8 *passim*, 104;
Carlyle accuses Coleridge of
obscurity, 42, 46, 71–2, 73
and Lewes, 22, 23, 67, 90–1, 106,
113, 118, 131, 146; influence of
Carlyle on Lewes, 105, 110–12
passim, 123, 131; Lewes dedi-
cates his *Life of Goethe* to
Carlyle, 80; Carlyle criticises
the *Life*, 143
and other Germanists; helped by
Crabb Robinson, 12; and De
Quincey, 16–17; importance of
his writings for Mill, 25, 64, 90,
98, 106, 177; importance of his
writings for Sterling, 21, 64, 80,
90, 103, 106, 107; fame in
Germany, 78; influence in
America, 19, 21, 98; underrates
other Germanists, 68–70 *passim*
Chapman, John, 154, 155
Clarkson, Thomas, 46
Coleridge, Henry Nelson, 108
Coleridge, Samuel Taylor, 1–21
passim, 22, 24–5, 27–66 *passim*,
68, 69, 100, 101, 106–8 *passim*,
148, 175, 177, 178n1, 210n41,
211n58, 218n3
and Germany, 27–35 *passim*; trip
to Germany, 29, 32, 42–3,
188n10, 189n28
and German philosophy, 1, 3–4,
17, 18, 178n1; and Kant, 2–4
passim, 25, 29, 32, 36–48
passim, 49–51 *passim*, 53–4, 58,
66, 72, 92, 95, 97, 160, 178n5,
187n4, 190n61, 192n86,
193n97, 194n110; Coleridge
and Schiller similarly interested
in Kant, 35, 36, 42, 49, 51–3
passim, 194n111; and Spinoza,
24, 25, 55, 127, 156, 196n138;
and Boehme, 55, 74, 196n138;
and Fichte, 53–4, 58, 195n130;
and German 'mysticism', 18, 58,
73–4, 75, 101, 107, 199n34;

238

INDEX

Eliot, George, *cont.*

tion of *Das Leben Jesu* from Rufa Hennell, 148; dislikes the work, 148–9, 150, 151–2, 159; and Spinoza, 25, 155–9 *passim*, 166, 167; George Eliot translates Spinoza's *Ethics*, 24, 127, 156, 166; Spinoza's importance for her thought, 157–8, 159, 166, 167; and Feuerbach, 4, 25, 153, 158, 159–66 *passim*; George Eliot enjoys translating Feuerbach, 159, 160; her criticisms of Feuerbach, 165–6; Feuerbach's importance for her thought, 160–1, 162, 164–5, 169–70, 223n76

and Goethe, 4, 25, 166–73 *passim*; on *Wilhelm Meister*, 82, 134, 167–71 *passim*, 172, 173; on *Wahlverwandtschaften*, 134, 136, 166, 167, 168, 171, 173; and Lewes's *Life of Goethe*, 133, 134–5, 166–7; and Retzsch's illustrations to *Faust*, 61

and German genius, 24, 173–7 *passim*; and Heine, 166, 173–4, 175; and Jean Paul [Richter], 174; and Lessing, 175, 182n41; and Schiller, 147

and German philosophy, 150–1; and Kant, 25, 151, 167, 176, 226n120; and transcendentalism, 153

and Coleridge, 24, 147, 156, 186n93; and Carlyle, 22, 79, 94, 147; and Dr Cumming, 153, 160; and Mackay, 154; and Richard Holt Hutton, 164–5, 173, 223n79; and Comte, 157, 158, 161, 169–70, 222n69; and Gruppe, 150–1, 160; and the *Westminster Review*, 154, 161, 174

Scenes of Clerical Life, 159, 173; *Adam Bede*, 159, 173; *Mill on the Floss*, 173; *Romola*, 164–5, 222n69, 223n79; *The Spanish Gypsy*, 222n69; *Middlemarch*, 153–4, 157, 158, 170, 173; *Daniel Deronda*, 61, 170, 172; *Theophrastus Such*, 176, 223n76

Ellis, G., 6

Emerson, Ralph Waldo, and Carlyle, 19, 94, 106, 204n121; arranges publication of *Sartor* in America, 103; and transcendentalism, 98, 205n136

Empson, William, 70

Espinasse, Francis, 19–20, 94, 103

Ferrier, James, 187n4, 195n131

Feuerbach, Ludwig, 24, 152, 155, 175, 176, 186n93, 224n82; George Eliot and, 4, 25, 153, 158, 159–66 *passim*, 169–70, 223n76

Fichte, Johann Gottlieb, 107; Coleridge and, 53–4, 58, 195n130; Carlyle and, 4, 89, 95, 96–7, 100; Lewes and, 128

Foreign Quarterly Review, 16, 78

Foreign Review, 64, 78, 95, 106

Fortnightly Review, 127

Fouqué, Friedrich de la Motte, 3, 179n7

Fraser's Magazine, Carlyle's articles in, 70, 88; *Sartor Resartus* in, 19, 100, 103

Frere, J. H., 6, 30

Frothingham, O. B., 3, 98

Froude, James Anthony, 106; *Nemesis of Faith*, 22–3, 155, 173, 186n89, 186n90; on Spinoza, 157, 214n109

Fruman, Norman, 28, 187n4

Fuller, Margaret, 19, 218n186

German aesthetics, 1, 2, 3–4, 14, 49, 51, 55–6, 179n9, 193n103, 194n116; Coleridge and, 3–4, 48–56 *passim*, 66; Carlyle and, 75, 94; Lewes and, 55, 110, 111, 112–26 *passim*, 132; Kant and, 4, 14, 49–51 *passim*, 114, 115

German drama, 1, 5–10 *passim*, 13, 14, 25, 31, 33, 63, 64, 148, 180n20, 180n21, 180n22, 188n22; 'Sturm und Drang', 7, 58, 68, 135; *Anti-Jacobin* attacks on, 6–8 *passim*, 30, 68; 'Schicksalsdrama', 15

German 'mysticism', 18, 37–8, 177; Coleridge and, 18, 58, 73–4, 101, 107, 199n34; Carlyle and, 68, 70–1, 73–5 *passim*, 93, 95–6, 101,

240